# Millennium Rage

**Survivalists, White Supremacists, and the Doomsday Prophecy**

# Millennium Rage

## Survivalists, White Supremacists, and the Doomsday Prophecy

### PHILIP LAMY

PLENUM PRESS • NEW YORK AND LONDON

Library of Congress Cataloging-in-Publication Data

Lamy, Philip.
    Millennium rage : survivalists, white supremacists, and the
  Doomsday prophecy / Philip Lamy.
        p.    cm.
    Includes bibliographical references and index.
    ISBN 0-306-45409-2
    1. Survivalism.  2. Millenialism.  3. Millenium.  4. Judgment Day.
  5. Militia movements.  6. White supremacy movements.   I. Title.
  HM206.L26   1996
  301--dc20                                                    96-32896
                                                                   CIP

ISBN 0-306-45409-2

© 1996 Philip Lamy
Plenum Press is a Division of Plenum Publishing Corporation
233 Spring Street, New York, N.Y. 10013-1578

10 9 8 7 6 5 4 3 2

Printed in the United States of America

AJM1436

I t was in the early 1980s, while studying punk rock and its subculture, that I first became interested in the millennial myth. In the punks' disdain for the values of the dominant culture, I had discovered a worldview that was strangely apocalyptic. The punk look—black, torn, disfigured, a montage of fashions and styles—was the look of mass destruction. It was what everyone would be wearing after "they" dropped the "big one." Punk faces made up in the gaudy and grim starkness suggestive of death itself became the famous punk "faces of doom." Through their music and in their art, the punks rendered the entire social and value structure of modern society as repressive, decadent, and obsolete.

They viewed the dominant society as corrupt and its popular culture—exemplified by disco and synthesized music—as insipid examples of a mass cultural decay masquerading as "art." And so they sang anthems of social collapse, the fall of civilization, and nuclear Armageddon. "We're the future, your future!" screamed Johnny Rotten, lead singer of the Sex Pistols, punk's most famous band, in their first and only hit single, "God Save the Queen." In an odd sort of way, the punks were prophets of the apocalyptic age that had already begun. From the marginal terrain of underground rock 'n' roll, the punks were voices crying out in the wilderness, telling us that, as best they could make out (with tongues planted firmly in their cheeks), the end times were near.[1]

Many of the apocalyptic themes I had seen in punk music and literature I began to see elsewhere, especially in the popular culture and mass media. The 1980s—the decade John Mitchell

(1983) dubbed the "doomsday decade"—was especially steeped in apocalyptic thought and millennial movement.[2] The conservative morality of the "Reagan revolution" was aided in part by the prophetic and evangelical fervor of the religious right. In the American heartland, white "Christian" supremacists melded with paramilitary antigoverment extremists, producing groups such as "The Order" and "The Covenant, the Sword, and the Arm of the Lord," which engaged in shoot-outs with law enforcement agencies.

Meanwhile, New Age consciousness, heavy metal and Christian rock bands, and "cyber-punk" apocalyptic films were other examples of a "pop apocalypticism" that permeated American culture throughout the 1980s and into the l990s. Even George Bush employed apocalyptic language to frame the Persian Gulf War as an effort to build and preserve a "new world order"—a theme that was to appear a few years later, and with a very different meaning, in the rhetoric of militias and the "America first" platform of presidential candidate Patrick Buchanan.

Doomsday visions were also being manifested through survivalism, the main focus of this book. Survivalism addresses the physical survival of nuclear war (or some other major societal disaster) through crisis relocation, the stockpiling of food and weapons, and the practice of survival strategies. Survivalism is a practical and secular approach to disaster preparedness. Many survivalists feel strongly that the current social and world order is moribund, and so they have taken steps to prepare for its imminent demise.

Much of this doomsday prophecy derives from the millennial myth. The millennial myth originated in ancient Hebrew and Christian apocalyptic prophecies concerning the ultimate destiny of the world and the cosmic cataclysm in which God destroys the ruling powers of evil and raises the righteous to life in a messianic kingdom that will last for 1,000 years—the prophesied millennium. For the past several years I have followed the evolution of the millennial myth as it has been manifested in survivalism and the subculture of the paramilitary right. I have interviewed dozens of survivalists in major metropolitan areas (such as greater Boston), many of whom maintain caches of water, food, camping equipment, and weapons locked in the closets and/or cellars of their homes or apartments. One, a former public school teacher, began practicing survivalism shortly after becoming a born-again Christian. I also have spoken with rural-based survivalists and members of survivalist communities or compounds who have devoted great time and expense to surviving the collapse of society.

Survivalism provides a modern site where the millennial myth has "fractured"; its symbols and meanings have been reproduced and redefined in our popular culture through the mass media and within new social movements. In certain ways, survivalism reflects the severe downside of the millennial myth. Like the nihilism of punk, the survivalist philosophy speaks of mass destruction and death. It is not interested in reforming the system; the collapse of civilization is imminent. However, it does offer a plan of action, a kind of "redemption" or "salvation," in the manner of surviving the great destruction of the current order and living on to build a new one. The fusion of survivalist ethic and millennial belief is the subject of this book.

This fascination with the end times continues to filter through American society and, increasingly, the world as we approach the year 2000 and the next millennium, producing a wide array of apocalyptic expressions and movements. More recently, millennial expressions can be found in revitalized messianic movements like the Branch Davidians and the Aum Shinrikyo of Japan—the millennial cult linked to poison gas attacks in the subways of Tokyo, and even in the rock'n roll messianism of the "Church of Elvis." However, millennialism also appears in unusual, seemingly secular, groups and individuals as well, such as survivalists, the Unabomber and, most notorious of recent years, the paramilitary and antigovernment "militia movement." The "apocalyptic" war with the government "beast" can be discerned in the militia- and survivalist-inspired Timothy McVeigh and Terry Nichols, the alleged Oklahoma City bombers; it is present in the "common law" philosophy and "Identity" religion of the Montana Freemen, who, refusing to abide by state and federal law, prompted a spring 1996 stand-off with federal law enforcement; and it fueled the terrorist plot of the Arizona "Viper Militia," of whom twelve members were arrested in July 1996 for allegedly plotting to bomb buildings housing the FBI, ATF, IRS, the Phoenix Police Department, and the Arizona National Guard, among others.

A number of things are converging to create a resurgence of millennialism—widespread social change, relative deprivation, the end of an era. Many of these are the same things that have occurred throughout the myth's long history. What is different now, however, are the numerous and often contradictory ways the millennial myth is expressed in American culture. Millennial symbols and images not only belong to radical religious and secular movements and cults but are part of the dominant American culture as well.

As the millennial myth continues to evolve, certain groups come to interpret current events through the lens of cultural myth. In the past, millennial movements often arose during periods of intense social change, coinciding with the end of an age or era. In many ways contemporary expressions of millennialism reflect the major social changes that the world has been undergoing at the close of the second millennium A.D. They reflect the "tribulations" and "plagues" of our age—rapid and widespread social, cultural, and technological changes that are transforming the world into some form of new world order of the twenty-first century.

# Acknowledgments

Many people have helped me throughout the development and preparation of this book: family, friends, colleagues, students, and staff. I thank them all for their suggestions, support, and caring. The research for *Millennium Rage* began back in the 1980s, while I was a graduate student at Northeastern University in Boston. At that institution Drs. Jack Levin, Ronald McAllister, Christine Gailey, Herman Gray (now at the University of California, Santa Cruz), Susan Setta, and Alan Klein were instrumental in the development of my interest in the sociology and anthropology of millenarian movements. Other colleagues and associates who have contributed important suggestions include Arnold Arluke, Wilfred Holten, Debra Kaufman, Maureen Kelleller, the late Pat Golden, Thomas Koenig, and Judith Perrolle of Northeastern University; Bill Kuehn, David Ellenbrook, Luther Brown, Natalie Duany, Linda Olsen, Brad Hunt, Ann Bartol, Victoria DeRosia, Paul Cohen, and Joe Mark of Castleton State College; Henry Paar of Springfield College; John Forster of SUNY, Cortland; Robert Granfield of the University of Colorado, Denver; Christian Appy of the Massachusetts Institute of Technology; Thomas Robbins; Augie Diana; Bob Quinn; Joe Cultrera; Henry Ferrini, and Peter and Lynette Brand.

I also acknowledge the research assistance of Hermino Miranda, whose skill in navigating the Internet provided a wealth of important data for this book; CSC librarians Sandra Duling, Frank Moulton, and Nancy Luzer; Jean Blair, Mary Giordano, and the Leavenworth secretarial staff of CSC; Ennis Duling of CSC's Office of Public Information; Andrew Bacchi, Gayle Morris, Charles Davis, and Ritika Rao of Computer Services; the Castleton State College Alumni Fund for research support; and the many students I have had over the years at Castleton and Northeastern University who contributed in many ways to the evolution of my sociological perspective and the ideas that appear in this book.

Finally, I wish to thank my children and most of all, my wife and best friend, Whitney, who endured the many hours I spent away from our family with great cheer and selfless love and support, as well as insightful commentary on the manuscript. This book is as much hers as mine.

An earlier version of Chapter 3—"Tribulation: Survivalists and Soldiers of Fortune," appeared in the *Journal for the Scientific Study of Religion*, with the title "Millennialism in the Mass Media: The Case of *Soldier of Fortune* Magazine." Any errors that may be found in this book are mine.

Dedicated to the memory of my parents, Louis and Cecelia.

# Contents

# Chapter 1

# Millennium Rage

*For when they shall say "peace and safety"; then sudden destruction
cometh upon them, and they shall not escape.*

1 Thess. 5:3, King James Version (KJV)[1]

*And I saw a star fallen from heaven to earth, and he was given the
key to the shaft of the bottomless pit; he opened the shaft of the bottomless pit, and from the shaft rose smoke like the smoke of a great
furnace, and the sun and the air were darkened with the smoke from
the shaft. And in those days men will seek death and will not find it;
they will long to die, but death will elude them.*

Rev. 9:1–2, 6, Revised Standard Version (RSV)

At the start of 1990 the world seemed to be on the verge of
a "new age" of world cooperation. Almost overnight the Cold War
disappeared as the Soviet Union collapsed, the Berlin wall collapsed, and Eastern Europe was feeling free. The United States and
the former Soviet Union agreed to reduce and destroy their chemical
and nuclear weapons. Economic powers were emerging in Europe
and East Asia to compete with those in North America. Nonviolent
"velvet revolutions" in Czechoslovakia, "peace dividends" from the
halt to the arms race, and a "new world order" of international
cooperation and global "democratization" excited hope for a
new and optimistic future.

But in Paradise Valley, Montana, during the week of March
11, 1990, thousands of members of a survivalist religious sect
called the Church Universal and Triumphant were excit-
edly preparing for the "end times" and a different sort of new

world order—the biblical millennium. Elizabeth Clare Prophet, known to followers as "Guru Ma," which in church language means "the teacher who is mother," had called out a warning that a Soviet attack on the United States was imminent. Claiming that she spoke as a medium for God, Prophet warned that recent international events were the result of deception by the Soviet Union designed to lure the United States into complacency. Prophet, age 51 and a wife and mother, admonished followers to prepare for "nuclear Armageddon."

Around the country church members and sympathizers were reportedly cashing in savings accounts, moving out of urban centers, stockpiling food and weapons, and preparing to move into underground bomb shelters. At the church's 30,000-acre property and state-of-the-art survivalist compound and retreat bordering Yellowstone National Park, residents paid up to $10,000 for a plot or $200,000 for a specially designed survival condominium. During the church's countdown to Armageddon, 750 staff members (including 250 children) and 2,000 close followers gathered with Prophet to pray and prepare for the beginning of the end.[2] The "signs of the times are everywhere," said Prophet, appearing on a 1987 segment of the Phil Donahue Show. Alluding to the hole in the ozone layer, increasing volcanic activity worldwide, and the population "bomb," Prophet argued that we can and should do nothing to head off Armageddon. Instead we must prepare to survive into the new era about to begin.

Local authorities were especially apprehensive about the excitement at Paradise Valley. In the fall of 1989, Edward Francis, husband of Elizabeth Clare Prophet and vice president of the church, was convicted of illegally purchasing $100,000 worth of semiautomatic weapons and handguns and 120,000 rounds of ammunition under a false name.[3] Among the weapons confiscated were eight Barrent .50-caliber rifles, several uzi machine guns, and a rocket launcher with a six-inch shell designed to pierce armored personnel carriers. Francis was sentenced to one month in jail and three months probation at home with an electronic ankle bracelet. The combination of apocalyptic prophesy with military-style weapons caused some to question the meaning of the Church Universal and Triumphant.[4]

On the day Prophet had predicted the likely outbreak of nuclear war, a judge in nearby Livingston ordered a halt to construction at the site of a huge underground bomb shelter as cleanup crews worked to remove more than 31,000 gallons of diesel fuel and gasoline that had leaked from storage tanks near the shelter. Environmental officials feared that the spill would damage a prime spawning creek for trout and threaten land in Yellowstone National Park. Montana officials said the construction project undertaken by the church "had resulted in substantial environmental harm."[5]

Founded in 1957 by her late husband, Mark L. Prophet, who died in 1973, the Church Universal and Triumphant is now headed by Mrs. Prophet. Her beliefs are a loose blend of Eastern and New Age religions, Christianity, and survivalism, or "disaster preparedness." Assuming the mantle of "prophet" left to her by her husband, Mrs. Prophet says ,"I am a messenger speaking on behalf of God." Members of the church also believe that Prophet, a political science graduate of Boston University, is divinely inspired by a host of "ascended masters," including Merlin the Magician, Hercules, William Shakespeare, Jesus Christ, and the Archangel Michael. Blending elements and characters from a variety of religious and mythical traditions, and fitting these to the character and disposition of the current age, Mrs. Prophet has become a prophet of the postmodern Apocalypse.[6]

While the theology of the Church Universal and Triumphant draws from diverse religious traditions, it is primarily apocalyptic because it professes a belief that the end of the world is at hand and that it is being supernaturally engineered by God. Apocalyptic beliefs are rooted in ancient Jewish and Christian literature concerning the destiny of the world and the cosmic cataclysm in which God destroys the ruling powers of evil and raises the righteous to life in a messianic kingdom that will last for 1,000 years—the prophesied millennium. The apocalyptic belief—or *millennial myth*, as I refer to it throughout this book—teaches that we are living at the end of human history.

Perhaps the most famous example of the millennial myth is the Christian Apocalypse, or the Revelation to Saint John the Divine. What makes Revelation special is that its prophecies are eschatological—about the "end times." The final chapter of the New Testament, or Christian Bible, Revelation was probably written during Roman Emperor Domitian's reign in 95 B.C., when Christians were being persecuted for their refusal to worship the deified emperor. Revelation represents the Roman persecutions as the beginning of a universal war between the forces of good and evil. Like apocalyptists of the Jewish era, John, the book's author, sees the Messiah appearing amid a series of catastrophic events culminating in the near success of the Antichrist—the figure of the "false prophet" or satanic opponent to Christ. The Messiah destroys the Antichrist, brings redemption for the chosen, and establishes a new Heaven and a new earth for 1,000 years of spiritual bliss.

Because of its highly cryptic language, Revelation has no single, indisputable meaning, and its ambiguity has left it open to numerous interpretations, imbuing it with the power and persistence of myth. The millennial myth is a powerful and flexible religious worldview that adapts easily, although unevenly, to changing social and cultural conditions. The myth explains the "big picture" of human history and destiny, and it exists on a transcendental plane, where a kind of "superconsciousness" with absolute and sacred values guides human behavior and directs human history.

Throughout the history of the Middle Eastern and Western civilizations, and in non-Christian religions as well, the millennial myth has accompanied the rise and fall of many societies and has spurred the development of numerous revolutionary and utopian movements, most notably during the Crusades and the Reformation.[7] This has been true throughout the history of the United States as well. In its American form, the myth renders America as a uniquely millennial land and Americans as a chosen people. The millennial myth helped guide Columbus' discovery and exploration of the New World; it was embedded in the lamentations and "fire and brimstone" sermons, or jeremiads, of Puritan ministers;

and it underlay both the manifest destiny and political demonology that has molded nationalist ideology in the United States since its inception.[8] The millennial myth has played a prominent role in American history and culture and it continues to do so.

The Church Universal and Triumphant represents just one recent example of the ever-evolving millennial myth. More interesting, and perhaps more disturbing, is the practice of survivalism as part of the church's apocalyptic theology. The millennial myth is a sacred belief system whereby salvation comes to the individual or group through faith in God. Survivalism addresses the physical survival of nuclear war (or some other major environmental or societal disaster) through crisis relocation, the stockpiling of food and weapons, and the practice of survival strategies or "disaster preparedness." Survivalism is a "practical" and secular approach to the fear of disasters—natural, man-made, or supernatural. For Prophet and members of her church, apocalyptic and survivalist tendencies are fused into a single belief system—a kind of yin and yang of contemporary millennial culture. Survivalism becomes part of salvation, which, in the early months or years of the Apocalypse, means disaster preparedness.

While Prophet acknowledges that it will be God during the Last Judgment who decides who will ultimately "survive," she and her followers want to be present for the plagues and destruction that mark the period called the tribulation, which, according to Prophet and her followers, is the time we are now living through. They also hope to be present for the Second Coming of Jesus Christ, to fight on His side against Satan and the forces of evil during the Battle of Armageddon and to witness the birth of "a new Heaven and a new earth" in the millennium. Tribulationists like the Church Universal and Triumphant believe they may be able to survive the coming plagues, wars, and other forms of destruction unleashed by God on the world by being spiritually and physically "prepared." Disaster preparedness and survival training during the tribulation become part of church belief and practice—a form of "Christian survivalism."

When the prophesied crisis did not occur during the week of March 11, 1990, and the sun continued to rise in the days after, Prophet and her church proclaimed that their prayers and faith helped stem the apocalyptic tide, at least for the time being. It was a strategy millennial groups have used in the past when their prophecies failed. The Millerites, for example, a nineteenth-century millenarian sect, also predicted the end of the world in late 1843. When the Apocalypse failed to arrive, they claimed their prayers had temporarily prevented it. The Jehovah's Witnesses firmly believed that Armageddon had begun with the onset of World War I, only to find disappointment when peace was achieved. Later many thought World War II was truly the "war to end all wars," but they were proved wrong again. Other predictions (1972, 1975) have come and past. As a result of these miscalculations, the Witnesses are now cautious about specific dates; however, they continue to believe that the end times are near.[9]

While many were disappointed that Armageddon did not come as planned, faith in Prophet and membership in her survivalist church remain firm. The millennial myth remains strong in American culture as well, and it continues to evolve and merge with a growing survivalist subculture.

*And I saw when the Lamb opened one of the seals, and I heard as it were the noise of thunder, one of the four beasts saying, Come and see. And I saw, and behold a white horse: and he that sat on it had a bow; and a crown was given unto him: and he went forth conquering, and to conquer.* (REV. 6:1–2, KJV)

*God, Guns and Guts Made America: Let's Keep All Three* (BUMPER STICKER, *SOLDIER OF FORTUNE* CONVENTION AND EXPOSITION, 1990)

The battle against tyranny raged on at the 15th anniversary *Soldier of Fortune* (*SOF*) Convention and Exposition held at the Sahara Hotel and Casino in Las Vegas in September 1990. The convention occurred at a propitious time. Iraq's Saddam Hussein had invaded his small but oil-rich neighbor Kuwait one month before. By September more than 100,000 American troops were stationed in Saudi Arabia and throughout the Persian Gulf. The United States stood on the brink of war with Iraq. Consequently, the *Soldier of Fortune* Convention was especially charged given the threat of international war with a notable tyrant. The best-selling item at the *SOF* Exposition was a two-dollar, two-foot target of a smirking Saddam with a bull's-eye centered on his nose. The most popular T-shirt showed a turbaned figure riding a camel while fixed in the gun sight of an attacking Air Force fighter plane. The caption read, "I'd walk 10,000 miles to smoke a camel."[10]

Posters and banners further expressed American outrage at "the international terrorist" Saddam Hussein. Covering half of the wall in the convention headquarters hung the familiar *SOF* logo: the special forces beret atop crossing knives and the slogan "death to tyrants" underneath (Figure 1.1). On this day, however, "tyrants" had been crossed out with red tape and "Saddam" inserted. "'Death to Saddam' has a nice ring to it," an older man in fatigues chuckled. Other familiar tyrants, such as Fidel Castro, Muammar Gadhafi, and Daniel Ortega, were also available for purchase at the exhibition center on T-shirts and on posters for target practice (in 2 x 2 posters or life size). And there were American heroes as well. Posters and paintings of Davy Crockett, Robert E. Lee, George

FIGURE 1.1. "Death to Tyrants/Saddam." *SOF* logo and slogan, *Soldier of Fortune* convention, Sahara Hotel and Casino, Las Vegas, September 1990.

Patton, Ronald Reagan, and the "Vietnam Vet" hung alongside Hollywood soldier John Wayne, Clint Eastwood's "Man with No Name," and Sylvester Stallone's "Rambo." Also on exhibition was a poster portrait of Adolf Hitler with the caption, "When I come back, no more Mr. Nice Guy" (Figure 1.2). There also were several booths that specialized in World War II-era German and Nazi memorabilia, including Nazi flags with the swastika, German Lugars, medals, uniforms, and posters.

For seven days and nights the Sahara Hotel and Casino played host to hundreds of camouflaged conventioneers as they attended meetings on international military conflict in the morning, fired machine guns in the afternoon, and discussed the politics of the new world order over drinks and blackjack in the evenings (Figures 1.3 and 1.4). During the week, gun enthusiasts competed in "the world's premier three-gun shooting match," testing participants' facility with different weapons and shooting situations. Other conventioneers competed in pugil stick fighting over a hotel pool and ran a desert obstacle course called "Operation Headhunter."

In the hotel minibus taking conventioneers to the firing range 10 miles outside of the Vegas strip, 24-year-old ex-Marine Gordon Willoughby looked forward to the afternoon's firepower demonstration, where military weapons experts test fire a wide assortment of vintage and modern machine guns and small cannons.[11]

FIGURE 1.2. Adolf Hitler photo: "When I come back, no more Mr. Nice Guy."

FIGURE 1.3. Firepower demonstration, *Soldier of Fortune* convention, Las Vegas, September 1990.

Gordon had decided to become a survivalist after his military tour of duty. He was "disgusted" with the military and the government, but he would "support our men" if they fought in the Gulf. "And they'll kick butt too," said Gordon, "if they're not bogged down by some wormy multilateral command that won't let us lead." Gordon, an avid reader of survivalist literature, recommended to me two survivalist book series: Barry Sadler's *Casca: The Eternal Mercenary* and Jerry Ahern's *The Survivalist*—both fictional accounts of survivalism.

Sadler, who wrote the popular Marine anthem "Ballad of the Green Beret," the theme song for the 1968 film *The Green Berets*, starring John Wayne, was also a novelist, musician, mercenary, and contributing editor to *SOF*. Of the numerous fiction in this genre, the *Casca* series is unique, as it blends war and mercenary activity with Christianity and the millenial myth. *Casca: The Eternal Mercenary* (1979) is the first of a series of books (some 20-odd) that tells the story of a Roman centurion, Casca, who participated in the crucifixion of Christ. While near death on the cross, Christ condemns Casca to never-ending death as a soldier and mercenary.

FIGURE 1.4. The author test fires an uzi machine gun, Las Vegas, September 1990.

Ultimately Casca becomes a Christian soldier fighting the "good Christian fight" until Christ's Second Coming.[12] Sadler was killed by left-wing guerrillas in Costa Rica while acting as a hired mercenary for the Costa Rican government in 1989.

With more than a dozen books in his series, Jerry Ahern's *The Survivalist* is more typical of survivalist fiction. *The Survivalist* begins when

> . . . World War III is now a bloody page in American history. With nuclear holocaust killing more than a quarter-billion people worldwide and the United States just a memory, John Thomas Rourke, ex-CIA covert operations officer, weapons expert, and survival authority is enduring the ultimate test.[13]

Copies of both these survivalist book series, and many other titles, could be purchased at the convention's week-long product exhibition. At the firepower demonstration, survivalist Lou Cameron from Nova Scotia test fired an uzi machine gun. Lou, a construction foreman, had recently built himself a "a nice little bunker" on Pictou Island, between northern Nova Scotia and Prince Edward Island, in the Northumberland Strait. Lou supported the secession movement in Quebec and hoped it would spark a trend in which more Canadian provinces would secede from the nation. He was also a staunch defender of Native American sovereignty and regularly spent time with Indian friends among the Kahnawake of Quebec—"the original survivalists," Lou called them.

Throughout the convention, workshops were given in the use of combat knives, impact weapons, evasive driving, personal defense, and emergency medical care. The survivalist and weapons industries were well represented at the exposition. Las Vegas' own Survival Store displayed all manner of military and paramilitary weaponry and gear, including knives, gas masks, and Geiger counters. At a neighboring booth a real estate broker in fatigues hawked isolated properties in the Ozarks. Paladin Press—"the action library"—displayed dozens of their best-selling books, including *Fallout Survival; Better Read, than Dead; The Survivalist Medicine Chest; Combat Survival;* and *Beat the Odds.* Representatives of *American Survival Guide* magazine solicited new subscribers and displayed over 100 different small arms advertised in their magazine (Figures 1.5, 1.6, and 1.7). An advertising representative for *American Survival Guide* said that "business was very good, and Saddam has brought out a lot of people."

During the convention, seminars and briefings were conducted by freedom fighters from Laos and Vietnam. *SOF* journalists reported on their sojourns with anticommunist rebel factions in Mozambique and Vietnam. An *SOF* contributing editor spoke about Soviet special forces in his talk "Spetsnaz: The Dark Side of Perestroika." The speaker, Major William Northacker, warned that, "With the erosion of communism does not come the dismantling of the KGB or the Soviet military's special force operations."

The *Soldier of Fortune* Exchange booth sold all manner of *SOF* paraphernalia, while staffers and other representatives raised money for "Refugee Relief" and the "Afghan Freedom Fighters Fund." Also for sale and support of freedom fighters were the unusual "Contra crosses." Created by Nicaraguan Contras to help fund their cause, Contra crosses are bullets in cartridges that have been fashioned into the Christian sign of the cross. The crosses are then sold to Americans through an *SOF* "operative" in Central

FIGURE 1.5. *American Survival Guide* display, *SOF* Convention and Exposition, Sahara Hotel and Casino, Las Vegas, September 1990.

FIGURE 1.6. Weapons exhibit. *SOF* Convention and Exposition, Las Vegas, 1990.

FIGURE 1.7. Survivalist booth, *SOF* Convention and Exposition, Las Vegas, 1990.

America. At a neighboring booth, a civilian defense organization called The Texas Civilian Material Assistance Group displayed survival manuals and civil defense plans. Tito, a Mexican-American representative, spoke to an interested group of conventioneers on the need for strong citizen defense and disaster preparedness. He also warned of worsening U.S.–Mexico border problems and of the flow of illegal immigrants and drugs into North America from the south. With slides, photographs, documents, and a petition, the group advocated "citizen defense" and "traditional community survival."

*Soldier of Fortune Magazine*: *The Journal of Professional Adventurers* brings together an odd assortment of characters, including mercenaries, survivalists, militiamen and militiawomen, and all manner of paramilitary patriots, antigovernment zealots, and would-be Rambos. With over one million subscribers worldwide, *Soldier of Fortune* is the most popular periodical in the industry and subculture of survivalism. Published out of Boulder, Colorado, *SOF* is a venture begun by Robert K. Brown. A former Army special forces team leader during the Vietnam War and a lieutenant colonel in the Army Reserves, Brown is an active member of the National

Rifle Association and an ardent American nationalist and anticommunist. His magazine reflects these interests. Blending state-of-the-art weapons with military action, espionage, survivalism, and right-wing politics, *SOF* now dominates an extensive paramilitary and survivalist literature and has become a main player among gun magazines. In addition, it has infused new energy into the subculture of American survivalists.

Survivalism is a loosely structured yet pervasive belief system and set of practices focusing on disaster preparedness. Many survivalists feel strongly that the current social and world order is moribund, and so they have taken steps to prepare for its imminent demise. The degree to which people practice survivalism varies greatly. Some people may read survival magazines like *Soldier of Fortune* or play survival games only on weekends. Others stockpile water, canned goods, medical supplies, and guns. Still others purchase isolated rural property, enroll in survival training programs, or belong to survival communities and organizations. Survivalists are people who are prepared to survive the devastation—whether economic, societal, or nuclear disaster, brought on by nature, humankind, or God—by breaking away from society and becoming self-sufficient. At one end of the spectrum are "boy scout" survivalists, who claim only to be "prepared" for potentially difficult times; at the other end are white supremacists, antigovernment zealots, and apocalyptic cults.

This is the market that *Soldier of Fortune* caters to, but it is more than a catalog for American gun enthusiasts and doomsayers. Like many members of the survivalist subculture, *SOF* expresses a uniquely American view of the world: Soldiers of fortune fight the never-ending battle against "tyranny"; citizen soldiers practice survivalism in defense of the "American way" and in preparation for social collapse or "nuclear Armaggedon." *Soldier of Fortune* expresses an American form of the millennial myth, though not necessarily a purely religious one. While *Soldier of Fortune* is not generally mistaken for a religious tract, apocalyptic symbols and images permeate its pages. From reports of military conflicts around the world to advertisements and classifieds and most recently the *SOF* home page on the Internet, *SOF* sees the world as caught in "cosmic war" and on the verge of massive destruction and death. In Revelation—the quintessential apocalyptic scripture—the classic image of the carnage that is to accompany the end times is the Four Horsemen of the Apocalypse (Rev. 6.1–8). Bearers of conquest, slaughter, famine, and death, these Four Horsemen often ride through the pages of *SOF*.

Especially in advertisements and on T-shirts and posters, the symbols and images of the Apocalypse provide the millennial message of *Soldier of Fortune*. A T-shirt shows the Fourth Horseman cloaked in a hooded black robe and clutching a smoking uzi: "Liberty or Death" the caption reads (Figure 1.8). These symbols are fragments of the American millennial myth, and they provide a symbolic context in which *SOF* expresses its unique mythology of world conflict and American destiny. In these ways, *Soldier of Fortune* can be read as an apocalyptic script.

While *Soldier of Fortune* and survivalism focus on the dark side of the millennial myth, the part that speaks of war, destruction, and death, it also sees America as the primary defender of freedom in the world, whose crusade is the battle against tyranny and the benevolent expansion of the American way of life. Ultimately, redemption for Americans will come in fighting the great tyrants and evil forces in the world and surviving into the next millennium, where every individual fends for himself in a world dominated by "survival of the fittest" values and practices. If a new world order is to be built, it will be the "fit" who will build it.

While less overtly religious than the Church Universal and Triumphant, the survivalist worldview of *Soldier of Fortune* is also tribulationist. The times they see are bad times, and the future does not look bright. World instability is likely to increase, and military and paramilitary conflicts will continue into the so-called new world order. At home, crime also continues unabated, and government intrusion into the lives of ordinary citizens, through the steady erosion of gun rights, for example, will further undermine the domestic order and our faith in the nation's leaders. There's a bad time ahead, *SOF* tells its readers, and you must be prepared.

FIGURE 1.8. Grim reaper with uzi. *SOF* T-shirt image.

These secular millennial interpretations allow the *Soldier of Fortune* subscriber to read his or her own marginal social status and position into the confusing and rapidly changing events of the day. The *SOF* worldview can be understood as a set of organizing principles for interpreting current events and a mythology for making sense of a world that for some is out of control.

While the momentous changes brought on by the end of the Cold War were also reflected in a positive light in *Soldier of Fortune*—as "successes of the forces of good in the great cosmic effort"—these events did not mean the end of war or the start of a utopian new world order. In March of 1990, a subscriber writes in the "Flak" section (letters to the editor) that "The 'end' of the Cold War does not end the terrorist war, the drug war, or various regional conflicts that may affect the continental United States." In the April 1990 issue, Robert K. Brown suggests that since "'The Soviet Evil Empire' is crumbling we can focus our attention on matters closer to home. Let's start with a rat eradication program; identify key cartel drug lords, and exorcise them through the use of military force."[14]

And there are those in *Soldier of Fortune* who worry that, far from being neutralized, the Soviet Union is as dangerous as ever. A February 1990 letter to the editor reads: "Destabilized, demoralized, and broke, but still a superpower with atomic weapons, the Soviet threat has only increased with the erosion of Eastern Bloc communism, and we must be ever vigilant towards it." More recently, intense disdain for the American government, federal law enforcement, and "internationalist" organizations have surfaced as key elements in *SOF*. In *Soldier of Fortune* the great cosmic effort is far from over.

That much was proved when Saddam Hussein invaded Kuwait on August 2, 1990. He had been there all along, of course, slowly accumulating scud missiles and T-72 tanks, smuggling in parts for his long-range "doomsday gun," bankrolling terrorists, and gassing his own people. Still, just about everyone seemed caught by surprise at the boldness of his invasion of Kuwait. Bush called Saddam "another Hitler" and said the invasion was "tyranny and a naked act of aggression."[15] For the United States and its allies the stakes were high. A ruthless tyrant threatened to take control of Kuwait and 25 percent of the world's oil supply. If he ever captured Saudi Arabia, he would control 45 percent. He had even threatened to "burn half of Israel" with chemical weapons in the process.

In the following month, George Bush began speaking about the preservation of the new world order as the justification for going to war with Iraq. Whether consciously or not, by using the phrase "new world order" as a metaphor for a nebulous future of global peace and harmony, the president (or his speech writers) had plugged into the millennial myth. It was there when he addressed the Council of Christian Broadcasters, calling the war with Saddam "a moral and just war to defeat the tyranny of Saddam—a madman who threatens the burgeoning new world order."[16] It was there on September 12, when Bush told a joint session of Congress that the new world order meant that "the rule of law supplants the rule of the jungle, [and] nations recognize the shared responsibility for freedom and justice."[17] The phrase "new world order" reflected a new optimism during the final decade of the twentieth century. "We stand at a defining hour," the president said, "the winds of change are with us now."[18] Saddam Hussein provided the new world order its first test.

Metaphorically, of course, when U.S.-led military forces attacked the war machine of Saddam Hussein, the fourth largest in the world, other elements of the millennial myth were fulfilled as well. One of these was the certainty that the "wrath of the righteous" would rain down upon a wayward and "lost people" as a punishment for their wicked ways. Saddam Hussein and Iraq had become a symbol of Babylon, the archetypal enemy of God's people and the symbol of Satan's worldly power. The destruction of a "fallen away" people is an important theme in both the Hebrew and Christian bibles. In Revelation the destruction of the "harlot" Babylon is the metaphor for the final destruction of the world that ushers in the millennium.

Coincidentally, the ruins of ancient Babylon lie in what is now Hillah, located less than 50 miles south of Baghdad in central Iraq. Thus it was fitting that George Bush's war for the new world order was fought on the soil of ancient Babylon. The metaphor of Babylon for George Bush was that Saddam Hussein and Iraq represented the decaying old world order, a world that must be wiped out—if not by flood, then by the fire and brimstone of "smart bombs" and "Patriot missiles." So while President Bush would call the war a crucial test of the new world order (the secular millennium), Saddam Hussein would call it "the mother of all battles" (the secular Armageddon). The Babylonian metaphor was not lost on the hundreds of conventioneers at the *SOF* Convention. A popular T-shirt showed an Army tank rolling over a map of Iraq with the caption "Babylon or Bust."

The crisis in the Gulf became the key issue for discussion throughout the *Soldier of Fortune* Convention. Speculating on the outcome of the Gulf crisis, keynote speaker Dr. Ray Cline, chairman of the conservative U.S. Global Strategy Council, sounded the millennial trumpet when he spoke of "crumbling dictatorships and new U.S. strategic goals." "In today's world," said Cline, "the United States is the only potential world leader and if we play our role correctly, by the end of the decade there could be a new world stability."

But in the lead editorial of the *Soldier of Fortune* 15th anniversary issue (Oct. 1990), handed out free at the exposition, Robert K. Brown cautioned about such utopian thinking. "There are those who . . . . maintain the major upheavals in the Soviet Bloc mark 'the end of history,' a time in which war will be obsolete. . . . That's a pleasant delusion, but it doesn't square with the facts." Brown goes on to list the numerous wars, both declared and undeclared, that wage on across the globe. And on the erosion of authoritarian communism, Brown remarks, "No one has told the New People's Army in the Phillipines, the Sendero Luminoso in Peru or the FMLN in El Salvador that communism has failed." Finally, says Brown, "History has not ended, nor will it. We will be there as it is made. . . . We stand with those who fight for freedom. We will be at the sharp end."[19]

*I say the Feds know they are under siege, and have warehoused children in the hopes that their enemies would be more squeamish than they are about blowing up innocent children. Unfortunately, for their children, the thugs in that building had made just too many enemies.* (ANONYMOUS INTERNET POSTING, APRIL 23, 1995)

*There is no doubt in my mind that this was NOT orchestrated by anything (quote-unquote) "domestic" with regard to the people, or with regard to "terrorists," per se. But rather it is another foot-stomp on the part of the New World Order crowd to manipulate the population. And, of course, we all know.* (MARK KOERNKE, APRIL 23, 1995, INTERNET POSTING).

Timothy McVeigh was at the "sharp end" in the Persian Gulf War and later outside of Oklahoma City when he was arrested in connection with the April 19, 1995, bombing of the Alfred P. Murrah Federal Building. He and friend Terry Nichols are purported to be responsible for the deaths of 167 people, including 19 children, in one of the worst acts of domestic terrorism the United States has experienced. The bombing in Oklahoma City focused attention on paramilitary extremists of the far right, including the so-called militia movement with which McVeigh and Nichols allegedly had been associated in Kingman, Arizona.

In the next few weeks Americans learned a lot about the militia movement: that members were armed, organized, and practiced in survivalism and that they were angry at the U.S. government for eroding the rights of American citizens. Militia leaders pointed to Ruby Ridge, Iowa, where a white supremacist named Randy Weaver had resisted arrest on illegal weapons charges and had been "attacked" by U.S. marshals. During a shootout and subsequent standoff, Weaver's wife, his 14-year-old son, and a U.S. marshal were killed. There also had been the tragic events in Waco, Texas, which began on February 28, 1993. An apocalyptic cult called the Branch Davidians, led by David Koresh, a man who claimed to be the Messiah, came into fatal contact with the FBI and the Bureau of Alcohol, Tobacco and Firearms (ATF), once again over the alleged possession of illegal firearms. During the initial raid, four ATF agents and six members of the Branch Davidian church were killed. Fifty-one days later on April 19, in a televised event carried live around the world, the large, compoundlike home of the Branch Davidians erupted into flames as federal agents tried to tear gas the building and evacuate its inhabitants. In the fiery "apocalypse," 74 adults, including David Koresh, and 21 children died.

Militia leaders blamed both tragedies on overzealous federal law enforcement agencies. It was the logical outcome of a government that was hell-bent on disarming Americans at all costs. Ruby Ridge and Waco had become rallying cries for a new subculture of Americans who were losing patience with their government and were taking up arms and joining paramilitary organizations such as the militias. The Oklahoma City bombing, occurring on April 19, 1995, the second anniversary of the Waco fire, was one of the more spectacular examples of this domestic paranoia. Seething with apocalyptic notions, the antigovernment fear and anger continues to appear and sometimes to explode into our daily lives. The beliefs and actions displayed by the terrorists in Oklahoma City demonstrate how the millennial myth is being used as an ideology for violent resistance and "counterattack" by some members of the survivalist right.

In various ways the shoot-out at Ruby Ridge, the Waco incident, and the Oklahoma City bombing all bear witness to the power of the ever-evolving millennial myth in the United States. Indeed, the bombing in Oklahoma City has more in common with the Branch Davidian tragedy than with extremist fears of government intrusion on the (gun) rights of private citizens. Like the message of the messianic figure of David Koresh (who, along with his followers, also dealt in weapons and practiced survivalism), the extremism of the Oklahoma City bombers was motivated by delusions of societal collapse and great cosmic battles between the "forces of good" (themselves) and the "forces of evil": In both cases that evil was embodied in the U.S. government. The Oklahoma City bombers acted on those beliefs in a kind of self-fulfilling prophecy.

In the millennialism of the "survivalist right"—the movement that spawned Timothy McVeigh and his comrades—evil comes in various guises: the government, especially the IRS, the FBI, and the ATF; the media; Jews; and the greatly feared new world order. The Oklahoma City bombing also closely resembles the Tokyo subway gassing that killed 12 people and sickened more than 5,000 others in the March 20, 1995, attack, which occurred one month before the Oklahoma City incident. That domestic terrorist incident has been linked to self-proclaimed messiah Shoko Asahara and his apocalyptic Aum Shinrikyo (Sublime Truth), who also view themselves in conflict with an evil, tyrannical government and world. The existence of Aum Shinrikyo also points to the global reach of the millennial myth.

While we have yet to see the depths of Timothy McVeigh's and his colleagues' religious and ideological beliefs, we have much evidence from the subculture of survivalism in which both McVeigh and Nichols participated to see the connection to a white supremacist form of millennialism. One of the strongest connections can be found in the way millennial movements often demonize other peoples or institutions, committing murder and genocide in the name of religion and ideology, in order to fulfill their prophecies. In this way, religion and apocalyptic prophecy were used by the Catholic Church and the monarchies of medieval Europe to justify the Crusades and legitimize the actions of European crusaders against non-Christian "heathens" in the European attempt to "recapture" the Holy Land.

Behind America's "manifest destiny" also lay the millennial myth, which sanctioned the mid-nineteenth-century imperialistic expansion of the United States at the expense of Native American land, culture, and lives. While not especially religious, Hitler also saw the value of the apocalyptic script and employed it to demonize certain groups such as the Jews and to justify their extermination and his imperialistic designs. The millennial myth exists within the ideology of the survivalist movement as well. On one level survivalism has become home to a belief system imbued with racist, anti-Semitic, and apocalyptic notions—a new (secular) religion for white supremacy.

In the 1980s the demonizing of African Americans and Jews reasserted itself in the merging of millennial and survivalist tendencies. Spurred by the farm crisis, massive factory layoffs, and fears of declining American power in the world, right-wing survivalist groups and communities began to develop across the rural areas of the country. Spouting the rhetoric of the Jewish world conspiracy as the root of America's problems, some of these groups became linked to paramilitary and survivalist training centers and to vigilantes, the Ku Klux Klan, the Aryan Nations, and the militia movement. With the rise of the survivalist right and the bombing in Oklahoma City, we are witnessing the violent results of a white supremacist, apocalyptic subculture now engaging in confrontational actions.

The plan for those actions and, it seems, for the bombing in Oklahoma City is contained in the novel *The Turner Diaries*, written in 1978 by William Pierce, a member of the neo-Nazi National Alliance (see Chapter 5). The story begins in 1991, when white supremacist survivalists start a guerrilla war against ZOG (the Zionist Occupation Government, which rules in Washington). In an attempt to overthrow the government, the rebellious survivalists assassinate federal officials, lawmen, and politicians; purge the country of Jews and minorities; and destroy Israel with the nuclear arsenal inherited from ZOG. If this sounds unbelievable, consider that federal authorities believe that certain pieces of the bombers' plan (such as the target, dates, and timing) accord so closely to material in *The Turner Diaries* that the book may have provided both motive and method in the bombing of the federal building in Oklahoma City.

Today millennial expressions are found not only in revitalized messianic movements like the Church Universal and Triumphant, the Branch Davidians, and the Aum Shinrikyo, but also in groups that appear, at least on the surface, not to be religious in orientation, like *Soldier of Fortune* magazine and the paramilitary "militia movement." At its margins, survivalism is a haven for white supremacists, antigovernment zealots, and apocalyptic cults—sometimes all rolled into one. Combining survivalism with apocalypticism, as doomsayers take up arms, is an increasingly popular and combustible mix.

*I Love My Country, But I Hate My Government* (BUMPER STICKER, *SOLDIER OF FORTUNE* CONVENTION, LAS VEGAS, SEPTEMBER 1995)

The twentieth anniversary of *Soldier of Fortune* magazine was held at the Sands Hotel and Casino, Las Vegas, in late September 1995. The temper of the *SOF* Convention seemed quieter than the 1990 convention, held during the Persian Gulf War, but it also seemed angry and bitter. The April 19 Oklahoma City bombing had brought an intense focus on the militia movement and related organizations like *Soldier of Fortune*. A congressional hearing was underway regarding possible FBI abuses in the 1992 shoot-out at Ruby Ridge. And there was Waco; the April 1993 tragedy is viewed by many on the survivalist right, including many at the *SOF* Convention, as a vicious and murderous attack on a small, independent American church by fascist law enforcement forces of the American government.

For the past 20 years it was tyrants like Muammar Gadhafi, the Ayatollah Khomeini, Saddam Hussein, and the former Soviet Union that infected the world, according to *Soldier of Fortune* magazine. But today world-class tyrants are in short supply, apparently, so *SOF* has turned its sights increasingly inward—at the U.S. government, federal law enforcement agencies, and especially the FBI and the ATF. Distrust, anger, and fear of the government was evident throughout the convention. In every conventioneer's packet was a warning from publisher Brown that "the ATF and the Clinton Administration are bitterly and dangerously hostile to the law-abiding gun owners of this country. At Waco and elsewhere they have demonstrated an entire lack of concern for legality and the Constitutional rights of the ordinary citizen." Brown fears that the *SOF* Convention may be seen by government as an ideal setting for a sting or entrapment. He admonished conventioneers to "Always, always, always keep in mind that the person with whom you are talking may be an employee of a Federal or other law-enforcement agency. You don't have to explain what you didn't say. Just because you're paranoid doesn't mean that they aren't plotting against you"[20] (Figure 1.9).

A seminar called "The Militarization of Law Enforcement" focused on a possible military takeover of law enforcement agencies. *SOF* reporter James L. Pate (who briefly negotiated with the anti-government Montana Freemen during the spring 1996 standoff) pointed to the collapse of the Soviet Union and America's large, expensive, and outdated military as the root of the problem. A defense lawyer for the Branch Davidians showed photographs taken at Waco ("never seen by the public") that purported to show military vehicles methodically tearing down the Branch Davidian compound in a "seek-and-destroy" military mission. Panelists concluded that at Ruby Ridge, Waco, and elsewhere, paramilitary police groups have routinely used military tactics to handle domestic crime situations with disastrous results. Said one member of the audience, "Our law enforcement agencies have turned on the

FIGURE 1.9. Book exhibit, *SOF* Convention and Exposition, Sands Hotel and Casino, September/October 1995.

American people. Along with gun control this is the next step in the emergence of an American police state."

At a seminar entitled "Regaining the Pioneer Spirit," survivalist and radio talk show host Bob Speer said that "the U.S. government has become the new Evil Empire, and it looks to me like the entire social order is going to unravel." He had taken on the "ministry" of talk radio to teach survival skills and values. Called "The Preparedness Hour," Speer's radio show is carried on the USA Patriot Network. At the exposition center, the Militia of Montana (MOM) had an exhibit featuring an extensive book, pamphlet, and video library. Books included *The New World Order: Takeover America, Blueprint for Survival,* and *Citizen Soldier.* Available videos included *The Countdown Has Begun, The True Story of Waco,* and

*Millennium 2,000.* There were Militia of Montana baseball caps with the signature "MOM—the Mother of all Militias." And there were MOM T-shirts—one stated simply, "Angry White Guy." Bumper stickers proclaimed, "Don't Let Clinton Gore Your Gun Rights," "I Love My Country, but I Hate my Government," and "The U.N.—Peace through Terror."

The Oklahoma City bombing, *Soldier of Fortune* magazine, and the Church Universal and Triumphant are all examples of an apocalyptic undercurrent that has surfaced in the United States and the world in the final decades of the twentieth century. Throughout the 1980s a "pop apocalypticism" permeated American culture in seemingly disparate trends such as survivalism, New Age beliefs, religious cults, Christian rock bands, and cyber-punk, postapocalyptic films like the Mad Max trilogy, starring Mel Gibson as the "road warrior," who must fight sadistic punk motorcycle gangs to survive a future world devastated by nuclear war. Even George Bush employed, whether knowing or not, apocalyptic language to frame the Persian Gulf War as an effort to build and preserve a "new world order." This fascination with the end times filters through American society in increasingly violent ways as we approach the year 2000 and the next millennium.

A number of factors are converging to create a resurgence of millennial activity in the United States; these include rapid social change both here and abroad, the relative economic decline of the United States, the ending of an age or an era (the end of Soviet communism, a perceived end of the American era, and, foremost, the end of the twentieth century). These kinds of social, economic, political, and even numerological changes have always driven the millennial myth.

What is unusual about contemporary forms of apocalyptic activity are the multiple and often contradictory forms they take. Millennial expressions are found not only among revitalized messianic cults like the Church Universal and Triumphant and the Branch Davidians, but in unusual secular (or seemingly nonreligious) practices as well, such as the militia movement, survivalism, or among a group of planetary colonizers called the Synergetic Civilization, who plan to colonize the Moon or Mars in the near future as the earth's ecosystem decays. For these groups the apocalypse will most likely be man-made—brought about by social and economic collapse, environmental degradation, or civil or nuclear war. Salvation may not be in the hands of a savior but in the preparations of the individual.

Secular forms of the millennial myth differ from the classic forms because they lack supernatural elements, most importantly the belief that the Apocalypse will be engineered by God and that the millennium will be ushered in by the Second Coming of Christ. Instead, secular millennialists build an organization of ideology, politics, and an alternative plan for society. However, secularists can adopt religious imagery and ideology in the way *Soldier of Fortune* magazine does. On the other hand, religious millenarian movements can and do adopt secular ideas. Some Christian fundamentalists confidently predict the millennium will be ushered in by nuclear war, economic collapse, environmental destruction, or a combination of them all, "if that's God's will."

In an important book on millenarian movements entitled *Primitive Rebels* (1959), historian Eric Hobsbawn suggested that between the "pure," or classical, millenarian movement and the more secular kind, "all manner of intermediate positions are possible."[21] This appears to be the case in American culture today, where elements from the classical apocalyptic tradition merge with modern and secular ones, producing a strange array of millennial phenomena. The Branch Davidians can be viewed in this way—as Christian survivalists who stockpiled food and weapons in anticipation of the end times.

As the millennial myth continues to evolve, certain groups come to interpret current events through the lens of cultural myth. In the past, millenarian movements often arose during periods of intense social change, coinciding with the end of an era, as happened in the United States between 1830 and 1850 during the "Age of Reform," which saw the eruption of numerous millenarian groups, including the Shakers, the Oneida, and Christian Scientists, in response to the secularizing influences of the Industrial Revolution and the transformation of the agricultural way of life. In many ways contemporary expressions of the millennial myth reflect the major social changes that the world is currently undergoing. The United States and much of the world do seem to be at a turning point as old nations crumble and new ones arise from their ashes, as a global economy evolves and the physical and cultural borders that separate nations erode, and as the destructive power of modern warfare and environmental pollution continue to threaten life on the planet. The fact that all this is occurring with the end of one numerical millennium and the beginning of another may be only coincidence, but it helps to fulfill the apocalyptic prophecy that the old world is in decline and a new world order is emerging.

While the millennium may be an arbitrary mark on the calender, religiously significant only to a narrow band of Christians who—in the absence of any hard biblical evidence—are pinning the Second Coming of Christ to the end of the second millennium, the date is nonetheless pregnant with historical symbolism and mythical power. Some have made the argument that the next millennium does not even begin until 2001, so there is no real millennial significance to the year 2000. While they too may be right, it makes little difference to everyone else, millennialist or not, who are enthralled with the "great event"—2000 is a big round number, teeming with prophetic and apocalyptic significance for the beginning of a new age.

Indeed, the world is different now. It is only since World War II that the possibility of world annihilation, whether through nuclear war or environmental pollution, "has come to pass." Both the destructive potential of world-scale social problems and the mass communicability of their images are factors prompting the millennium rage. Disasters, crime, economic decline, globalization, war, terrorism, pollution, AIDS, famine, earthquakes, and "twisters" have become the common fare of television news, film drama, and popular literature, not to mention social movements. They are the "tribulations" and "plagues" of the late twentieth century. Apocalyptic visions are all too real at the end of the twentieth century, and one does not have to be on the millennial fringe to appreciate them. Massive disasters are no longer solely natural but are often manmade; they are no longer bound to a single town or locality but are universal in scope.

Many say we live in a period of globalization, where the world is becoming a smaller place. The walls that used to separate us have fallen and our global interactions have increased manifold. We swim in a sea of information, provided by the "knowledge industries," connected to us by the "global superhighway" of the Internet and Worldwide Web. Globalization also means that, at the same time the world is becoming smaller, it is also becoming more diverse, marked by more differences, more changes, more "multiculturalism."[22] These changes are reflected in social problems such as illegal immigration, hate crimes, distrust in government, and fear of the future.

Politically, the world is changing too. Conflicts between nations affect more than those nations. Because economies and cultures have become more tightly linked, conflicts are more widely felt. But that is no assurance to working things out. Those who fear some organized new world government, as many in the survivalist movement do, should look to Bosnia and the conflict in the former Yugoslavia to see that such a world government is unlikely. Still, all of this change increases the anxiety of many people over the future of their families, their nation, and the world. The world moves so fast and seems so chaotic. People's lives are so filled with work, family, and responsibilities that they seldom see the big picture, if there even is one. The millennial myth, however, provides the big picture through a mythology derived from the Bible that is familiar to many. It provides an explanation and tells the story of our trials and tribulations and the future.

This book is about those groups, paramilitary and apocalyptic, that make up the subculture of survivalism. It is also about their beliefs and their practices, which are steeped in doomsday predictions and apocalyptic symbolism. Survivalism can be viewed as a modern but fractured expression of the millennial myth because it expresses some (but not all) of its central features. These fractured expressions also become altered in form and meaning, reflecting the temper of the times and the nature and context of their expression. Through the symbolic and thematic content of survivalist expressions, threads of the classical millennial myth become rearranged into modern configurations.

This apocalyptic view, especially the American version, I call the millennial myth, though it derives from ancient Hebrew and Christian apocalyptic prophecies concerning the ultimate destiny of the world and the cosmic cataclysm in which God destroys the ruling powers of evil and raises the righteous to life in a messianic kingdom that will last for 1,000 years—the prophesied millennium. Primary elements of the myth, such as tribulation, Babylon, Armageddon, the Messiah, and millennium, are powerful and flexible religious symbols that adapt easily, although unevenly, to changing social and cultural conditions (see Chapter 2). Today, as in the past, we are witnessing a revitalization of the millennial myth—this time, as our modern culture interprets it. From the Branch Davidians to *Soldier of Fortune* magazine to the militia movement, numerous groups of diverse interests and backgrounds have organized around the Apocalypse.

For millennialists the year 2000 looms, and we are already witnessing an increase in apocalyptic activity. There are those who suggest that classical myths are self-fulfilling. As were David Koresh and the Branch Davidians, who helped engineer their own apocalypse, an educated guess would suggest that the bombers in Oklahoma City were acting on their interpretation of the myth, thereby justifying their beliefs and practices. Clearly, we can no longer ignore such marginal expressions of the millennial myth.

# Chapter 2

# Apocalypse

## A History of the End of the World

*This is the blood of the new testament, which is shed for many . . . I will drink no more of the fruit of the vine, until that day I drink it new in the kingdom of God.*

MARK 11:24–25, KJV

*The Revelation of Jesus Christ, which God gave unto him, to show unto his servants things which must shortly come to pass; and he sent and signified it by his angel unto his servant John.*

REV. 1:1, KJV

On the afternoon of the first day of the week following his crucifixion, Jesus of Nazareth, having risen from death that morning, appears to his 11 apostles in a house in Jerusalem, just as they are discussing the rumors of Jesus' resurrection. After chastising them for their doubt, he says to them, "Go ye into all the world and preach the gospel to every living creature" (Mark 16:15). In the following decades, disciples of the Messiah took to heart their teacher's final words, and went forth into the world to preach the Gospel, or "good news," to all nations. Facing persecution, arrest, imprisonment, and often execution, the early Christians faced tremendous obstacles as they spread out across the Middle East, further east to Asia, and west to Europe, spreading "the word," making converts, and building the early church based on the New Covenant, or New Testament, introduced by Jesus at the Last Supper (Mark 14:22–25; Matt. 26:26–29). The New Covenant was a contract between God and believers of all nations who embraced the revelations made by his son Jesus Christ. The covenant superseded the old Mosaic covenant made between God and Moses in which the Jews would be the "chosen people."

Sometime around the year 95, during the reign of the brutal Roman Emperor Titus Flavius Domitianus (81–96), a Christian by the name of John was arrested for preaching the beliefs of the heretical sect called Christianity and for publicly proclaiming Christ as King and refusing to worship the deified emperor. John was exiled to the Greek island of Patmos in the Aegean Sea, northeast of Crete. With an area of 16 square miles, bordering Turkey and Asia Minor, Patmos was a place for criminals and other threats to the Roman Empire, including early Christians. One day while "in the Spirit of the Lord's day," presumably the Sabbath, John heard "a great voice as a trumpet, saying 'I am the Alpha and the Omega, the first and last: and what thou seest, write in a book, and send it unto the seven churches which are in Asia'" (Rev. 1:10–11). Revelation is the book based on the visions that engulfed John, as revealed by "one like unto the Son of God" (Rev. 1:13).

In composing this remarkable literary work, John borrowed many of his primary symbols, images, and theology from numerous books of Hebrew scripture (Old Testament), including Daniel, Ezekiel, Joel, Zechariah, and Jeremiah. In his visions John saw the Messiah appearing amid a series of catastrophic events culminating in the near success of the Antichrist, the evil false prophet who, during the final days, rises in leadership to deceive the world. The Messiah destroys the Antichrist, brings redemption for the chosen, and establishes a new Heaven and a new earth. Revelation presents the Roman persecutions of Christians as the beginning of a universal war between the forces of good and evil.

While a great number of volumes have interpreted the vast complexities of Revelation, some of the more outstanding visions and striking symbols can be summarized under the following themes: tribulation and the Four Horsemen of the Apocalypse; the demonic dragons, beasts, and the Antichrist; the corrupt Babylon; the coming of a Messiah; the saints and heavenly hosts; the Battle of Armageddon; the Final Judgment; and the millennium. Throughout Revelation, John employs the number seven both as an organizational device and to denote a particular series of visions or symbols in the story: For example, the seven seals, the seven visions of the dragons' worldly rule, the seven visions of Babylon's fall, the seven bowls of divine anger, and the seven visions of the end of Satan's power.[1]

In the vision of the seven seals, John is shown "a Lamb, as it had been slain" who is the only one worthy to open the seven seals. Many Christians have seen in the slain Lamb one of the several incarnations that Jesus embodied in Revelation. The Lamb begins to open the seven sealed scrolls, and as each scroll is broken, disasters and tribulations of famine, disease, earthquakes, and war begin to occur on earth (Rev. 6:1–8:6). Tribulation refers to the plagues and "bitter sorrows" that mark the decay of the world and the onset of the Apocalypse (Rev. 1:9, 2:9–10, 22, 7:14). They are the "signs of the times," which foreshadow the end of human history and reveal the terrible disasters and mass destruction to be unleashed upon the earth.

Opening the first four seals unleashes the Four Horsemen of the Apocalypse, often defined as war, revolution, famine, and death (Rev. 6:2–8). Breaking the fifth seal reveals Christian martyrs crying out from their graves for vengeance (Rev. 6:9–11). The sixth seal discloses earthquakes and other natural disasters that wrack the earth, humbling all of nature to God's power (Rev. 6:12–17). Before the opening of the seventh sealed scroll, 144,000 spiritual Israelites and a "vast throng" are taken up to Heaven in an event later Christians refer to as the "rapture" (Rev. 7:1–17). The breaking of the seventh seal introduces the vision of seven trumpets, in which additional plagues beset the earth (Rev. 8:7–11:19).

Revelation is also populated by terrible demons, including the beast, or Antichrist, and the dragon—different personifications of Satan. Of particular interest is the "great red dragon, having seven heads and ten horns, and seven crowns upon his heads" (a composite of apocalyptic beasts) who persecutes a pregnant women dressed in the sun, the moon, and the stars (Rev. 12:1–17). Identified as Satan, the "serpent of old" (Rev. 12:9, Gen. 3:1, 14–15), the red dragon is a Judeo-Christian embodiment of the ancient Mesopotamian myth concerning Tiamat, the monster of chaos. As Marduk, the Mesopotamian creator-god, vanquishes Tiamat and brings order to the universe, so the Archangel Michael, the traditional spirit prince of Israel (Dan. 11:1), defeats the dragon, thus allowing a new cosmic order to appear (Rev. 12:9). The victim of the dragon's attack, a woman who gives birth to a male child destined to rule "all nations," apparently represents heavenly Israel, as well as Jews and Christians on earth.

Two distinct beasts appear in Revelation. The beast that rises up out of the sea, "like unto a leopard" with "the feet of a bear" and "the mouth of a lion," probably symbolizes Rome, the earthly focus of Satan's power (Rev. 13:1–2). The two-horned beast that comes up out of the earth and "spake as a Dragon" may represent the Roman priesthood that helped to enforce emperor worship (Rev. 13:11–17). The second beast, who causes those on earth to worship the first beast, is mysteriously identified by the "number of the beast" (666), signifying a man's name, and now commonly thought to stand for Nero Caesar, whose name in Hebrew letters has the numerical value of 666 (Rev. 13:18). John may also be referring to a popular first-century legend that Nero was still alive and would return from the east heading a conquering army.

The next set of visions (Rev. 17:1–19:10) predict the fall of the great harlot and Babylon, both symbolizing Rome. The metaphor of Babylon is twofold: She is the harlot who prostitutes her body and soul for earthly pleasures, but in the end will be punished, just like the ancient city of Babylon, depicted in Revelation as a rich, cosmopolitan city that had become sinful and had fallen away from God. Babylon was used by the early church as a symbol of Rome, and the Roman emperor was seen as the Antichrist. The destruction of a "fallen away" people is an important theme in the Hebrew and Christian Bibles. Interestingly, the myth of this destruction is most pronounced at the beginning of the Hebrew canon (Genesis) and at the end of the Christian canon (Revelation). In Genesis, the supernatural destruction of the world is told in the story of Noah and the flood, and in the destruction of Sodom, Gomorrah, Babylon, and other "wicked" cities. In Revelation the destruction of the "harlot" Babylon is the metaphor for the final destruction of the world that ushers in the millennium (Rev. 14.8, 16.19, 18.2, 10.21).

After promising salvation for those who worship the Lamb and damnation for those who worship the beast (Rev. 19:11–21:8), John reviews the horrors destined to afflict the earth before the climactic battle of Armageddon (Rev. 15:1–16:16). Armageddon expresses the militaristic and moral imagery of great battles and a final war between the forces of Christ and those of Satan. In Revelation (16:16), Armageddon is also the site where the cosmic battle occurs. While the most generally accepted location of Armageddon (or Har-Megiddon) is in Israel, another explanation finds in the word a survival of a Mesopotamian place-name where the gods of ancient Babylon were believed to have defeated the dragon Tiamat and other evil spirits in Mesopotamian legend. Metaphorically, Armageddon is the site of the ultimate war between the forces of good and evil, and it is the conflict itself, both the military and ideological battles, that will usher in the end times.

A Christlike figure appears throughout Revelation, though in different guises. Early on he reveals himself as the angel who first appears to John, clothed in "a golden girdle" with his hair "as white as wool" and his "eyes . . . as a flame of fire" (Rev. 1:13–14). It is he who tells John to write in a book the revelation he is about to witness and to send it to the seven leading Christian churches in Asia Minor. A short time later, John is shown "a Lamb as it had been slain, having seven horns and seven eyes, which are the seven spirits of God sent forth into all the earth" (Rev. 5:6). The Lamb stands in the midst of "four and twenty Elders," as John enters through the door to Heaven (Rev. 4:1–4). A short time later the Lamb opens the seven seals for John (Revelation, 6, 7, 8). Still later, the Christ figure becomes the Messiah, or savior, transformed into the rider called "Faithful and True," sitting upon a white horse leading the armies of Heaven at his own Second Coming. He arrives just as Satan and his army are about to annihilate the world. Leading his crusaders in the final battle of Armageddon, the Messiah destroys the Antichrist and the dragon, throwing them into the pit for 1,000 years (Rev. 19:11–21:8). He also brings redemption for the chosen and resurrection for the saints, and he restores the earth's former beauty, instituting the millennium (Rev. 20:2–7).

The Christ, or Messiah, figure refers to the Second Coming of Christ. Also called messianism, the Second Coming includes the notion of Final Judgment and salvation—the belief that a savior will bring redemption for the chosen and damnation for the wicked. This Christ of Revelation is quite different from the Christ of the Gospels. More like the God of Genesis in his harshness and unforgiving nature, he is both savior and executioner as he lays out the rules for who will survive into the millennium. In one last anticlimactic moment following the millennium, Satan is released for a short time to deceive the nations until his final annihilation, at which time there occurs the final resurrection and judgment of all souls and the creation of a "new heaven and a new earth, from which all pain and sorrow are to be excluded" (Rev. 21:1). Following a vision of a celestial Jerusalem, described metaphorically as a city of gold and jewels (Rev. 21:9–27), John hears Christ inviting all to drink "the waters of life" (Rev. 22:1–17).

In the Old Testament Book of Daniel, the prophet Daniel is given a similar series of visions, interpreted for him by the Archangel Gabriel and revealing the events that would culminate in the end of the world. John borrowed a great deal of these symbols and images to fill out the tale of Revelation. As the biblical scholar Stephen L. Harris has noted, while Gabriel told Daniel to seal up his visions until the time of the end, which was not specified (Dan. 12:4), John is instructed to leave his scrolls unsealed because "the hour of fulfillment is near" (Rev. 1:3). John seems to expect that his vision of apocalypse will be realized momentarily. This is the way apocalyptic movements have continued to operate.[2]

The Revelation of John has become the most famous version of the millennial myth. Also called the Apocalypse—which in Greek means "unveiling"—Revelation is the final chapter in the Christian Bible (New Testament, or New Covenant) and one of its most enduring and influential legacies. Classical examples of the millennial myth, like Revelation, derive from Hebrew and Christian apocalyptic writings from 200 B.C. to A.D. 150. Although there is a history of disagreement over which literature truly represents the genre, most contemporary scholars accept those books deemed authoritative as Holy Scripture by believers (i.e., canon) as the most reliably apocalyptic. These include the Book of Daniel, the Epistles to the Thessalonians, the "Little Apocalypse" of the synoptic Gospels, and the "Great Apocalypse," or Revelation of John.[3] Numerous other texts—some canonical, some not—also are apocalyptic in whole or in part. What makes these texts apocalyptic is that they are prophecies about the final events leading up to and including the end of the world.

Most reputable scholars do not believe that John of Patmos was Jesus' "beloved disciple" John, the presumed author of the Fourth Gospel. John the Elder, a prominent church leader who lived in the Aegean seaport town of Ephesus in Asia Minor about A.D.100, has also been identified as the apocalyptist. Other leading Christians by the name of John have also been considered. While all are subject to debate, it is generally agreed that John's supernatural visions and the remarkable story he penned—The Revelation to Saint John the Divine—are perhaps the greatest in a long line of end times prophecies dating back more 2,000 years before Christ. The apocalyptic thread is woven into the mythologies of Sumerian, Mesopotamian, and other ancient Middle Eastern civilizations and cultures, including that of the Jews. In the Babylonian *Epic of Gilgamesh*, for example, can be found one of the earliest tales of the supernatural destruction of the world. Inscribed on tablets uncovered in 1872 by British archaeologists excavating a site at Nineveh, one of the buried cities of Mesopotamia, the *Epic of Gilgamesh* includes the fantastic story of a great flood caused by Enlil, the god of wisdom. With remarkable parallels to the story of Noah's ark in Genesis, Utnapishtim, an ancestor of the ancient Mesopotamian hero Gilgamesh, is told by Ea to build an ark (a box-shaped boat) to preserve the lives of his family from the coming flood. With his family, servants, and various animals, Utnapishtim survived the seven-day flood and replanted the seeds of his people in the newly cleansed land.[4]

Over the centuries, visions of the apocalypse have continued to appear to countless individuals and groups, especially since the time of Jesus Christ. The revelation to John at Patmos represents the quintessential millennial myth: a cosmology or worldview explaining the birth, life, death, and rebirth of a people and their world. All myths are symbolic forms of belief that act as metaphors for real human events. Myths provide cosmologies for believers—metaphysical explanations for the "way of the world." However, myths are more than mere abstractions with no basis in reality. In fact, they are based on the events of history and of everyday life. Prophetic myths explain the present and predict the future so well because they are drawing on the past, and on events that have already occurred. As long as the past repeats itself, in whatever ways, myths will provide guidance for believers and inspire some to action. Myths are relevant to everyday life, and they provide a context in which to interpret current events and give meaning and direction to people's lives. Myths are not stagnant legends; they are dynamic in their nature and can have a force over people.[5] That was the purpose of Revelation 2,000 years ago—to inspire faith and give direction to the faithful in the darkest of times—and that is its purpose today.

Some scholars see myth in a positive light: as a way to make sense of the senseless, as a meaningful metaphor for those alienated or confused by society or their position in it, and as a rallying point for social change or even revolution.[6] But myth can be viewed critically as well, especially when it is used for ideological control or delusional practice that may serve the interests of an oppressive individual, controlling group, or dominant culture. For example, myth may obscure or cushion reality and teach people to accept a bad situation uncritically.[7] Either way, myths can be viewed as repositories of ideology. The significance of the millennial myth lies in its enduring and spectacular ability to interpret and explain the meaning(s) of life. The millennial myth is like a floating framework for explaining the big picture. It exists on a transcendental plane where the experience of the sacred gives birth to the idea that there are absolute values that guide human beings and give meaning to human life and all of history.

Throughout the history of the Christian Church the millennial myth has played a considerable role, even when the great theologians have opposed it. By the second and third centuries, Christianity had split into two separate religions. The official Christianity was preached from pulpits and kept pure by popes, bishops, and priests. It was concerned with canonical authority, the minutia of liturgy (the body of rites prescribed by the church for public worship), and control of the populace. The popular Christianity was swept along by the fervor of the masses, blending official church dogma with beliefs drawn from their own experiences and lives, much of it based in long-standing pre-Christian pagan practices. This split would widen in the later Middle Ages, as oppressed peoples formed rebellious movements that would identify nearly every great authority or opponent—including the popes and the hierarchy of the Catholic Church—as the Antichrist.

Apocalyptic thought has permeated the theologies of many sects and cults in the Hebrew and Christian tradition and has accompanied the development of numerous rebellions, revolutions, and utopian communities. For most lay people Revelation continued to be the beacon of millennial light, especially its fantastic images of horror and evil, resurrection, and everlasting life. Indeed, death and resurrection make up the core of Christian eschatology, the branch of theology dealing with the final events in the history of humankind. As historian Michael Grant insists, "every thought and saying of Jesus directed and subordinated to one single thing . . . the realization of the Kingdom of God upon the earth."[8] In the first centuries after Christ, apocalyptic cults proliferated. Late second-century bishops such as Iranaeus of Lyons and theologians such as the Egyptian Origen vigorously preached the imminent demise of the world. Where Iranaeus believed that the chosen would be rewarded with a paradise on earth, Origen believed that the Christian's only hope is the hope of Heaven, not on this earth, but in the soul. For the paradise of "gold and precious stones," Origen substituted a kingdom of spirit.

Such apocalyptic beliefs, often contradictory, were handed down from generation to generation through the teachings of the religious hierarchy. There they mingled with the beliefs and experiences of the peasant and commoner, beliefs that were often steeped in a folk culture that might be quite different from official dogma and might include such practices as nature worship and pagan rituals. Such a diffusion and evolution of ideas produced an explosion of religiously inspired movements. Montanism, also known as the Cataphrygian Heresy and the "new prophecy," is one example of a heretical apocalyptic movement.

Founded by the prophet Montanus, who arose in the Christian Church in Phrygia, Asia Minor, in the second century A.D., Montanism flourished in the West, principally in Carthage under the leadership of the Latin church father Tertullian (c. 160–c. 230) in the third century A.D. According to legend, a Christian convert by the name of Montanus had appeared in the town of Ardabau in Phrygia around the year 156. He fell into a trance and began to prophesy under the influence of the Spirit. Two young women, Priscilla and Maximilla, joined Montanus and also began to prophesy. Engaging in deliberately induced states of ecstasy, Montanus and the women began to speak in strange tongues and utter words they claimed were the "spirit of truth."

The essential principle of Montanism was that the spirit of truth that Jesus had promised in the Gospel according to John was manifesting itself through Montanus and his prophetesses. They also believed that the heavenly Jerusalem was soon to descend upon the earth on a plain between the two villages of Pepuza and Tymion in Phrygia. Many Christian communities were abandoned as villagers followed the prophets to await the descent of the New Jerusalem. When it failed to appear, Montanism did not die. Instead, it grew and spread throughout Asia Minor where many towns were almost completely converted to Montanism. While Montanism originated within the church, it was later deemed heretical and a threat to church authority. Montanus and his followers were excommunicated and became a separate sect, though legislated against by the dominant church. Under Emperor Justinian I (reigned 527–565), Montanism was nearly destroyed, but it continued on and survived into the ninth century.[9]

Referred to as "millenarian movements" by historians and anthropologists, apocalyptic groups such as the Montanists tend to arise in periods of rapid social and cultural change, often creating friction with the dominant culture, as happened in the early Christian era.[10] In tracing the early history of Christian eschatology and its representations in medieval Europe, it becomes apparent that millennialism survived on the fringes of mainstream Christianity, breaking out with almost predictable regularity under the impact of social change and discontent. Millennial movements sought to cut through a seemingly hopeless situation with the promise and optimism of a utopian vision. Although their beliefs were often grounded in religion, the reality of their visions were reflected in their own experiences and in the sometimes momentous events that marked and changed their lives. It was obvious to most Christians in the first millennium that the Roman emperor was the Antichrist and the earthly incarnation of the whore Babylon that sat on the beast with the seven heads, which stood for the Roman Empire. But when the Roman Emperor Constantine (c. 280–337) converted to Christianity in the fourth century, it became difficult to see Rome as the personification of apocalyptic evil, and it was no longer heretical for Christians in the Empire to be loyal to the emperor and his armies. Constantine took a forceful role in reconciling the church with its feuding sects. Perhaps it was inevitable that some people would come to see Constantine as divinely appointed.

This role was created for him and popularized in the Sibylline Oracles, a collection of prophecies inspired by apocalyptic traditions handed down for over 1,000 years and based in the ancient Greek prophetess Sibyl. Sibyl, or Sibylla, was a prophetess of ancient Greek legend, depicted as a wise old woman who would enter into ecstatic frenzy and utter fantastic predictions. Until the fourth and fifth centuries B.C., Sibyl was referred to in the singular and was believed to have lived in Asia Minor. In the late fourth century B.C., many Sibyls began to appear at famous oracle centers and holy shrines throughout Asia Minor, especially in association with the Greek, and later Roman, god Apollo—the god of prophecy, poetry, and music. By the fourth century after Christ, a collection of apocalyptic prophecies descended from second century Jewish and Christian writers appeared in Greece and were reported to have been confirmed by a Sibyl. These became the Sibylline Oracles, and they accommodated the first Christian Emperor Constantine to their prophecies in the legend of "the Emperor of the Last Days."[11] The Emperor had a role, and so did the Empire. The oracles promised that the Christian Roman Empire would be everlasting. While often fueling rebellion and revolution, millennialism can be a stabilizing force as well, and may serve to secure and make legitimate the current social order and its power structure.

*Kill them all! God will recognize his own.* (ARNAUD-AMALRIC, PAPAL COMMANDER AND RULING ABBOT TO THE CISTERCIANS)[12]

In the summer of 1209, during the birth of the French Inquisition and the Albigensian Crusade, a skirmish between French crusaders in search of heretics and a crowd of hostile residents of the southern city of Béziers erupted into a massacre of the entire community. Arnaud-Amalric, the papal commander on the scene and ruling abbot to an austere Benedictine monastic order called the Cistercians, was greatly impressed with the crusading spirit of his soldiers. As one contemporary cleric noted, these soldiers had no fear of death and killed and massacred everyone they encountered. According to legend, when asked by new recruits, "Lord, what shall we do? We cannot distinguish the good from the wicked," Arnaud-Amalric replied, "Kill them all! God will recognize his own." At one point crowds of men, women, and children barricaded themselves in the town's church to pray and sing requiem hymns for the dead and dying. The crusaders set fire to the church and watched as all who took refuge inside were incinerated in the inferno. Arnaud-Amaric's famous words illustrated the whole spirit of the campaign and became what Otto Friedrich has called "a thoroughly admirable statement of Christian faith."[13]

The Crusades generally refer to the organized expeditions and battles waged by western European kingdoms against the Muslim powers beginning in 1095. Their main purpose was to take possession or maintain control over the holy city of Jerusalem and other sacred lands and shrines associated with the earthly life of Jesus Christ. Between the late eleventh century, when the first crusade began, and 1291, when the last Christians were finally expelled from Syria, historians have counted eight major expeditions.[14] Many additional, though smaller, expeditions continued into the next century, largely to win back lands lost by Christian crusaders, and sometimes in quixotic adventures in search of the Holy Grail, the Ark of the Covenant, or other sacred relics. The 200-year period of the Crusades was also a time of significant social, economic, and institutional change in western Europe. In turn, each of the Crusades reflected these changes, as well as the particular conditions prevailing in their regions and cultures.

Politically, western Europe in the eleventh century comprised several feudal kingdoms. At the end of the tenth century Europe was beginning to feel the impact of an exploding population that would continue to grow well into the thirteenth century. Simultaneously, an economic revival was in full swing. Forests were being cleared, frontiers opened or pushed forward, markets organized, and the Muslim control of the Mediterranean was challenged by Italian shipping. Nobles, bourgeoisie, and peasants were all seeking new outlets for trade and prosperity. Unless one married advantageously or entered the religious life, more people than ever before were disposed to adventure—organized or otherwise.

The eleventh century also witnessed a widespread religious revival, including mass pilgrimages to the holy lands or to holy shrines. Especially significant for the Crusades were the sweeping changes occurring in the ecclesiastical structure of the church, which enabled the popes, bishops, and other clerics to assume a more active role in politics and society. In the closing years of the eleventh century, western Europe was abounding with confidence and energy. It was also evident from early victories such as the Norman conquest of England that Europeans possessed the capacity to launch a major military undertaking. Why this energy was channeled into a holy war seems to be based in the religious and cultural turmoil in the West itself and in the widespread and rapid social changes that were going on—especially the religious and economic challenge from Islam, which by the eleventh century was moving south and west into Iran and north toward southern Europe from Africa.

The religion of the layperson in medieval Europe was probably unsophisticated in its interpretation of the Bible, which was generally reserved for the church. Ordinary people were probably moved more by the tales spun by local soothsayers and oracles and attributed natural disasters to supernatural forces. They were more likely to be impressed with celestial signs and wonders in the night sky and the divination of future events from homespun magic than by the increasingly detailed and distant ritual of the church, growing in complexity and power. At the same time, laypeople were not indifferent to the abuses of the church, especially those of the local clergy. There were many instances of townspeople agitating against the church by attacking clergy whom they regarded as unworthy or oppressive or by resisting church mandates and destroying church property. While the idea of a holy war against Muslim "infidels" in the holy land had been raised for over 100 years in Europe, Pope Urban II's call to arms in 1095 against Turkish expansion in Asia Minor that was threatening the West was the first officially sanctioned Crusade. Defending Christian society from the heathen and winning back the holy land were not only justifiable and pleasing to God, but also necessary because of the need to convert the "great unwashed" of the world in advance of the end of the world.[15]

Central to the popular religious belief system of the time was a widespread expectation—associated with both the Crusades and the pilgrimages to Jerusalem and the holy land—that the end of the world was imminent. While earlier historians thought the millennial upheaval was associated with the year 1000—the end of the first millennium—scholars now tend to discount so precise a date and suggest that Europeans maintained the millennial idea well into the eleventh century and after. Furthermore, in certain late eleventh-century portrayals of the end of the world, the "last emperor" (now associated with the "king of the Franks"—the final successor of Charlemagne) was to lead all the faithful to Jerusalem and there await the Second Coming of Christ. Jerusalem, as the symbol of the heavenly city, figured prominently in Western consciousness well beyond the first millennium. As the number of pilgrimages to Jerusalem increased in the eleventh century, Europeans were making economic inroads to the East but feeling the threats—economic, political, and religious—from the Muslim world. With religious clerics now more centrally involved in politics and war, the idea that they might be living during the final days helped to fuel the Crusades and organize the masses into nationalist fervor.

The Crusades represent a period of time in which the millennial myth served to galvanize the kingdoms of Europe in fervent pursuit of a holy war. Apocalyptic and millennial expressions now served to support the institutions of Christendom rather than challenge them. Clerical and monarchal powers played to the longings of the populace by fueling apocalyptic beliefs and directing them toward political and military ends. In this way the church and state monopolized the primary medium of communication and worldview so that millennialism became a means of ideological and social control. The merging of religious and secular aspirations underline the adaptive power of the millennial myth. Secular millennialism differs from the classical form mainly in its lack of supernatural elements. During the Crusades, for example, official church doctrine downplayed the Second Coming of Christ, probably so the crusaders would not be distracted from the great nationalist work at hand.

The focus on the Messiah, or messianism, is downplayed in many later millennial movements as well, especially when the myth becomes combined with the authority of the state, or political order, where more secular concerns take precedence over the spiritual. In addition, because the Messiah had failed to return so many times before, more practical applications of the myth were sought. For many believers, this problem was also solved by reasoning that Christ had already come, or would come prior to the millennium. (This is the doctrine of *premillennialism*. The belief that Christ would return after the millennium had been established on earth is sometimes referred to as *postmillennialism*.)

While the Crusades continued to occupy monarchs, popes, and peasants well into the thirteenth century, the medieval populace continued to be impressed with apocalyptic prophets, would-be messiahs, and end-of-the-world cults. Given the numerous social upheavals that befell much of Europe at the time, this is not too difficult to imagine. From the thirteenth through the sixteenth centuries, Christian Europe was feeling increasingly threatened from several sources. "Barbarian hordes" of Muslims advancing as far as Morocco and Spain continued to threaten Europe and Christianity. The crusading spirit of the church took a domestic turn in the hysteria and mass killings of "heretics," "witches," and other "pagans" directed by the powerful Catholic Inquisitions in Italy, France, and Spain. Perhaps most apocalyptic of all was the Black Death, a combination of bubonic and pneumonic plagues that is believed to have wiped out a quarter of the population of Europe, or about 25 million people, in the thirteenth century alone. By the end of the fiteenth century, however, a new day was dawning as a "new world" was being discovered.

*Therefore, let the King and Queen, our Princes, and their most happy kingdoms, and all the other provinces of Christendom render thanks to our Lord and Savior Jesus Christ, who has granted us so great a victory and such prosperity. Let processions be made and sacred feasts be held and the temples be adorned with festive boughs. Let Christ rejoice on earth, as he rejoices in heaven in the prospect of the salvation of the souls of so many nations hitherto lost. (*CHRISTOPHER COLUMBUS*)[16]*

Christopher Columbus first proposed to Ferdinand and Isabella, the Spanish monarchs of Aragon and Castile, the idea of funding and leading a crusade on Jerusalem to liberate it from the Muslims. In August of 1492, the day before he set sail on the first voyage, Columbus confided to his regal patrons that he would bring gold from the East Indies for that future epic venture. While he never realized that he had truly discovered a "new world," and not a new route to the Indies (India), he fervently believed that he was participating in and, indeed, helping to engineer events leading to the end of the world. Columbus viewed his own life in apocalyptic terms and believed his destiny was a sacred mission.

Just before his third voyage, of 1498–1500, Columbus wrote a will. It directed that part of the income from his estate each year should support efforts to liberate the Holy Sepulcher in Jerusalem, the alleged burial chamber of Jesus. While in Brazil, he declared the Orinoco River to be one of the Garden of Eden's four rivers. Back in Spain, Columbus wrote a scriptural commentary that was both mystical and apocalyptic. "He call it *The Book of Prophecies*, and in its introduction claimed that his decision to sail west came not from all his learning but from the Holy Spirit."[17]

At the time Columbus wrote, Muslims maintained control of the holy land. Columbus was convinced that one of the conditions for the end of the world was the Christian conquest of Jerusalem. To Ferdinand and Isabella he wrote, "Not unworthily nor without reason, Most splendid Rulers, do I assert that even greater things are reserved for you, when we read that Joachim the Calabrian Abbot predicted that the future ruler who would recover Mt. Sion would come from Spain."[18] As part of his plans to liberate Jerusalem from the Muslims, Columbus announced that David and Solomon had built the first Temple from stones quarried in Panama. With the discovery of Solomon's legendary mines, he could rebuild the Temple with the original stone.

In 1501 Columbus announced that he himself was the Messiah prophesied by Joachim, a twelfth-century Italian mystic and apocalyptist. Columbus believed his discovery of a direct route to the East Indies (which, of course, it wasn't) was the climax of the 15 centuries since Christ. The next climax in history would be the last crusade to lead the Christian armies and reclaim Jerusalem in preparation for the Second Coming. Columbus allowed 155 years for all of humankind to be converted to Christianity, then the world would end.

The picture of Columbus that is now commonly understood by historians is that of a religious visionary, strongly influenced by centuries of Hebrew and Christian apocalypticism, who, as Bernard McGinn writes, "thought that his own divinely inspired mission to open up a new path to Asia . . . would herald an age of universal conversion that would precede the End of the World."[19] The start of the sixteenth century marks an important turning point in the apocalyptic tradition: the diffusion of the millennial myth to the American continent. Columbus was perhaps the first European to interpret the discovery of the New World in the light of a millennial vision of the dawn of a more perfect age.

By the end of its first thousand years, Christianity was confined to a small part of southern Europe and northern Africa. In the Gospel of Mark, Jesus instructs his apostles following his resurrection to "go into all the world and preach the Gospel to all living creatures" (Mark 16:15). For crusading missionaries, soldiers, and explorers like Columbus, Revelation (9:7) provided the inspiration. At the breaking of the sixth seal, John saw the 144,000 saints taken up from among the tribes of Israel. He then saw a "great multitude," clothed in white robes from "all nations and kindreds, peoples and tongues." For this much larger group to be saved they had to be converted first. The idea provided a logical and theological rationale for the Crusades and a force easily tapped. The "Age of Discovery"—the four centuries from 1100 to 1500, when Europeans began to systematically explore the world—was spectacular for the development and diffusion of European and Christian culture and control.

*For the Lord had said unto Abraham, get thee out of thy country, and from thy kindred, and from thy father's house, unto the land that I will show thee. And I will make of thee a great nation, and will bless thee, and make thy name great, and thou shalt be a blessing. I will bless them also that bless thee, and curse them that curse thee, and in thee shall all the families of the earth be blessed. (GEN. 12:1–3, RSV)*

The study of millennialism in American culture is especially pronounced in the literature of Puritan New England. Many historians have linked the Puritan New England "sense of mission" and the sacredness of liberty to a millennial streak found in the religious and political doctrine of the time and rooted in apocalyptic European traditions. These traditions were cast in the mold neither of liberalism nor democracy, but in the apocalyptic tales spun by Puritans, Quakers, Congregationalists, Calvinists, Unitarians, and other Christian sects that formed in the aftermath of the Protestant Reformation.

The Reformation was a sixteenth-century religious revolution in the Western church—its greatest leaders being Martin Luther and John Calvin—that rejected much of Roman Catholic doctrine and practice and established the Protestant churches. One of the most important of these early sects, and significant to American millennialism, were the Puritans. Puritanism was a reform movement within the Church of England that sought to purify the church by ridding it of any remnants of the corrupt Roman Catholicism. Puritans had rejected the ceremonial worship and religious authority of the Church of England as unscriptural. Like the Israelites' pact with God, in which the Jews became the "chosen people," the Puritans hoped to renew the covenant between God and the people of England. They based this belief on revelations made to them by one of England's earliest Protestants, William Tyndale (c. 1494–1536). They also hoped to transform the nation from a profane to a holy one and to make their own lifestyle of a rigorous and fundamentalist moral conduct the pattern for the nation.[20]

The Pilgrims who would form the first English settlement in New England at Plymouth were Puritans from East Anglia, England. In 1609 this group moved to Leyden, Holland, where they formed an English separatist church and remained for 10 years. Due to local hostility toward them, they decided to go to America, and secured a land patent from the Virginia Company of Plymouth—one of two joint stock companies organized by English merchants and chartered by King James I in 1606 for the purpose of colonization.[21] On November 11, 1620, as their ship *The Mayflower* floated idly within the curve of present-day Cape Cod, mutinous words began to be uttered among some of the passengers. The voyagers had sailed dangerously outside the jurisdiction of the Virginia Company of London and its settlement in Jamestown, Virginia, and the ship's authority was being challenged. Led by Captain Miles Standish and William Bradford, the future governor of Plymouth colony, 41 men aboard the ship signed a compact binding themselves to one another and in submission and obedience to their God and king, in order to quell a potential uprising and further the glory of the Christian faith.

> In the name of God, Amen. We . . . the loyal subjects of our dread sovereign lord, King James, by the grace of God, of Great Britain, France, and Ireland, King, Defender of the Faith, . . .
> Having undertaken for the glory of God, and advancement of the Christian faith and honor of our king and country, a voyage to plant the first colony in the northern parts of Virginia, do . . . solemnly and mutually, in the presence of God and one of another, covenant and combine ourselves together into a civil body politic, for our better ordering and preservation and furtherance of the ends aforesaid. . . .[22]

To the Puritan mind the migration to the New World was viewed as an "errand into the wilderness," in which God's chosen people, the Puritan "pilgrims" of England, were cast into the American wilderness to spread the word of Christ and build the heavenly New Jerusalem.[23] The sacred mission of the Puritans would continue to infuse the thought and actions of early European colonists in the New World, especially in the sermons and writings of New England ministers who created an entire theological genre called the "jeremiad." In *The American Jeremiad*, Sacvan Berkovitch defines the apocalypticism of the jeremiad "as a ritual designed to join social criticism to spiritual renewal, public to private identity, the shifting 'signs of the times' to certain traditional metaphors, themes, symbols."[24]

The jeremiad derives in part from the Book of Jeremiah, one of the major prophetic writings of the Old Testament, which concerns the life of the Prophet Jeremiah (c. 650–570 B.C.). Jeremiah's prophecies announced the coming destruction of Judah and Jerusalem because of the people's defection from God's laws. The only way to avert the imminent disaster, preached Jeremiah, was through repentance, conversion, and renewing the covenant between Yahweh and his chosen people. In the sermons and religious tracts of Puritan ministers the American jeremiad became a constant reminder to renew the covenant between God and his newly chosen people, the Puritans, and later Protestant sects in New England. Among Calvinists like Peter Bulkeley, a preacher and one of the founders of Concord, Massachusetts, the "Gospel covenant" assured New England colonists a special relationship with God, one in which they were called upon to form a political and religious community wholly dedicated to God's works. However, God's graces would only accrue to the colonists if they remained true to the covenant and emphasized "right living." In a famous jeremiad entitled "A City upon a Hill," the Reverend Bulkeley admonishes the faithful to live up to their calling:

> And for ourselves here, the people of New England, we should in a special manner labor to shine forth in holiness above other people . . . . we are as a city set upon a hill, in the open view of all the earth, the eyes of the world are upon us, because we profess ourselves to be a people in covenant with God, and therefore not only the Lord our God with whom we have made covenant, but heaven and earth, angels and men, that are witnesses of our profession, will cry shame upon us if we walk contrary to the covenant which we have professed and promised to walk in.[25]

Berkovitch argues that the jeremiad has been a major influence in the evolution of the American millennial myth because of its capacity to "clothe history as fiction" and cause people to become actors in history.[26] The jeremiad was a distinct and powerful literary genre that survived long after the Puritans, persisted through the eighteenth century, and helped sustain a national dream through 200 years of turbulent change. The millennial visions of the Puritans and other Protestant sects who later immigrated to New England survived from colony to province, and from province to nation.[27] The myth of the millennial kingdom in America did not die with the decline of Puritanism, but grew with the great migration west of the Mississippi to manifest American destiny. The millennial visions the Puritans brought to the New World went on to play a significant role in the development of what has become the American millennial myth: the notion that America is a promised land and Americans are a chosen people.

*Beyond these glooms what brighter days appear.*
*Where dawns on mortals heav'n's millennial year.*
*In western wilds what scenes of grandeur rise,*
*As unborn ages crowd upon my eyes;*

*A better area claims its destin'd birth.*
*And heav'n descending dwells with man on earth.*[28]

Through the centuries Americans have grabbed on to the millennial myth, adapting it to their needs, particularly during periods of rapid change or national crisis. For example, the millennial aspirations of the early westward and southern expansions have been noted by historians of the American West in terms of the "frontier thesis" of American history. Early twentieth-century historians such as Frederick Jackson Turner spoke of the frontier as the "thin red line" that recorded the dynamic element in American history up to recent times. Just as numerous as the prospectors in search of gold were bands of Christian pilgrims in search of the promised land.[29] Herbert Bolton, who called the frontier the "rim of Christendom," saw in the spiritual wanderings of groups such as the Mormons, and in the many Christian missions that became frontier institutions, the true representatives of America's "manifest destiny."[30]

Many historians have attacked the frontier thesis of American history, especially because of its neglect of the North American Indian heritage. However, Native Americans also played a role in the American millennial myth in several instances. From Columbus' time on, they were demeaned as savages and often enslaved. As the emerging American culture came to dominate the land through exploration, missionary activity, westward migrations, and war, the natives were alternately "cast out" as wicked demons or "redeemed" as new Christian and American converts. The belief in demons and other satanic characters from Revelation easily made the passage from Europe to America via the millennial myth.

American pioneers and explorers like Davy Crockett and Zebulon Pike were drawn to the wilderness for more than just romance. They were politically driven as well by the early forms of manifest destiny that triggered the westward movement. The exploration and acquisition of gold and land for personal benefit and nationalist pride and the belief that the white man was superior to the red man, and so the natural inheritors of this "wilderness," imbued many of the early pioneers with a moral imperative and legal license to dehumanize native peoples. In the wake of increasing contact between the white man and the indigenous cultures on the rim of Christendom, new millennial forms began to appear among some native groups. Sometimes referred to as "nativistic" or "revitalization" movements, these millennial groups blended missionary teachings and native traditions to explain the arrival of the white man and the subsequent destruction of native culture. Their tales often espoused a belief in the coming of a warrior-hero who destroys the evil white man and institutes a new age where the traditional way of life is revitalized.[31]

One example of the power of the millennial myth on Native Americans can be found in the genesis of the Handsome Lake cult in 1799. By the end of the eighteenth century the Iroquois confederacy of New York, which consisted of the Cayuga, Mohawk, Oneida, Onondaga, and Seneca tribes, had been adversely affected by British colonialism and war and the people dispersed among several small reservations. In the previous decades the Iroquois had increasingly suffered at the hands of the white man. Through policies dictated by the law and with the inspiration of manifest destiny, the U.S. government waged physical and psychological warfare on the natives, allowing the theft of their lands based on the white man's superior claims to it. Many died from diseases, such as smallpox and measles, that would later wipe out hundreds of thousands of Native Americans across the continent. During the Revolutionary War the Seneca had supported the British against the colonists. Afterward, the newly born Americans sought revenge on the Seneca and killed many of them.[32]

Seneca men had been proud warriors, hunters, and fur traders, but were now confined to reservations, living in poverty and disease and wracked by war and death. As on many other Indian reservations, alcoholism ran rampant, devastating families. Neighboring peoples once subject to the Seneca and the League of the Iroquois ridiculed them. On the reservation accusations of witchcraft spread, causing further conflict among the Seneca. Many women lost their desire for children or took medicines to induce abortions or cause sterility. The Seneca culture, an entire way of life, was dying.

In 1799, a Seneca man called Handsome Lake lay close to death. He would later claim that during his drift toward the spirit world he received a series of supernatural messages from three angels that he was to share with his people concerning their future. Miraculously, Handsome Lake recovered and reported that the Creator was saddened by the condition of the Seneca people but blamed them for their sorry fate. They had become a weak and slovenly people, having fallen away from their traditional beliefs and practices. Handsome Lake's first visions emphasized the need to return to traditional Iroquois way of life, and many of the symbols he used derived from traditional Iroquois culture. The Seneca must repent of their deeds or surely face destruction, he warned.

A second set of visions predicted that there would be an apocalypse in which great drops of fire would fall from the sky and destroy the world. All would be consumed unless the people heeded the words of Handsome Lake, which demanded confessing their sins, such as witchcraft and drinking. A third set of visions, however, contradicted his earlier ones. Handsome Lake now told his people that to survive they must abandon their old ways in favor of the white man's ways. They must take up the farming and marriage patterns of the white man. While the fiery apocalypse never materialized, the end did come for the Seneca, as beliefs and traditions became transformed by the adoption of the white man's culture. Between 1803 and his death in 1815, Handsome Lake continued to preach temperance. He said the Creator had forbidden Indians to drink whiskey. He continued to preach peace with whites and urged Indians on the scattered reservations of the Seneca tribe to reunite so that the people could live as one again.[33]

Handsome Lake and his followers eventually brought order and purpose to the tribes and helped form the basis of a new church and a new religion in New York and Ontario that has members to this day. While the Handsome Lake cult did not preserve a traditional culture, it revitalized a dying one. Like his own "resurrection," Handsome Lake rekindled a new spirit and a new people from the ashes that was the Seneca tribe, a people molded of native and colonial culture and of the changes brought by western religion, disease, and war. As a result of this "revitalization" movement, the Iroquois survived in a radically changed environment. Millennial cults like Handsome Lake's were unintentional products of western missionary and cultural imperialism. Such millennialism often develops among colonized peoples and becomes the "religion of the oppressed," which, under certain circumstances, can unite formerly disparate groups.

The tensions that arise among indigenous cultures—most significantly the challenge to cultural integrity—can stimulate millennial or revitalization forms. After all, such cultures may indeed be experiencing the demise of their way of life. The main theme in such movements becomes moral regeneration and the creation of a new kind of person and society. Such aspirations are most often articulated in a savior or returned hero who will crush the interlopers and raise his people to their past glory. But they also may serve to support, even legitimate, their own decline. Rather than challenge a new and powerful threat to its existence, a movement may abandon the old ways and, like Handsome Lake, embrace the new order.

Native Americans were the first of such peoples to be demonized by the newly implanted Christian European culture. As the new American culture and history was written, so was its book of demons. The Christianity imposed on black slaves produced even more permutations of the myth. Among the "invisible" churches that dotted the pre-Civil War culture of slavery in the South, there evolved an apocalypticism in which blacks would overturn the evil structure imposed upon them and create a true heaven on earth that lived up to the one promised in the white man's Bible. Black spirituals were the songs of the oppressed searching for divine inspiration and intervention to overturn the existing evil order of slavery. At times these longings would erupt in millennial excitement, as in the slave revolt led by "the Prophet," Nat Turner.

Nat Turner was born a slave to a rich plantation owner in Virginia on October 2, 1800. His mother, an African slave, instilled in her son a passionate hatred for slavery. As a young boy Nat learned to read and write from the sons of his master. He especially absorbed the religious instruction and developed an affinity for Scripture. In the early 1820s, Turner was sold to a neighboring farmer. In the next decade his religious persona grew almost to fanaticism, and he began to see himself as God's messenger, called upon by the heavenly Father to lead his people out of bondage. Other slaves became attracted to his charisma and biblical acumen. They began to call him "the Prophet."

In 1831, after being sold again, Turner received a sign in the sky—a solar eclipse—telling him that the hour of emancipation was near. Turner contrived to attack and capture the armoury in Jerusalem—the county seat. He and his followers would then move on 30 miles to Dismal Swamp, where they would hide out and plan their holy war against the whites. On the night of August 21, Turner and seven of his followers launched their rebellion. Beginning with the murder of Turner's owner and family as they slept, the revolt moved on to Jerusalem, where in the next two days, 51 people were murdered by the slaves. Resistance in the form of a 3,000-man militia pursued the rebellious slaves. In the hysteria that followed, many innocent slaves were killed. Eventually, all involved in the Nat Turner rebellion were killed or captured, including Turner, who eluded the militia for six weeks but was finally caught, tried, and hanged in Jerusalem, Virginia, on November 11, 1831.[34]

For Nat Turner and his followers, the teachings of the Bible and the real chains of their oppression became the inspiration to resist and destroy a system that was evil. The slaves saw themselves in the Jews, who had been denied the holy land, and in the early Christians, who were persecuted by the Romans. They transformed Christianity from a religion imposed upon them to a religion of liberation. Seeing the demons not in themselves but in the white man, slaves in the South and abolitionists in the North fought to eradicate this scourge on the land. In the antislavery movement, the millennial myth becomes the inspiration for revolutionary action.

*Mine eyes have seen the glory of the coming of the Lord. He is trampling out the vintage where the grapes of wrath are stored. He hath loosed the fateful lightning of his terrible swift sword. His truth is marching on.* (JULIA WARD HOWE, THE BATTLE HYMN OF THE RE-PUBLIC)

The "apocalyptic trumpet" sounded some of its clearest notes during the Civil War. *The Battle Hymn of the Republic*, written by Julia Ward Howe and first published in February 1862, has become, as Ernest Tuveson points out, "the most popular hymn of wars and moral crusades of English-speaking people."[35] While rationalist thinkers of the Enlightenment began to criticize slavery on the basis of its inhumanity toward man, challenging the slave system aroused little serious and widespread interest until the early nineteenth century. Between the 1830s and 1850s, during the so-called Age of Reform, many abolitionists were already involved in the various social reform movements that emerged in the aftermath of the American Revolution and the Industrial Revolution, including crusading for temperance, child labor laws, and public education. By midcentury slavery had become the burning issue for social reformers of many stripes. William Lloyd Garrison, founder of the American Anti-Slavery Society and editor of *The Liberator* (1831–1865), was one of the most aggressive of the abolitionists. Famous abolitionists include former slaves Frederick Douglass and Williams Wells Brown and writers John Greenleaf Whittier, James Russell Lowell, Lydia Maria Child, and Harriet Beecher Stowe, whose antislavery novel *Uncle Tom's Cabin* (1852) convinced many of the immorality of slavery.

While the agitation of secular abolitionists was significant for the cause of emancipation, the dynamics of the antislavery movement were largely religious. In Britain and America, the Quakers were the first sustained voice in opposition to slavery. Evangelical religious groups, especially, condemned slavery as brutal, sinful, and unchristian, and it is probable that the greater force of abolitionism drew from evangelical roots. Theodore Dwight Weld and his "Seventy Apostles" were a tremendous force for the antislavery crusade as they carried the gospel of emancipation to the pulpits throughout the North with the millennial zeal of evangelism.

But most Americans, even in the North, were distrustful of the extremism of the abolitionists and the virulent white supremacist opposition. Abolitionists were often met with violence and ridicule. For example, Owen P. Lovejoy, an antislavery newspaper editor, was murdered by a mob of antiabolitionists in Alton, Illinois, in 1837. By the 1850s militancy pervaded both sides of the slavery issue, as armed factions began to act on their convictions in violent ways. Around 1849, while living with his family in the Negro community of North Elba, New York, John Brown, "an abolitionist," became obsessed about the idea of armed resistance to the slave system and winning justice for black peoples still in bondage. With his five sons, Brown moved to Kansas Territory to join up with antislavery forces struggling for control and soon became an antislavery guerrilla leader. After a sack of antislavery forces in Lawrence by a mob of slavery sympathizers on May 21, 1856, Brown concluded that he had a divine mission to take vengeance on the enemy.

With 21 other men (16 whites and 5 blacks) Brown organized a guerrilla band in an old farmhouse not far from the federal armory at Harper's Ferry. On the night of October 16, 1859, Brown and his men attacked and captured the armory, as well as 60 local men whom they took as hostages. They held off the local militia for almost two days until a force of Marines arrived, overpowering the guerrillas, wounding Brown, and killing 10 of his men, including two of his sons. Tried for murder, slave insurrection, and treason, he was convicted and hanged on December 2, 1859. While Brown failed to start a general movement among the slaves, his sensational exploits and high moral tone would help to immortalize him as a martyr for the cause of emancipation. His exploits would also hasten the start of the war that would end slavery. Union soldiers adopted the song of "John Brown's Body," whose "soul goes marching on," as part of their inspirational arsenal.[36]

The bloody raid on Harper's Ferry caused the South to fear that its way of life, based in an agricultural economy and a racial supremacy, was being threatened. The election of President Abraham Lincoln (November 1860) further convinced the South that a war for survival was imminent, and led to the secession of the Southern states and to the Civil War (1861–1865). The war turned Lincoln into an abolitionist and led him to emancipate the slaves in the areas in rebellion in 1863 and to free all slaves through the Thirteenth Amendment to the Constitution in 1865. The Civil War began as a fight to preserve the Union, but resulted in the emancipation of almost 4 million slaves. Once Lincoln accepted that slavery had to go, it became easier for him to render a moral justification for war through an apocalyptic script. The "fit" between the Civil War and the millennial myth is clearly drawn from Lincoln's second inaugural address—a speech permeated by the language of the King James Version. Borrowing freely from the Gospel according to Matthew (18:1), the document becomes a logical and legitimate justification for the war.

> The Almighty has his own purposes. "Woe unto the world because of offences! for it must needs be that offences come." . . . Fondly do we hope—fervently do we pray—that this mighty scourge of war may speedily pass away. Yet if God wills that it continue, . . . until every drop of blood drawn with the lash, shall be paid with another drawn with the sword, as was said three thousand years ago, so still it must be said "The judgments of the Lord are true and righteous altogether."[37]

In this regard, the "civil religion" thesis is an important contribution to the study of American millennialism. Civil religion refers to a secular or "public religion" that expresses a strong tie between a deity or religious set of ideas and a society's way of life.[38] It is another example of how the millennial myth takes on secular elements in adaptation to the current age. Lincoln chose to frame his words in apocalyptic language in order to provide biblical justification for going to war with the confederate states and emancipating the slaves, just as the evangelical abolitionists did. The terrible death and destruction that must be waged was the crucible from which a new and better America would be born. Lincoln spoke of the nation's interests and goals in terms of a "covenant" or pact with God, and he called on Americans to renew that pact in the moral crusade of civil war.

Historian Ernest Tuveson, in his book *Redeemer Nation*, distinguishes between the different forms of American millennialism in the American notions of "progress." Tuveson identifies two forms of progress—progressivists and separativists.[39] Only among progressivists is there a true "cult of revolution," where millennialism seeks to overturn the existing society while abetting its transformation. Progressivists motivated the Northern drive to preserve the Union by emancipating the slaves and pushing forward the industrial development that was eroding the earlier agricultural way of life but heralding a new "modern" age. The progressivist form of millennialism also underlay the American Revolution to overturn the tyrannical monarchy of King George and England and create a new, free, and sovereign nation.

Separativists, however, do not attempt to overturn and replace the old order, but break away from the dominant society to practice an alternative, often times communal, lifestyle or quietly await the coming of the millennium or new age. Separativists, says Tuveson, are not truly millennial because they are not revolutionary. I'd disagree. Many eighteenth- and nineteenth-century utopian religious movements, such as the Millerites, the Shakers, and the Hutterites, were inspired by the revolutionary changes taking place in America, especially during the Civil War and the Industrial Revolution. In reaction to the spreading values of economic competition and individualism, they sought a world of human cooperation and spiritual renewal. Many were also motivated by intense millennial expectations.[40] The Millerites, for example, expected the Messiah to establish the millennium after evil had reached its peak in the world. The role that Scripture told them to play was to "lay low," keep the faith, and wait for the Savior's final glory. The same might be said for survivalists, who also appear to be laying low and are much less concerned with reforming the world than with preparing for and surviving its destruction.

Such groups may not agitate for social change in "this world," yet they are still apocalyptic in the biblical sense when they come to view their world and orient their lives according to the millennial compass. More importantly, their separation from the larger society may actually be self-prophetic. The major changes that mark their world, creating painful social problems and conflicts for society, may be viewed by them as evidence of the end times and justification for not doing anything about it. This is also mirrored in the contemporary survivalist movement, which sees the collapse of civilization as imminent, and thus preparation for that eventuality is the only course of action. Again, the dynamic relationship that exists between millennial religious belief and secular society is crucial here, for no social group, however separativist it may profess to be, can fully extricate itself from the clutches of the dominant society. As the society continues to change and affect people's lives, the beliefs and actions of certain groups, such as millennial ones, may change as well. The dominant society may come to feel threatened by alternative, separativist groups, and may lash out at them and try to bring them back into the fold. In turn, such groups may resist or fight back and, in the process, become transformed into progressivist or revolutionary movements.

In conclusion, we can say that millennialism tends to arise in periods of intense social change. Anthropologists and historians have demonstrated that cultural contact, diffusion, and a loss of social and political sovereignty often result in millenarian activity.[41] Millennial elements can be discovered in a wide range of phenomena: from conservative or political religious groups that employ apocalyptic language to support the dominant culture to revolutionary groups that seek to overturn the existing social and political order. It is important to recognize the religious and secular dimensions that millennialism may take. In these ways, the millennial myth is able to transcend time, place, and circumstances. The American forms of millennialism discussed here reflected an interpretation of apocalyptic prophecy that looked to America as the promised land and "redeemer nation."

Thus, as the American frontier expanded westward to the Pacific and south into Spanish America, where it encountered other versions of Christianity and melded with other native traditions, the millennial myth continued to evolve with it. The twentieth century was to be the "American century," as American economic and political might grew and its armies went overseas to fight tyranny and dictatorship and preserve democracy for the world. In Europe and Asia, where the roots of the myth are deeper and even more tangled than in America, secular, even atheistic, forms of millennialism had evolved in the political revolutionary movements of Marxism, communism, and fascism.[42]

# Chapter 3

# Tribulation

## Survivalists and Soldiers of Fortune

*So prepare and make yourself ready, and all of your family, and be on guard against the enemy.*

EZEK. 38:7, RSV

*I really don't know if I'd shoot someone who was coming after my last Snickers Bar—but I might.*

ABE, 25-YEAR-OLD URBAN SURVIVALIST[1]

Abe is an urban survivalist who does not embody the image of the survivalist portrayed in our media or popular culture of an armed and embittered right-wing zealot crazed by racist, religious, or conspiratorial delusions—the images many now have of David Koresh, Timothy McVeigh, and the militias. Yet Abe does represent what is perhaps the most common type of survivalist: an individual not allied to any organized group or religion and not fanatic or apocalyptic in the classic sense. Concerned mainly with the negative effects of a rapidly changing world, including a deteriorating society and way of life and the potential for major social disruptions in the near future, Abe preaches "disaster preparedness"—the mantra of the "boy scout survivalist."

Although raised in the city, Abe describes himself as an outdoorsman—hunter, environmentalist, and survivalist—and he has spent many years hiking and hunting in northern Maine.

In a large walk-in closet in his bedroom, which is always locked and bolted, Abe keeps his "hock": food rations, medical supplies, camouflage clothing, skin-diving gear, outdoor cooking utensils, sleeping bags and tents, a small gasoline generator, compasses, binoculars, fishing lines, survival knives, and about a dozen guns. "And that's only half of it," says Abe.

Abe is tall, husky, unkempt, and what a friend describes as "a good-natured redneck." In Abe's case, looks can be deceiving. Having earned a B.A. in psychology and a B.S. in clinical psychology at a university in Boston, Abe is currently finishing up a master's degree in social psychology. In addition, he is a graduate student instructor and a substance abuse counselor at the university. Upon completing his master's thesis, Abe plans to take a brief vacation in the Maine woods, marry his fiancée, and then return to his studies to pursue a Ph.D. in psychology.

Abe sublets a comfortable condominium in a middle-class suburban neighborhood. Adjacent to his upstairs bedroom is his office—a small cluttered space with desk, personal computer, two small bookcases, and two wooden filing cabinets. Aside from an innocuous-looking poster of a fleet of hot-air balloons, the rest of the office decor is vintage Americana, with a decidedly military bent. On a wall hangs a framed black-and-white photograph of John Wayne as the colonel from the film *The Green Berets* (1968). Another photo depicts Clint Eastwood as the gun-slinging "man with no name," and there is a small, framed Civil War photograph of Abraham Lincoln and two Union officers standing outside a military tent.

On opposite walls facing each other hang the Union Jack—the flag of the rebel South during the Civil War—and Old Glory. Neatly ordered on the shelves of a small bookcase are miniature toy soldiers and military vehicles. Scattered throughout the room, on a desk and filing cabinets, are miniature tanks, trucks, jeeps, cannons, aircraft carriers, German submarines, and small armies of toy soldiers. Abe takes one of the tanks and hands it to me. The gray head of a gray toy soldier peers from the gray cockpit. "They're German," he says, and he quickly rattles off the technical names of the tanks and other miniature war machines. Abe is building a

World War II "battle panorama" with American and German armies. "Were you ever in the military?" I asked. "No, never even considered it. But I love military history. It's one of my hobbies."

Because of his eloquence and wit, I have decided at this point to let Abe speak at length, as he often does during the several tape-recorded discussions I had with him at the start of the 1990s. Without interrupting Abe's commentary with my questions, I have taken the liberty of connecting relevant parts of Abe's commentary from several interviews, so that there is a logical and consistent portrayal of his beliefs.

In the middle of Abe's desk lies the Tom Clancy novel *The Hunt for Red October*. "Great book," he says, "full of mind games. But they couldn't duplicate it on the screen." I asked him if he thinks *Red October* may be the last Cold War movie, as some critics contend. "I seriously doubt that," he said, "since a new cold war might just be beginning." I asked Abe to explain, and this is what he told me:

Well, it's pretty clear to me that something is going on. There's some big changes coming, worldwide changes I think. Shit, they've already begun—the economy, the politicians, the environment—they're all in the toilet now. But I think a real bad time is coming too—25 or 30 years, the next generation, maybe sooner. Our world—and I mean the U.S.A.—is going to change, and there's not much we can do about it. If we don't die from all the shit that we put into the environment, then we'll suffer from the ways we've lost control of our economy, and the fact that we're at the mercy of each other and the rest of the world.

But I'm a rational person, and that's why I'm a survivalist. I don't want to have to rely on anybody, least of all the government. Still, I support the U.S., when I think they're right. And I'm a God-fearing, tax-paying, Middle American. I'm nationalist, capitalist, and antisocialist. But I'm not a fanatic. I think survivalism is an important thing to consider if you want more than half a chance at surviving the things that could happen—not because you think the end of the world is coming, but because it's important to always be prepared. Of course, that's the Boy Scout motto, but it's true and it's an important American value too, one that I think is at the heart of America.

The first Americans—the Pilgrims, the frontiersmen, the mountain men—they were your classic Americans. They were self-suffcient individuals. They didn't need anybody. The mountain man was the epitome of the American individual. All he needed was his hock and rifle, and he could cross the Mississippi on a raft he built or explore the Rockies, and never see another individual, and yet survive just fine. In the case of Hollywood, the frontiersmen and mountain men are always fighting Indians and Mexican bandidos or each other. Some of this happened, obviously, but most of the time survival was a quiet, natural way of life. Most of the time you didn't see a whole lot of people. If you look at it in the historical sense, you see that for a few hundred years—from about the 1600s to the late 1800s—there were lots of people who had to survive by their own wits and guile in the wilderness. And they all did it basically the same way—by honing a kind of survival instinct. I mean, Davy Crockett was a survivalist. And people like Jeremiah Johnson, Zebulon Pike, and Daniel Boone—they're your classic survivalists, but there were thousands of people living that way in the American wilderness, with nothing except what they carried on their backs and they learned to survive.[2]

At that time there were all kinds of nasty things happening—the mountain lions, the Indians, the land—so they had to make it, and they did. There was really very little threat to man from man—I mean, not like now. For most of the people alive then there were few external threats—that is, threats from civilization. The threat that existed was internal to their immediate situation. It was a real thing—nature—nature versus man. Even the Indians were thought of as part of nature and the "wilderness." And you can bet the Indians thought of the pioneers in the same way. They could be a threat like a grizzly bear or a rattlesnake. And they were right about that. So it was survival of the fittest in its most basic form. What happened to the Indians was sad, but it had to happen.

Closely related to the survivalist instinct, I think, is a belief in God. Jeremiah Johnson was a very religious man, and God was important to his survival. Because of his religion he refused to fight in the Mexican War, so he took off. Basically, he was a passive resistance kind of guy. He didn't want to go off and kill Mexicans, so he went off and killed Indians instead—because he had to, not because someone else told him to because it was pleasing to God.

Still, the early survivalists, the people who pioneered the country, were God-fearing Americans. I don't think there could be an atheist survivalist. God is a natural part of staying alive. I'm a fairly religious Roman Catholic myself, but by no means fanatical about it. I carry around my rosary beads and my Bible. I've even got a special water-resistant copy for my hock—Revised Catholic Edition. One of the main things that any survival manual will teach you—in fact it's rule number one in Nesbit's *Survival Book*, the bible of survivalism if you ask me—is, and I quote, "It is imperative that a man have hope." And it says it in here maybe a hundred times. The second you give up hope you're a dead man. To a survivalist hope means trust and faith. So if you have something to hope for, or have faith in, it brings you that much higher up on the ability to survive. Believing in God helps you to do that. You have a very strong link between survivalists and religion there. And even though most survivalists aren't fanatics, we all know that "there are no atheists in foxholes."

After instinct and God, it's the practical things that are most important—knowledge, experience, your cache, plans, and your degree of survivability. In a word, preparedness. The old Boy Scout motto again, but it's key. I'm an urban survivalist, which means my main concern is surviving disaster in the urban environment—city survivalism, that's what I'm prepared for. But I'm prepared for other situations too, and could, if need be, survive in the woods or on a deserted island. Jungles, deserts, the sea—I might be in trouble, but I'm concerned with that too and I'm developing those dimensions of my preparation.

I've been studying Air Corps survival manuals. They're the best, the most comprehensive because they train for all disasters, including nuclear war. I just bought a Geiger counter—I'm rational; Seabrook (a New Hampshire nuclear power plant) is not far away.[3] Flexibility in survival—and that means preparedness—is essential. You know preparedness relates to religion too. God helps those who help themselves. I've read that many times in survival books. But you'll never read, "The meek shall inherit the earth" in a survival book.

Always being prepared for the least or the worst is rational thinking. So when the environment has been massively disrupted—a major industrial disaster, an earthquake or hurricane, a terrorist incident, a war—and a whole bunch of people get trapped in the middle, where they're on one side or the other, or they're not on anybody's side, who will be the survivors?

Basically you have three types of survivors: those who didn't prepare at all and so are in big trouble; your lucky people, who just happened to be in the right place at the right time, and so have something left, like their lives; and the people who did prepare, and who have the ability to survive long term. They have the food, water, clothing, shelter, medical supplies, guns. They can last weeks, months, years—whatever it takes to survive. And that's the way I look at it. I'm in the last of those three groups. I think that if the need arose—I'm not saying it will—but if it does, my skills, my hock, my philosophy would get me through it. It's always better to have it and not need it, then to need it and not have it. That's my philosophy.

Weapons, that's another thing. I'm an avid hunter but I've never pointed a gun at another human being in my life. I refuse to play paintball, which is a survivalist sport. The way I see it, if you point a gun at an individual you pull the trigger and you kill him. Because the only reason you point a gun at someone is when your life is threatened. But some of these hardcore people use it as practice. They hone their skills in cover and concealment, tracking, killing, and revenge.

But then—and I state the obvious—a paintball gun is very different from a real gun. However, it does have one very nasty characteristic. When you encourage people to point a loaded gun at someone, even a paintball gun, and you tell them to shoot, you give them the thrill of combat and the rush of a near-death-like experience. And even though it's a game, ultimately some people become desensitized to shooting people. So that's why I'm opposed to paintball games (see Chapter 8).

I own several weapons. I have a couple of pellet guns, a Saturday night special, a working German Luger, and two large bore heavy hitting rifles—assault weapons. I refuse to think—and this is the way the military teaches it—to think on instinct: to have an instinct to pull that trigger, to have an instinct to slash, to have an instinct to jab, to have an instinct to knock a person down, to have an instinct to kill a person without thinking. To encourage that kind of behavior outside the military is wrong, because it isn't a game. We do operate on instinct, but we also have the most developed sense of intelligence. That's what makes us different from animals, right?

If you give a 20-year-old kid a paintball gun, and you teach him to shoot at another person, without thought, he gets a feel for what it would be like to shoot a real gun at a real person. He might just come to enjoy it. Just like the little kid watching cartoons. He thinks, Ya, but it's not real, it's fun. Like a kid, he becomes desensitized to the real violence in the game, and maybe he even becomes more violent himself. I think paintball games can do that. Survivalism is serious business. Making a game out of it is an oxymoron.

Then you come to the question of, How far am I willing to take it? Am I really under the surface fanatical about it? I really don't know if I'd shoot someone who was coming after my last Snickers Bar—but I might. It would depend on how bad the situation was. But the hardcore guys would kill you in an instant because you're not one of them, or you're not part of their organization, or worse, you're Jewish. They don't think you deserve to survive over them, so therefore, they've thrown out any ethics of human relationships. Now it's survival of the fittest. They're going to win no matter what.

They probably won't waste a bullet on you if they don't have to because they need the bullet. But if you give them any reason to think you're a threat to them, then one bullet is well spent. I mean, I don't look at survival that way. I must admit if it were a situation of me and mine against you and yours, and I didn't know you, and you were coming up the street and begging food off of me after some natural disaster, and I wasn't sure help was coming, I'd have to think pretty hard on it. But I wouldn't shoot you outright. The hardcore guys wouldn't think twice. You'd be dead before you hit the ground. That's the difference between someone like me and them. And it's a great big difference.

The survivalists who are the white supremacists believe, by some perversion of the imagination, that the black, the Jew, the Catholic—anybody who's not white, Anglo Saxon, Protestant, Southern Baptist is going to rise up and crush them. So they're prepared for that, in a military sense. OK, I don't see it happening. I don't think they have too much to worry about. Even if they did, the way they're going about it is a little insane. In their mind God was white and therefore their cause is right, and white is right, and might makes right. To them survival means the ability to procreate at a future date to resupply the race. Crap! OK fine, if that's the way you look at it. That's one thing. But preparedness for individual survivalists, for people who consider themselves survivalists in the Boy Scout sense, being prepared for the worst is a very different idea. Survival means staying alive. It means you kind of like breathing and getting up in the morning—that kind of thing.

And those guys (Abe points to a recent issue of *Soldier of Fortune* magazine). The "heroes" I call them; they're fanatics too—mercenaries and white supremacists. They're the ones you've got to worry about. Believe me, I know some. Friends of friends of mine in Maine are religious survivalists. These guys believe the Apocalypse has already started. They're interesting as all hell to talk to, and I go hunting and fishing with them sometimes, but I wouldn't want to get too close to them.

*And he that overcometh, and keepeth my works, unto the end, to him will I give power over the nations: And he shall rule them with a rod of iron; as the vessels of a potter shall they be broken to shivers: even as I received my Father.* (REV. 2:27, KJV)

Survivalism is a loosely structured yet pervasive set of philosophies, practices, and expressions in American culture.[4] The degree to which people practice survivalism varies greatly. Some people may read survival magazines or play survival games only on weekends. Others stockpile water, canned goods, medical supplies, and guns. Still others purchase isolated rural property, enroll in survival training programs, or belong to survival communities and organizations. More or less, survivalists are prepared for all kinds of disasters—natural, supernatural, or man-made. In the event of a disaster, surviving the initial calamity, breaking away from centers of destruction, and becoming self-sufficient are the survivalist's major concerns.

Significantly, the end of World War II saw the interest in disaster preparedness and survivalism begin to develop. The period also witnessed the resurgence of American millennialism. The terrible destruction wrought by that war, reflected in the rise of fascism, the Holocaust, and the creation and use of atomic weapons, brought a new seriousness to apocalyptic thought. While many millennialists, such as the Jehovah's Witnesses, saw the war and its effects as another sign that "the final days were near," in others it created an appreciation, however metaphorically, of the potential for fulfilling apocalyptic scripture. Upon witnessing the first successful atomic bomb test, scientist Robert Oppenheimer described his feeling by quoting from the Bhagavad Gita, "I am become Death, the destroyer of worlds."[5]

In the 1950s, bomb shelters and survivalist preparations began as a fad but took on a new seriousness during the Cuban missile crisis. The military conflicts in Korea in the 1950s and Vietnam in the 1960s, both of which ended in heavy American losses and eventual withdrawals, did much to inspire the survivalist ethic. While still a marginal practice by the mid-1970s, survivalism was growing and spawning an industry devoted to disaster preparedness. By the 1980s survivalism had become the center of a widespread subculture and billion-dollar industry. It is unclear how many Americans are survivalists, since concealment of one's cache and identity is a part of survivalist practice. Federal agencies like the FBI and ATF and private groups like the Southern Poverty Law Center and the Anti-Defamation League of the B'nai B'rith keep tabs on extremist paramilitary groups of the "survivalist right" such as the Ku Klux Klan and Aryan Nations (see Chapter 5). However, the data are sketchy on what is certainly the far greater number of Americans who practice survivalism in a less sensational manner. While most survivalists try not to call attention to themselves, the complexity of the practice and belief system can be uncovered in the literature, media, and industry of survivalism.[6]

It was during the early 1970s, following the American withdrawal from Vietnam, that paramilitary literature focusing on survivalism and apocalyptic visions of social collapse or nuclear war began to appear. In many cases produced by and reflecting the experiences of the Vietnam vet, magazines such as *Soldiers of Glory*, *Mercenary*, *American Survival Guide*, and *Soldier of Fortune* were some of the early survivalist magazines to emerge within the literature and subculture of American survivalism. The literature reflected a dramatic change in the tradition of gun magazines with the emergence of a new paramilitary subculture blending an interest in state-of-the-art weaponry with survival preparations amid visions of a disintegrating world.[7]

Rather than hunting and marksmanship, the survivalist literature focused on espionage, vigilantism, the martial arts, war, and survival. The world was viewed as increasingly dangerous. International relations were depicted as becoming strained and polarized. On any given day dozens of military skirmishes, civil wars, and terrorist incidents were occurring around the globe. Famine in India and Africa, deforestation in the Amazonian rain forest, and massive oil spills in Europe were signs of environmental destruction. At home, drugs, poverty, crime, urban warfare, and corrupt politicians threatened America and the American way of life, and serial killers, mass murderers, and new deadly diseases like AIDS dominated the headlines.

In the survivalist literature citizens were told to take action—drastic action if need be—to protect themselves, their families and property, and their country. Stockpiling weapons and food and developing strategies of self-defense and counterattack were encouraged by the paramilitary and survivalist press. The literature also talked about changes in the nature of warfare and in the production and availability of modern weapons of war. Modern warfare had become defined by "guerrilla war" and "low-intensity conflict"—a focus on small, highly trained "special forces," paramilitary weapons and tactics, and secret operations. In the paramilitary and survivalist literature, contemporary military conflict involved not only the organized military forces of nations but paramilitary forces as well. Paramilitary soldiers could be mercenaries, terrorists, freedom fighters, vigilantes, and survivalists. While not an entirely new type of warfare (American revolutionaries are often credited with practicing guerrilla warfare against the British), low-intensity conflict came to define the present and future state of international war. Despite the relative peace the United States experienced since the eighties, the conflicts in Grenada, Nicaragua, Libya, Beirut, the Persian Gulf, Somalia, and Bosnia have put American soldiers in harm's way throughout the 1980s and 1990s.

*And Behold a White horse; and he that sat upon him had a bow: and he went forth conquering, and to conquer. (REV. 6:2, KJV)*

The literature of survivalism is extensive: It comprises books, manuals, newsletters, and magazines, as well as videotapes, computer networks, and "home pages" on the Internet. There are also gun shows, conventions, and political organizations whose focus is the new American paramilitary subculture and survivalist industry. With over one million subscribers worldwide, *Soldier of Fortune Magazine: The Journal of Professional Adventurers (SOF)* is the most popular survivalist periodical. Like the subculture it represents, *SOF* expresses modern, fractured elements of the classical millennial myth. Specifically, it expresses a uniquely American interpretation of the millennial myth: a world where "soldiers of fortune" fight the never-ending battle against "tyranny" and where citizen soldiers practice survivalism in defense of the "American way" and in preparation for social collapse and "nuclear Armaggedon." Through the symbolic and thematic tapestry of *SOF*, threads of the millennial myth become rearranged and redefined, and only some of the myth's main elements appear.

*Soldier of Fortune* can be located in the genre of American gun magazines (Table 3.1). That genre covers a wide spectrum of literature including sport, marksmanship, hunting, military, paramilitary, war history, and antiques. What makes them all "gun magazines" is their central focus on guns and the gun industry and subculture. In the 1950s and 1960s popular gun magazines like *American Rifleman, American Hunter,* and *Guns and Ammo* defined the subculture of American gun enthusiasts in terms of sport and leisure. The most common guns these magazines dealt with were rifles, pistols, and shotguns—guns for marksmanship and hunting. Articles stressed competition and gun mechanics and repair and reveled in the joys of the outdoor sporting life. How to bag an elk, track deer, or mount trophy antlers was the kind of hunting lore offered in the "gun-as-sport" genre.

Guns also are the principle focus of *Soldier of Fortune*. However, the types of guns displayed are of a far different quality from those in earlier gun magazines. Where hunting rifles, western-style pistols, and shotguns defined the weapons content of the gun-and-sport genre, ground-to-air missile launchers, compact uzi machine guns, plastic explosives, and "dirty tricks" define *SOF*'s content. The magazine is expressive of an American "warrior" culture and what sociologist James William Gibson, author of *Warrior Dreams*, has called the "new war."[8]

The survivalist right is fearful of a disintegrating "old world order" and declining American wealth and influence in the world. They are angry at their government for taking away their rights and their guns and for allowing "globalism" to take away their jobs and threaten their way of life. With a fetish for modern weaponry and war and a "survival-of-the-fittest" mentality, the paramilitary press has turned guns into totems of power and survivalism into a kind of secular apocalyptic philosophy and practice.

Table 3.1. American Gun Magazines[a]

| | 1st Pub. | Circulation |
|---|---|---|
| Type I: Sport/hunting magazines[b] | | |
| 1. American Rifleman[c] | 1959 | 1,733,679 |
| 2. American Marksman[c] | 1965 | 5,000 |
| 3. American Hunter[c] | 1973 | 1,534,423 |
| 4. Guns and Ammo | 1958 | 575,000 |
| 5. Gun World | 1960 | 130,000 |
| 6. Guns Review | ? | 19,728 |
| 7. Sports Afield[d] | 1940 | 530,000 |
| 8. Outdoor Life[d] | 1987 | 1,350,000 |
| Type II: Paramilitary/survivalist magazines[e] | | |
| 1. Soldier of Fortune[f] | 1975 | 104,593 |
| 2. Guns and Action[f] | ? | ? |
| 3. Mercenary Magazine | ? | ? |
| 4. Soldiers of Glory | ? | ? |
| 5. American Survival Guide | 1979 | 90,000 |
| 6. New Breed | 1980 | 68,000 |
| 7. Gung Ho | 1981 | ? |
| 8. International Combat Arms | 1983 | 126,000 |
| 9. Firepower | ? | ? |

[a]Publication and circulation information from *ULRICH's International Periodicals Directory*, 3rd ed., 1996.
[b]Most of the Type I magazines existed prior to 1960. All are currently published.
[c]NRA publications, American Hunters Group, Fairfax, Virginia.
[d]Guns are a significant part of these magazines.
[e]All Type II paramilitary magazines (it appears) came to print beginning in 1975 following the first publication of *Soldier of Fortune* magazine.
[f]Omega Group Publications, Boulder, Colorado.

Interestingly, *Soldier of Fortune* retains a sense of the sport and hunting feel of earlier gun magazines, only in *SOF* sport is defined in terms of warfare, and hunting in terms of humans. Articles report on "man trapping" and "war gaming" and frame war and survival as leisure time activities. A bumper sticker advertised in *SOF* reads, "War: Man's Oldest Contact Sport." A T-shirt depicts a soldier locked in the sights of a gun; "Viet Cong Hunting Club" is the caption on the front.[9] The notion of survivalism as sport is also apparent in an advertisement for The Ultimate Game—a paintball war and weapons game, where contestants can win "high cash profits."[10]

*And behold a pale horse: and his name that sat on him was Death, and Hell followed with him. And power was given them . . . to kill with the sword, and with hunger, and with death, and with the beasts of the earth.* (REV. 6:8, KJV)

*I am the Alpha and Omega, the beginning and the end. To him who thirsts I will give of the fountain of the water freely. He who overcomes shall possess these things, and I will be his God, and he shall be my son.* (REV. 21:6, RSV)

In the upper left-hand corner of every issue of *Soldier of Fortune* is the *SOF* logo: the special forces beret overlaid by crossing knives with the Greek symbol for omega (the ending) and the words "Omega Group Ltd." in the center. Omega Group may be named after the Cuban paramilitary exile group, the Omega Seven. In the late 1950s, *SOF* founder Robert K. Brown helped train anti-Castro exiles in the Florida Everglades. *SOF* ostensibly reports on national and international military conflict. But through symbols, images, and ideology it provides an apocalyptic frame of reference for its readers. Prophecies of war and tribulations of social decay and collapse are its primary messages. Like all apocalyptic literature, *SOF* (and Omega Group Publishing) is a prophetic text of the "end times."

America's Vietnam experience marked a watershed period in the founding of *Soldier of Fortune* and the paramilitary press. *SOF* and the survivalist industry emerged shortly after America's withdrawal from Vietnam. For *SOF* that war marked a major turning point for America. Not only did it introduce the future of international warfare—low-intensity guerrilla conflict—but it also exposed the evil of the communist threat and the vulnerability of American political and military hegemony.

In *SOF* Vietnam was a war of "good soldiers and gutless politicians," of heroic deeds and sinister designs. Most importantly, Vietnam was a war that America lost. Vietnam was a "sign." A popular T-shirt advertised in *SOF* depicts a battle-scarred soldier carrying an automatic weapon standing in front of a map of Vietnam. "Apocalypse" is its caption (Figure 3.1).[11] Another shows the Devil holding a pitchfork while looking over a map of Vietnam.

FIGURE 3.1. "Vietnam Apocalypse," *SOF* T-shirt image.

The caption reads, "The Land that God Forgot: I'm sure to go to Heaven because I spent my time in Hell."[12]

Providing the interpretations of "those who were there," the Vietnam legacy is central to the platform of *SOF*. The magazine is avowedly "pro-veteran" and dedicated to telling the "real" story of Vietnam. A regular column in *SOF* called "I Was There" provides the space for Vietnam veterans to recall their experiences and tell their personal stories of adventure and heroism. Part of that experience includes anger at the government for giving up on the war and its soldiers and ignoring the problems that many veterans had fitting back into a society that was often blind and sometimes hostile to their needs. Numerous articles, books, posters, and other paraphernalia in *SOF* recall the American Vietnam experience and provide a sympathetic worldview and therapeutic outlet for the sufferings of the Vietnam veteran.

In the revisionist and millennial history of *Soldier of Fortune*, Vietnam was a sign that the military and ideological balance of world power was shifting. But Vietnam was just the beginning.[13] So *SOF* encourages those Americans concerned with a dangerous future to take the offensive and assume a paramilitary role and ideology. Wars, terrorism, the nuclear threat, economic collapse, rampant crime, a deteriorating environment—these are today's realities, and tomorrow's look worse. It admonishes readers to "read the signs" and get involved. Americans can play an important role in the coming years, *SOF* suggests, by becoming "citizen soldiers" and survivalists.

Like the apocalyptic future prophesied in Revelation, the world foreseen by *SOF* is a world caught in "cosmic war" and on the verge of massive destruction and death. The classic image of the carnage that is to begin the end times is the Four Horsemen of the Apocalypse (Rev. 6:1–8). To many believers and scholars, the first horsemen of the Apocalypse represents war, as well as the destruction and death associated with it.

To the second horseman, all in red, was given power "to take peace from the earth, that they should kill one another" (Rev. 6:4). Often referred to as famine and poverty, the black horse is unveiled by the opening of the third seal, "and he that sat on him had a pair of balances in his hand" (Rev. 6:5). The fourth seal reveals a pale horse, "and his name that sat on him was Death, and Hell followed with him. To him is given power over one fourth of the earth, to kill with the sword, and with hunger, and with death, and with the beasts of the earth" (Rev. 6:8).

Bearers of conquest, slaughter, famine, and death, the Four Horsemen often ride through the pages of *SOF*. Especially in advertisements and on T-shirts and posters, the symbols and images of Apocalypse provide the millennial message.[14] One popular T-shirt shows the fourth horseman ("Death") galloping up behind a soldier of fortune clutching an AK-47. The right hand of "Death" is outstretched and guiding the head of the soldier. The caption reads: "Death Rides a Pale Horse" (Figure 3.2). A similar T-shirt image gleaned from Norse mythology depicts the "Ride of the Valkyries": the warrior maidens of Odin (the supreme god and creator of Norse mythology) on white horses galloping through the skulls and bones of fallen soldiers. In legend their job is to choose the heroes to be slain in battle and conduct them to Valhalla—the hall of the slain. Although the sources are different—in this case, Christian Scripture and Norse mythology—the images and messages are remarkably the same: images of war and "angels of death." In this example, fractured images of Apocalypse can come from different mythic traditions.[15]

FIGURE 3.2. "Death Rides a Pale Horse," SOF T-shirt image.

Further examples of death symbolism come from a T-shirt manufacturer. Mirroring the famous quote made by Arnaud-Amalric in A.D. 1210, "Kill them all! God will recognize his own," is a slogan on a shirt embossed with a winged skull wearing a green beret and the Army Air Corps slogan, "Kill 'em all, let God sort 'em out" (Figures 3.3 and 3.4). A reference to angels of death is expressed in a survival knife called the "Archangel I," designed "for people who drop out of airplanes."[16] Another company sells sterling silver skull rings bearing the names, "Death," "Grim Reaper," "Warrior," and "Revenge."[17]

FIGURE 3.3. Army Air Corps slogan, *SOF* T-shirt image.

FIGURE 3.4. Grim reaper T-shirts.

The skull and crossbones and grim reaper images of death in *SOF* derive from traditional biblical cultural images of death and the supernatural. They also reflect a deeper American past, the millennial past of seventeenth-century New England Puritans. Like the Puritans, for whom death was an integral part of everyday life, *SOF* suggests it is integral to the lives of all Americans now. Death is certainly an everyday reality for *Soldier of Fortune*. Photographs of the bullet-ridden bodies of freedom fighters from Nicaragua, Angola, Northern Ireland, Bosnia, and other international "hot spots" illustrate articles on military conflicts just as "Death" and the Apocalypse illustrate products. Although the content and meaning of gun magazines like *Soldier of Fortune* are vastly different from earlier gun magazines, they are not generally mistaken for religious tracts. However, religious symbols like the Four Horsemen of the Apocalypse and the Grim Reaper fill its pages. Such symbols and meanings are fragments of the American millennial myth, and they provide a context for *SOF* to express its mythology of world conflict and American destiny.

*And I beheld when he had opened the sixth seal, and, lo, there was a great earthquake; and the sun became black as sackcloth of hair; and the*

*moon became as blood; And the stars fell unto the earth . . . and every
mountain and island were moved out of their places . . . and every free
man, hid themselves in the dens and in the rocks of the mountains."*
(REV. 6:12–15, KJV)

*"We'll supply you 'til Doomsday."* (SALLY'S SURVIVAL OUTFITTER)

A multimillion-dollar industry has evolved to serve the apocalyptic fears of survivalists and feed the millennial myth. *Soldier of
Fortune* magazine sits at the center of the survivalist industry. In
fact, survivalism became such an important component of *SOF* that
in the mid-1980s a new magazine, *Survive* (later renamed *Guns and
Action*), was spun off and devoted entirely to the topic. Throughout
its history, however, survivalism has continued to be a primary
theme in *SOF*. Articles, advertisements, and the classified pages all
stress the importance of survival, while being couched in apocalyptic symbolism and imagery.

There is an extensive literature on survivalism, and many
publishers and booksellers advertise in *Soldier of Fortune*. Paladin
Press, an early venture of *SOF* founder Robert K. Brown, is a regular
*SOF* advertiser. Publishers of the "Action Library," Paladin has
become a leading publisher of survivalist and paramilitary books
and videotapes. A brief sampling of Paladin titles advertised in *SOF*
includes "how-to" books such as *Survival Poaching, Into the Primitive, Life after Doomsday,* and *The Survivalist Retreat.* Another survivalist publisher that advertises regularly in *SOF* is The Larder, a
publishing house with "something to offend everyone," including
*Saloon Survival, Make My Day, Up Yours,* and *Secret Freedom Fighter.*
In an advertisement for Ken Hale Survival Books, Ken commands
readers to "Be a survivor" and "Don't delay . . . My new catalog is
ready. Hundreds of titles, many new, including *Communist Guerrilla
Warfare* and *USMC Hand to Hand Combat.*[18] "We'll supply you 'til
Doomsday" is the motto of Sally's Survival Outfitter, a regular *SOF*
advertiser. An advertisement extols the virtues of the "M6 Survival
Gun," designed "for the retreatist-survivalist . . . one of your guaran-
tees against Doomsday . . . [and] a practical way to protect your urban

home or remote retreat from the present and senseless dangers threatening America."[19]

The subculture of survivalism is clearly expressed in the classified pages of *Soldier of Fortune*, where a survivalist network has evolved and where all manner of survival products are offered for sale. A list of such products gleaned from one issue of *SOF* included the following: survival guns and knives, camping and climbing equipment, clothing, books, newsletters, computer bulletin boards, Internet home pages, isolated rural properties, survival food, fall-out shelters, power generators, Geiger counters, medical kits, and wood-burning stoves.[20] All the survival information you might need is found in Mesa's "*Survival Encyclopedia*! Retreating, storage, weapons, solar bunkers, maps, plans, checklists, combat, power, disaster skills, demolitions, defense and decontamination equipment, shelters, survival chemicals, medicine. And more!" For those of limited means, Satan's Kingdom Press offers a "Day after Survival Card," a single wallet-sized card containing vital facts for nuclear survival, such as radiation measurement and shelter protection—all for under five dollars.[21]

There are many survival food and nutrition companies as well who regularly advertise in *SOF*. One company offers "Minutemen Survival Food Tabs:" "When emergency conditions require living off whatever food you can carry, Food Tabs save your life." Another survivalist food company offers a variety of "non-perishable survival foods . . . including meats, dairy products, breads, potatoes, and more." The ad offers "free literature and meat samples." Some classified ads hawk real estate or what is sometimes called "isolated rural properties." One ad offers "Nuclear War Survival Land in Australia," and another, an "Alaskan Wilderness Land Sale." For only $5,900 (easy monthly payments of only $133.86 with a down payment of $200) you can own 160 acres of virgin fertile land in the world's last unexplored lands. Just write Bolivian Land and Forestry Ltd. of Santa Cruz, Bolivia.[22]

For the ideal fallout shelter and retreat, "Harder Homes and Gardens" and "Architectural Resources" offer "bulletproof houses" and "practical nuclear shelter designs." And for the "Big

Dig," Underground Shelters International "specializes in the design and construction of reinforced concrete bomb shelters, steel blast chambers, and steel blast doors and hatches . . . For a free brochure send $2 to Underground Shelters International . . . San Jose, California."[23]

There are survivalist communities one can join as well. A call to join such a community appears in an ad from the Southern California area. The ad reads "Survivalist: You and your family can survive the impending nuclear threat. Join together with us. For free information, contact Families United." A contact person and California address are supplied.[24]

*Fear none of those things which thou shalt suffer: behold, the devil shall cast some of you into prison, that ye may be tried; and ye shall have tribulation ten days: be thou faithful unto death, and I will give thee a crown of life. (REV. 2:10, KJV)*

The tribulations unleashed by the seven seals and the Four Horsemen of the Apocalypse are metaphors for today's changing times just as they have been for 2,000 years. Survivalism retains many of the elements of the classical millennial myth, if only in a secular sense. Metaphorically speaking, the Apocalypse still comes riding on four horses to many survivalists. The first horseman, with sword in hand, is military conflict and war. The civil war and genocide that erupted in the former Yugoslavia following the collapse of the Soviet Union is the most recent example of the tribulations brought by the first horseman. The second horseman, a "favorite" of most hardcore survivalists, is social economic collapse: the unraveling of the monetary system, resulting in the exhaustion of food supplies and essential services, massive violence in the cities, spill-over rioting and looting, and civil war.

Floods, earthquakes, tornadoes, and other natural disasters, followed by poverty, starvation, and disease define the tribulations of the third horseman. Environmental problems are foremost on the minds of survivalists these days. Death, the fourth horseman, is thermonuclear war, accompanied by mass destruction and death—the theory being that since crisis relocation will not save lives, then survivalism beyond the fallout pattern will. For many survivalists the end of the Cold War and the reduction of American and Soviet nuclear arsenals did not lessen the threat of nuclear weapons proliferation. In fact, fear of rogue nations like Libya and Iraq or terrorist groups and individuals attaining nuclear weapons capability has heightened not only survivalists' fears of the fourth horseman but also those of many who are not survivalists.

The apocalyptic prophecy works by pinning current changes or major events, such as wars and environmental, economic, and political changes, to the millennial myth. Ever since John wrote down the Revelation at Patmos, millennialists have continued to interpret current events through the prism of the millennial myth. The most literal of these "tribulationists" today come from Christian fundamentalists, especially its evangelical wing. Throughout the 1970s and 1980s the Christian right became active in social and political issues. The Reagan revolution was aided in part by Jerry Falwell, Pat Robertson, and other members of the religious right, who continually called attention to biblical prophecy as keys to understanding domestic and international events and determining social and political policy.

The apocalyptic interpretations of Revelation by Christian author Hal Lindsey, for example, found a huge readership in the popular literature. *The Late Great Planet Earth* (1977) was one of the most popular nonfiction works of the 1970s.[25] By 1980 there were over 2 million copies in print. That book and its author spawned an entire industry devoted to pinning the events of the contemporary world to Scripture. Lindsey himself continued to write in this genre, publishing several other works in the same vein, including *There's a New World Coming* (1973), *The Terminal Generation* (1976), *1980s Countdown to Armageddon* (1981), *The Rapture: Truth or Consequences* (1983), *The Road to the Holocaust* (1989), *Satan Is Alive and Well on Planet Earth* (1992), and *Planet Earth 2000 A.D.* (1994). For religious millennialists the apocalypse entails inevitable and massive world destruction and collapse brought on by supernatural elements. AIDS, nuclear war, and a disintegrating environment all square well with the tribulations of Revelation.

The religious right sustained many setbacks to its crusades in the 1980s. The overbearance and overexposure of ministers like Jerry Falwell and his religiopolitical action organization called the Moral Majority caused many liberals and moderates to shudder at the thought of a Christian fundamentalist political movement. The extravagant lifestyles of rich and famous televangelists, such as the Reverend Robert Schuller and his multimillion-dollar drive-through Crystal Cathedral, and the high-tech marketing techniques televangelists employed in raising money brought in federal investigators and bad press. The financial scandals involving Jim Bakker and Oral Roberts and the sexual escapades of Jimmy Swaggert shook the faith of believers and all but destroyed the credibility of the movement in the eyes of the media and the public.

However, in the 1990s the Christian right is back, and it continues to be a factor in American culture, especially in politics, where it has been credited with helping to promote the agenda of Newt Gingrich, including his ascent to Speaker of the House, and the Republican majority of both the Senate and the House of Representatives for the first time in 40 years. In addition to a balanced budget, the conservative agenda includes many Christian aims, such as promoting prayer in school and rescinding abortion laws and laws protecting homosexual rights. From the ashes of the Moral Majority has arisen the Christian Coalition, a broad-based religious and political organization, largely supportive of conservative causes and leaders such as Pat Robertson, founder of the Christian Coalition, CEO of the Christian Broadcast Network, host of "The 700 Club," and former presidential candidate. Patrick Buchanan, CNN commentator, perennial presidential candidate, and champion of conservative causes, is another recent darling of the Christian right.

Concurrent with the religious millenarian revival of today is the development of new forms of secular millennialism. Tribulation refers to war, famine, disease, earthquakes, death, and other terrible signs that the end times are near. There are many signs today that can be accorded with the tribulations of Revelation, and one does not have to be on the religious right and millenarian fringe to appreciate them. The problems of today are no less than global.

Famine in Somalia, genocide in Bosnia, the destruction of the rain forests, ozone depletion, AIDS: These are the "tribulations" that scream from our newspaper and magazine headlines. Over the past few years the bestseller lists have been filled with secular dooms-day books on the "ecoapocalypse." *The Hole in the Sky: Man's Threat to the Ozone Layer, 5/5/2000: Ice, the Ultimate Disaster, Asteroid: Earth Destroyer or New Frontier,* and *The Coming Plague: Newly Emereging Disease in a World Out of Balance* are books that speak in varying degrees of apocalyptic language of planet-wide destruction due to a variety of environmental and ecological disasters.

The images and symbols of environmental, economic, and nu-clear destruction in our media often carry apocalyptic images and meanings. The revelations of recent years concerning the serious damage extant in the world's environment bring a wry smile to some environmentalists' faces. For example, environmentalist Eric Zency suggests that many of his peers seem to have assumed "Millerite" inclinations and derive a perverse satisfaction from all the bad news about our ecological predicament. "Yes," they say, "we were right all along. All that garbage spewing into the environment is finally having an effect and now everybody knows it."[26] Zency and others, like Spencer Weart, author of *Nuclear Fear*, fear that many environ-mentalists and antinuclear groups are becoming millennial by focus-ing too much on environmental decay and nuclear energy.[27] Ultimately they may become ineffectual in their abilities to initiate positive social change.

For example, a group of futurist planetary colonizers called the Synergetic Civilization have also come up with plans for surviving the impending ecoapocalypse. Other experiments with living in manufactured environments, whether under the sea or on space stations or "ecostations," include the Biosphere Project, designed in part for future planetary colonization. The "apoca-lypse" for these contemporary, secular, millenarian movements will most likely be man-made, brought about by socioeconomic collapse, environmental degradation, or world war. The deple-tion of the ozone layer, the destruction of the earth's rain forests, and other ecological problems are key to survivalist fears as well. The environment, of course, does need protection (the tempera-ture of the earth has risen in the last ten years), but environmen-talists should avoid overstating their case and lapsing into apocalyptic tirades that may do more harm to their cause than good.

In addition to environmental and ecological signs, other problems associated with global change include the social, economic, technological, and political changes that mark both the United States and much of the world. Economic doomsday bestsellers such as *The Coming Depression of 1990* by Ravi Batra also speak in apocalyptic terms about major social and economic changes.[28] Cyclical theories of the rise and decline of civilization, including Paul Kennedy's (1987) bestseller The *Rise and Fall of the Great Powers*, are apocalyptic to those looking for signs of tribulation and employing the millennial myth. Though neither book is overtly millennial in the classic religious sense, each speaks to issues of the relative military and economic decline of the United States, the ending of the "American era," and the major worldwide changes that are now underway. Such predictions may be true. History is filled with the rise and fall of great armies, such as those of ancient Greece, Rome, Great Britain, and the Soviet Union. Perhaps China, as some predict, will be the great power of the "Pacific century." Social problems based on economic and political change and the fragmenting effects of globalization all conspire to spotlight the dramatic and widespread "tribulations" that mark the end of the millennium.

Millennial symbols and themes also appear in the mass media and popular culture—on television and in film, in popular literature and music, even in toys and games. For example, the survivalist version of the millennial myth was most accessible to a large audience in the Hollywood action films of the 1980s. The Hollywood survivalist of the 1980s was very much cut from the cloth of the American survivalist, whose own stores of combat knives, automatic weapons, and other hardware rival the props for such movies as *Rambo: First Blood Part II* (1985), which grossed $75.8 million at the box office in its first 23 days.[29]

The survivalist character in American film can be traced back from Arnold Schwarzenegger, Steven Seagal, Chuck Norris, and Sylvester Stallone, to Clint Eastwood and Charles Bronson, to John Wayne, and even to Superman, who, to other superheroes, is a kind of ultimate survivalist (save for kryptonite). Frontiersman, gunslinger, war hero, or superhero, the survivalist character is a mythic American hero—the intrepid individualist, the killer with a conscience, the survivor.[30] Early television Westerns like *Daniel Boone, Davy Crockett, Wagon Train, Maverick, Cheyenne,* and even *The Lone Ranger* expressed this classic American character and his ability to succeed in all instances by way of a natural survival instinct and a wholesome American philosophy, honed in the backwoods or in the "wild, wild West."

Following upon the success of *Rambo: First Blood* (1982), a wave of mercenary and survivalist films appeared at the box office and later in videocassettes. Sylvester Stallone as *Rambo,* Arnold Schwarzenegger as *Commando* (1986), and Chuck Norris as the mercenary in *Missing in Action* (1984) were post-Vietnam soldiers of fortune who fought and won lost American battles against enemies that often included conspiratorial American bureaucrats in league with a foreign enemy. In a similar manner, the wave of 1980s Russian invasion films, including *Red Dawn* (1984), *Invasion USA* (1985), and the television miniseries *Amerika,* presented many of the same themes that drive the survivalist right. The narratives of the mercenary and Russian invasion films center on the sensational militaristic exploits of patriotic American citizens and mercenaries fighting to keep freedom and democracy safe from communist, or other outside deviant, influences.

The science fiction and fantasy film genres have also drawn on survivalist themes in the postapocalyptic visions of the future in the highly successful Mad Max trilogy (1980, 1982, 1986), *Blade Runner* (1982), *Terminator* (1984), and *Steel Dawn* (1984), to name the more successful. In these films similarities in genre, narrative, and setting are the most salient features. The films can be classified in the film noir genre because their narratives and settings are concerned with urban decay, the seamy underside of society, and the blackness of the postapocalyptic future. They are, of course, about nuclear war and its aftermath.

In *Mad Max* (starring Mel Gibson), the first of three successful Australian films centering on the postapocalypse, Max is a nomadic "road warrior" and a survivor of nuclear holocaust. He battles a devastated environment, punk motorcycle hoodlums, and other survivors for precious gasoline in this survival-of-the-fittest morality play. In the third film, *Mad Max Beyond Thunderdome* (1985), Max's antagonist and arch enemy is a woman (Tina Turner) who runs a "Babylonian" city of cutthroats where all disputes are settled in a Roman-style gladiatorial arena called Thunderdome. In the science fiction thriller *Blade Runner* (1982), starring Harrison Ford, the streets of a decayed and nuclear-devastated future Los Angeles are clogged with "River of Styx" hordes of lowlifes scurrying about their bases in a constant attempt to survive murderous rebel androids, corporate assassins, and the seething vermin of the postapocalypse. Much of the action in the film takes place on satellites orbiting the earth, drenched as it is by the poisonous rain of nuclear fallout.

These films present clear images of a nuclear-devastated future, an apocalyptic image that is shared by many survivalists, which may be why survivalist characters (paramilitary groups and punk hoodlums) and scenarios define the films. Thematically, films such as the Mad Max trilogy, *Blade Runner,* and *Steel Dawn* are all defined by nuclear devastation, a logical metaphor for the postmodern film noir. The apocalyptic scenario of mass destruction and Armageddon are central features in these films. Absent is the utopian vision of the millennium, the heaven on earth that will follow the great destruction. And there is no Second Coming. More survivalist than savior, the warrior hero may come to the defense of the defenseless, but he is an individualist who would rather go it alone; oftentimes he is a cynical Robin Hood, or a hardened loner with a soft spot in his heart. But he is not the Messiah.

Nuclear war and radioactive fallout in these films are the same expressions of the moribund (and survivable?) future that many survivalists envision and prepare for. However, implicitly they are also the symbols of Christian apocalypse and demonstrate the dimensions to which millennialism has been transformed in film narrative. The centrality of nuclear war and the postapocalypse in these films may represent secular transformations of the apocalypse and survival in the millennial myth. In fact, it is with the nuclear age that these nuclear symbols of apocalypse have gained ascendancy in our culture and have had much to do with the resurgence of survivalism and the modern millennial myth. Through these channels it also becomes accessible to a larger audience, although the source and meaning of its origin is not apparent.

*Too many cameras and not enough food, this is what we've seen.*
("DRIVEN TO TEARS," THE POLICE, 1987)

The apocalyptic myths of the last few decades have been projected on a global scale: world depression, world war, nuclear holocaust, overpopulation, ecological disaster. The "imagination of disaster" of a global catastrophe has become a worldwide fixation and, for some, an obsession. This is so because technology and the expansion of international transactions and communications now make it possible.

The master trends that most characterize our modern age are those involving the increasing reach and influence of international systems and technologies, such as the evolving world economy, mass communications and mass culture, international cooperation and conflict, and environmental concerns—the kinds of things that are creating a globalized world. Globalization, or the process by which the world is becoming a more highly integrated unit, is one of the the principle factors determining our current and future world. Globalization depends not only on the economy and the populations of the world, but on the communication media and popular culture as well.

In one way the revitalization of millennialism today is related to the increasing scale of many of the social and cultural trends that characterize our modern age. Images of disaster, mass murder, terrorism, and nuclear war have become the common fare of film, television news and drama, and popular literature. Such images help to fuel millennial expectations. Contemporary millennialism is no longer the simple consequence of relative deprivation—the inability to maintain the living standards customary in society.

Now the fear of deprivation can take the form of an imminent, absolute, and all-consuming environmental disaster. Because communication in our modern mass media can be instantaneous, drama and expectation is created that opens the way to milliennial interpretations.[31] The reporting on the Chernobyl accident, the war with Iraq, or Waco can excite millennial fervor when their images and meanings are plugged into the myth.

Survivalism provides a modern avenue for the symbols and meanings of the millennial myth to be reproduced and redefined. In certain ways survivalism reflects the severe downside of the millennial myth. Like the nihilism of punk, the survivalist philosophy speaks of mass destruction and mass death. It is not interested in reforming the system. The collapse of civilization is imminent, so why bother? It does, however, offer a plan of action—a kind of "redemption" or "salvation"—in the manner of surviving the great destruction of the current order and living on to begin again. The process evolves from a secularization of otherworldly apocalyptic elements into a self-salvationist credo based in this world. Salvation will come to those individuals and groups who have honed the "survival-of-the-fittest" instinct and ideology. The motto of the survivalist might as well be, "God helps those who help themselves." Survival may not in the hands of the savior but in the preparations of the individual. In this sense survivalism is "posttribulationist" in that survivalists don't believe that "the elect" or "the meek" will be raptured up into the clouds in some mass disappearing act before the return of Christ. Most are not counting on the Second Coming of Christ to bring them salvation anyway, at least not in the near future. Instead, they busily prepare for their physical security and survival during the times of tribulation to come. And if the Messiah does arrive, then they'll be there to greet him.

# Chapter 4

# Dragons, Beasts, and Christian Soldiers

*And behold a great red dragon, having seven heads and ten horns, and seven crowns upon his heads.*

Rev. 12:3, KJV

*Thou therefore endure hardness as a good soldier of Jesus Christ. No man that warreth entangle himself in the affairs of this life; that he may please him that hath chosen him to be a soldier.*

2 Tim. 2:3-4, KJV

Before the tragedy at Ruby Ridge, Randy Weaver had made enemies of many of his neighbors, who saw a foulmouthed man who was quick to anger. An avowed white supremacist, Weaver's sentences were littered with racist and anti-Semitic remarks. Weaver also claimed to be a survivalist, the kind that didn't join organizations but that was engaged in preparing for the collapse of society and the unraveling of the monetary system. He also subscribed to the white racist theology of Christian identity (see Chapter 5). He and his son Samuel regularly practiced shooting at their sprawling mountain home. Neighbors often complained that the Weavers were unconcerned about the noise and danger their shooting posed to the community. Weaver distrusted government in all of its guises—welfare, the public schools, the IRS, and law enforcement. He blamed liberals, Jews, and "internationalists" as the demons that threatened America.[1] He believed the government was out to get him. Little did he realize how prophetic his beliefs were—at least for himself and his family.

Weaver, 44, had been a fugitive since April 1990 when he failed to appear for a court hearing on weapons violations. He had sold two sawed-off shotguns to an ATF informant. A fugitive warrant for his arrest was issued and turned over to the U.S. marshals. Weaver retreated to his mountaintop refuge for the next 18 months, vowing he would resist government oppression. Holed up with Weaver were his wife, Vicky; his three daughters; his son Samuel; and a friend, Kevin Harris. U.S. marshals waited for months to bring a peaceful end to the siege; in the meantime they devised plans for a possible assault. That assault came on August 21, 1992. Weaver refused to allow the marshals on his property or near his house to execute their arrest warrants, at one point reportedly threatening them at gunpoint. Shortly after that episode, a gunfight broke out between the Weavers, Harris, and the marshals. Weaver's 13-year old son Samuel was shot and killed, as was Deputy Marshal William F. Degan.

The FBI quickly took over the operation. The next day a gunfight erupted between Weaver and Harris and agency sharpshooters, one of whom shot and killed Vicky Weaver as she stood in a doorway holding her infant daughter. Weaver, who was injured in the shoot-out, continued to hold out against federal authorities, but considered surrendering if he could be assured of a fair trial and allowed to have as a negotiator longtime friend James "Bo" Gritz. Like Weaver, Gritz was a Green Beret and a member of the same racist Christian Identity movement to which Weaver had paid allegiance. Gritz has been a third-party candidate for the presidency. Few soldiers returned from Vietnam more highly decorated. Sylvester Stallone's famous character Rambo was probably derived at least partly from Gritz. And after the Vietnam war had ended, Gritz led several trips back to Indochina, searching for POWs. But investigators have discredited his claim of having returned with human remains.[2]

Gritz felt uniquely qualified to understand and negotiate with Weaver, who at one point told him, "Bo, I can't get a fair trial in this Babylon court." Gritz eventually convinced Weaver to give himself up. In July 1993, a federal jury found Weaver guilty of failing to appear in court but acquitted him of the original weapons charge after Weaver's attorney, Gerry Spence, successfully argued that the ATF had entrapped his client. In July 1995, the courts awarded Weaver and his surviving family 3.1 million dollars for the death of his wife and son at the hands of federal agents.[3]

The August 1992 gunfight and standoff between white supremacist Randy Weaver and federal authorities at Weaver's Ruby Ridge, Idaho, ranch was a benchmark in the emergence of the militia movement and the reemergence of the Patriot movement, both with connections to survivalism and roots in American millennialism. The actions of the FBI, the federal marshals, and the ATF (though they played no direct role in the shooting) were viewed by many as terrorist and Gestapolike, designed to disarm Americans and take away individual rights in the name of law and order. Ruby Ridge literally became a call to arms for those on the far right—a new Alamo or Pearl Harbor. For years voices on the right had been warning of growing government abuse of power and intrusion into Americans' lives. The attack on Ruby Ridge showed just how far federal law enforcement was willing to go to disarm gun-owning Americans, even to the point of murdering innocent women and children.

Less than eight months later, the sensational incident at Waco involving the Branch Davidians and David Koresh would confirm fears—if Ruby Ridge hadn't already—that the U.S. government and law enforcement agencies especially were out of control and had become downright tyrannical. The shoot-out and subsequent 51-day standoff were the result of an aborted attempt by the ATF to issue arrest warrants on Koresh and the Davidians for accumulating weapons parts that could be used to transform semiautomatic weapons into automatic ones and stockpiling other illegal explosives. Koresh and his church had been under investigation for months, so on February 28 the ATF moved in.

Later investigations found that numerous mistakes were made by federal law enforcement from the start.[4] The ATF decided to use paramilitary force to deliver a warrant for Koresh's arrest even after they had lost the element of surprise. Koresh had been tipped off to the raid, and the ATF had discovered the breach. But they went ahead anyway and the raid turned into disaster. We may never know who shot first, but a shoot-out ensued in which four ATF agents and six Branch Davidians were killed. Koresh himself was shot in the arm during the attack and nursed the wound throughout the subsequent 51-day standoff. Through almost two months of telephone negotiations, in which the FBI eventually assumed control, authorities tried to understand Koresh and find a way out of the standoff. Finally giving up, the FBI devised a way out and convinced newly appointed Attorney General Janet Reno of their plan's feasibility. On April 19, the FBI ordered armored vehicles to punch holes in the building and shoot in gas canisters, which would force out the residents. Somehow the house caught fire, which quickly spread to other buildings until the entire complex was engulfed in flames. Regardless of how the fire began—by accident, set deliberately by Koresh and his followers, or set intentionally by federal authorities (as lawyers for the surviving Branch Davidians attest)—a conflagration consumed the Branch Davidian community at Mount Carmel, killing 135 members of the church, including 38 children (see Chapter 7).

Many questions have been raised in the aftermath of the Branch Davidian tragedy. Why had the ATF chosen to serve their warrant in such a violent fashion when so many innocent people, including children, were known to be present? Federal authorities also knew that Koresh left the Mount Carmel ranch on occasion. Why not arrest him off the ranch, away from the security of his church? Why had the FBI taken over negotiations from the ATF and local police authorities, who had developed a relationship and a degree of trust with the Davidians? And why were there no fire engines and other emergency vehicles present on the day of the gassing and subsequent fire? There was little doubt in the minds of many Americans that federal law enforcement authorities—from the ATF and the FBI to the attorney general—botched the incident, resulting in the terrible tragedy.

In the aftermath of Ruby Ridge and Waco, the survivalist and paramilitary subculture responded. In protests, editorials, letters to their representatives, and calls to radio talk shows, they attacked government law enforcers as brutal thugs who were stomping on the rights of ordinary Americans. Calls to "abolish" and "disarm" the ATF and to investigate the motives and actions of federal authorities, including those of Janet Reno, came from all quarters on the right.

Federal law enforcement agencies such as the FBI and the ATF are particularly loathed by the gun-toting paramilitary culture. Because they must enforce laws that many American gun owners find abhorrent, including the Brady Bill requirement for a five-day waiting period before purchasing a gun, the ban on assault rifles, and legislation in many states forbidding concealment of weapons, federal law enforcement agencies have come to be demonized as evil agents of larger sinister forces in government.

In the rhetoric and imagery of the subculture of the survivalist right, the U.S. government and select agencies have acquired the personas of the evil demons who populate Revelation, including the various dragons and beasts commonly identified as servants of Satan, if not the devil himself.[5]

To those who plug into the millennial myth, the U.S. government is the seven-headed Dragon. Its several heads are embodied in the ATF, FBI, IRS, EPA, and the whole alphabet soup of federal agencies that feed the ravenous appetite of the governmental beast. Some on the militant right have likened federal law enforcement to "jackbooted thugs," or to fascists or the gestapo—all references to Nazi police and storm troopers. Further down the road of right-wing fanaticism are skinheads, neo-Nazis, and white supremacists, who retain Nazi symbolism for themselves. They also attack the federal government and law enforcement, as well as "minority mud people" and "internationalist Jews," with a demonology derived from the mythology of the Third Reich and white Aryan supremacy.

The red dragon and the two-horned beast of Revelation are also demonic metaphors for international organizations like the

World Bank and the United Nations, who right-wing conspiracy theorists believe are set on undermining the power of the United States to impose upon it the dictates of a world government. The pregnant woman who is persecuted by the seven-headed dragon of Revelation, which stands ready to devour her child upon birth, personifies the heavenly city of Jerusalem and its saints, chosen people, and Christian soldiers. To those who maintain their faith in God and Christ and who are ready to fight the demonic foes of Christianity will be given the keys to the promised land. For the "true believer," the American government and its institutions—especially its law enforcement agencies and those groups that represent the new world order—have come to be seen as symbols of the evil of Satan's power unleashed in the world in the closing decades of the the second millennium.

*Michael and his angels battled against the Dragon and his angels and there was war in Heaven. (REV. 12:7, RSV)*

The bombing of the Alfred P. Murrah office building in Oklahoma City was a blatant attack on the federal government. The building housed various agencies of the government, including an IRS department, a registry of motor vehicles, and a day-care center primarily for the children of federal employees working in the building. Early reports of the first suspect arrested in connection with the crime, Timothy McVeigh, revealed that he was a Gulf War veteran and had allegedly been associated with the Kingman, Arizona, militia. A terrorist attack of the magnitude of the Oklahoma City bombing, possibly perpetrated by U.S. citizens, caused the public and the media to scrutinize the so-called militia movement and the other antigovernment groups on the militant right. In the weeks following the bombing, Americans learned a lot about militia members: They were angry, armed, and organized, and many practiced survivalism. They were angry at the U.S. government, apparently, for eroding the rights—particularly the gun rights—of average American citizens. Many of these Americans were also losing their jobs and seeing their lifestyles and values threatened by "globalism," "multiculturalism," and the "deindustrialization" of the American economy and way of life. Ruby Ridge and Waco became rallying cries for a subculture of Americans confused and angry at the current state of their lives and their country who were now lashing out at the government.

It is not known exactly how many militia members there are across the country. Daniel Junas, a researcher in Washington State, estimates that more than 40 states have militias, with a hardcore membership of at least 10,000 and still growing.[6] Local militias have existed for a long time in American society. One of the earliest and most famous was the Minutemen at Concord, whose "shot heard round the world" marked the first battle of the Revolutionary War. In Vermont, it was the Green Mountain Boys who held off the redcoats at Hubbardton in Vermont's legendary brush with Revolutionary War. Even the Alamo is remembered as a key event in the history of the American militia tradition by contemporary militia members. The militias use these examples to set forth a claim to the literal truth of the Second Amendment, which states that "a well-regulated militia, being necessary to the security of a free state, the right of the people to keep and bear arms, shall not be infringed."

They hearken back to the days when small colonial communities needed to defend themselves from Indians, redcoats, bandits, or rebellious slaves. Modern militia leaders brush aside arguments that the National Guard is the modern militia and cite the necessity of local militias being independent of the government, especially since militias may need to defend themselves from the government. To the "unalienable rights" of "life, liberty, and the pursuit of happiness" that are "endowed by their Creator" the militia would add the rights to bear arms and form local militias. The militias speak with reverence of the Second Amendment to the Constitution and to the words Thomas Jefferson wrote in *The Declaration of Independence:* "that to secure these rights, governments are instituted among men, deriving their just powers from the consent of the governed, that whenever any form of government becomes destructive of these ends, it is the right of the people to alter or abolish it. . . ."[7]

The militia movement presents many examples of the government infringing on the rights of gun owners, usurping more power for itself at the expense of average Americans. Ruby Ridge, Waco, and recent gun control laws have become rallying cries for the militia movement, proving government intrusion on private citizens, particularly since survivalist communities and others involved in collecting or selling weapons have been routinely targeted by the AFT. Before Ruby Ridge and Waco there were other highly publicized investigations of survivalist individuals and groups. Edward Francis, husband of Elizabeth Clare Prophet—"Guru Ma" to the survivalist and apocalyptic Church Universal and Triumphant—was convicted in the fall of 1989 of illegally purchasing $100,000 worth of illegal weapons.[8] Local and federal authorities continue to keep a close watch on the activities of the Church Universal and Triumphant.

Considered the "mother of all militias," or MOM for short, the Militia of Montana has been actively engaged in publicizing the philosophy of the militia movement and itself. Fifty-year-old John Trochman, his brother David, and nephew Randy run the Militia of Montana, a publicity-seeking outfit that has organized "militia support groups" and produces a wide assortment of books, pamphlets, videos, newsletters, and cassette tapes promoting its "product" and identity. All these products were on display at the *Soldier of Fortune* Convention and Exposition held in Las Vegas in the fall of 1995 (Figure 4.1).

*the new world order . . . . represents the latest chapter of a progressive conspiracy to replace God and Christianity with a godless man-centered world order.[9]*

When you peel back the layers of the government conspiracy to take rights from the American people, you find an even deeper conspiracy theory regarding international individuals and groups who supposedly conspire to destroy the sovereignty of nations so as to build a tyrannical new world government. In different versions of the theory the proponents of this new world government are centered in the United Nations and other international organi-

FIGURE 4.1. Militia of Montana (MOM) both, *SOF* Exposition, Las Vegas, September/October 1995.

zations, such as global think tanks, multinational corporations, and cultural or humanitarian organizations. The aim of the conspiracy is to build a new global order controlled by a cadre of powerful economic, political, and cultural elites bent on creating a global socialism. Global socialism will require Americans to share their wealth and resources more equitably with the rest of the world, inevitably resulting in the lowering of the living standards of Americans to that of the Third World. The laws and rules that govern the global order instituted by the new world government will take precedence over the federal government of the United States, and Americans will be taking orders from foreigners.

The terms "globalism" or "globalization" strike terror into the hearts of right-wing conspiracy theorists. They maintain that these

"internationalist" groups comprise elitists who believe it is necessary for highly educated and "globally aware" individuals from all
nations to rule the new world order. The conspiracy theory holds
that internationalists are born into wealthy and powerful families,
educated at elite schools, connected to the corporate and political
world, and are members of global organizations and clubs. In the
United States government the Council of Foreign Relations (CFR)
is the training ground for many new world leaders and appears to
head the drive for the new world government. Past and present
members such as George Bush, Gerald Ford, Henry Kissinger, and
David and Nelson Rockefeller are seen as members of the cadre of
internationalist conspirators. Conspiracy theory "historians" point
to former CFR member Alger Hiss as the model of global conspiracy. Hiss, who helped found the United Nations, was convicted of
espionage in 1950 during the McCarthy hearings and spent three
years in jail.

"Secular humanism" is the term used by many on the far right
to define the value system of the global conspirators. Secular
humanism refers to a man-centered and godless worldview, in
which moral and religious values are set aside in relations with
those whose beliefs and values are different. It also refers to the idea
that concern for, and improvement in, the human condition, or
"humanism," can be accomplished in the absence of spiritual guidance. Cultural relativism, the understanding and appreciation of
cultural diversity, and multiculturalism, the respect and tolerance
of ethnic, religious, or sexual preferences, are other important
values of the secular humanist. To many on the religious and
conspiracy-minded right, secular humanism is anti-Christian and
teaches that since religious and moral beliefs are relative, there is
no ethical or spiritual center. Ultimately, for some, the atheistic new
world socialist order of the secular humanist is inspired by Satan
himself.

Numerous institutions and groups, both national and international, came under attack in the aftermath of Ruby Ridge and Waco.
In the ideology of survivalists, militias, and Patriots, domestic
organizations like the ATF, the FBI, the Federal Reserve, the IRS, the

National Park Service, and the Environmental Protection Agency (EPA) all conspire against the individual's freedom and increase the wealth and power of the federal government. Other select international organizations like the Trilateral Commission (founded in 1973 by David Rockefeller as a way to better organize the economies of the United States, Europe, and Japan), the World Bank, and the United Nations compose the horns of the dragons of Revelation "set forth to deceive the nations."

The belief in the international conspiracy to build a new world socialist order is a central feature of the so-called Patriot movement. As its name implies, the Patriot movement espouses a strong nationalist philosophy and reflects the views of "superpatriotic" Americans, who see America as not just the land of the free and the brave, but as a Christian land promised to God-fearing Americans by the Almighty. Older and more broadly based than the militias, but organized in the same loose fashion, the Patriot movement has reached out in recent years to the emerging militia movement. Through networks created on the Internet; via an extensive literature that includes all manner of desktop-published books, pamphlets and newsletters, videos, and cassette tapes; and through talk radio programs and grassroots organizations, Patriots and militia members are finding common ground.

Many in the Patriot movement fear that America has reached a dangerous crossroads. The values that have made this nation great and a beacon to the world have weakened and are dangerously close to unraveling. America is becoming seduced by the values of a godless secular humanism, with its concern for multiculturalism, globalism, and cultural relativism, which Patriots believe will dilute and even obliterate the American ethic. Some Patriots fancy themselves "constitutionalists" and see themselves as latter-day Thomas Jeffersons, employing legal and constitutional analyses of the nation's founding documents, including the Constitution and its amendments, which they believe to be inspired by God. The Montana Freemen tried to use constitutional analyses and "common law" procedures and courts to sanction their flouting of local, state, and federal laws in their attempt to create a separatist and autonomous "township," resulting in the spring 1996 stand-off with the FBI. Threats to the Second Amendment protecting the right to bear arms is a key issue that has generated interest in constitutional analysis and discussion among Patriots and militia members.

Chief among the values that secular humanism is undermining is religion—American Christian Protestantism—which members believe rests at the heart of Western Christian civilization, American culture, and the Constitution. Many Patriots are strongly Christian and believe the Constitution was derived from the Bible and was given to the country's forefathers by God Himself. They fashion themselves as constitutional purists, holding to a strict interpretation of the Constitution in almost biblical terms. In fact, they often speak of the American Constitution as inspired by God and thus a sacred document. Patriots view the world in religious terms. The tyrannical factions of federal law enforcers and the engineers of the new world order are designing sinister plans to destroy the Constitution and American Christendom. They see themselves as the defenders of the nation's holy laws, the true believers of America's sacred destiny, the real American Patriots. Revelation speaks of the "called," the "faithful" and "true" to describe the true believers (Rev. 17:14), those who steadfastly hold to the laws of God, retain their faith in Christ, and are prepared to fight alongside the Messiah against the beast. We will see more of this religious rationality in the theology of the Christian survivalists (see Chapter 5).

While the Patriot movement has existed on the margins of American society for decades, Ruby Ridge, the Waco tragedy, the Oklahoma City bombing, the Freemen stand-off, and other recent events have brought their ideas into the mainstream and before a larger audience. While most Patriots condemned the attack on innocent people, including children, in the Oklahoma City bombing, many still intimated that they weren't surprised by the event given the viciousness of federal law enforcement actions in recent years. To them, the bombing demonstrated just how far Americans could be pushed. Some conspiracy-minded Patriots and militia members even suggested that federal agents may have executed the bombing themselves and blamed it on the militia to justify their crackdown on paramilitary groups.

Other factors in the spread of the Patriot movement include social and economic changes. While the Patriot movement provides a theory and politics for potential survivalist and militia members, increasingly it appeals to a broader American public as well. Many Americans are disaffected with government. Predominantly white, male, middle- and working-class Americans have been affected negatively by the changing American and global economy and its attendant restructuring, job losses, declining real wages, and social dislocations. This same sector sees its traditional privileges and status challenged and eroded by the liberal social movements of the 1960s and 1970s, which challenged the dominant social and economic institutions of society and opened up positions to women and minorities. They target feminism, minority rights, the gay and lesbian movement, and environmentalists as the bane of their existence.

In past decades the international threat of communism and the Cold War provided the best examples of the cosmic battle between the forces of good and evil for groups like the Patriots. The threat also provided a check on the antics of these groups, who still supported "America" with all her flaws. With the collapse of the Soviet Union and the widespread changes that continue to wash across Eastern Europe, the loss of the Soviet empire created a vacuum. Today world-class demons the likes of Hitler, Stalin, and the evil empire are in short supply, apparently, so the Patriots have turned their sites on the American government, its institutions, and the greatly feared new world order. Transfigured by the millennial myth, the institutions of political power have become symbolic representations of the dragons of Revelation and the agents of Satan.

*And the dragon was wroth with the woman, and went to make war with the remnant of her seed, which keep the commandments of God, and have the testimony of Jesus Christ. (REV. 12:17, RSV)*

*The federal government has abdicated Government here, by declaring us out of its Protection and waging War against us. The federal government has plundered our Seas, ravaged our coasts, burnt our towns, and destroyed the lives of our people.* (LINDA THOMPSON, "DECLARATION OF INDEPENDENCE," 1994)[10]

Of the many new faces to glow in the afterburn of Ruby Ridge, Waco, and Oklahoma City is Linda Thompson. Thompson, a lawyer and the leader of the Patriot movement of Indiana, gained national headlines in 1994 with her "Declaration of Independence," sent out over the Internet and mailed to hundreds of individuals and groups that compose the growing Patriot, militia, and survivalist movements. Subtitled "A Declaration by the Sovereign Citizens of the Several States within the United States of America," the document is written in the style of the original Declaration of Independence and uses similar language. For example, the first paragraph is the same as that penned by Thomas Jefferson in 1776:

> When in the course of human Events, it becomes necessary for one People to dissolve the Political Bands which have connected them with another, and to assume among the Powers of the Earth, the separate and equal station to which the Laws of Nature and of Nature's Laws entitle them, a decent respect to the Opinions of Mankind requires that they should declare the causes which impel them to the Separation.

Like the declaration of the founding fathers, the declaration of 1994 is a call for revolution. Because the current American government has usurped and abused its powers and has become destructive to the rights of citizens, Thompson writes, "It is the Right of the People to alter or to abolish it, and to institute new government." In her declaration, Thompson goes on to render the conspiracy at the heart of the U.S. government and the "long Train of Abuses and Usurpations, pursuing invariably the same Object, evidence of a Design to reduce them [Americans] under absolute Despotism." Thompson accuses all branches of the federal government of abusing the laws of the United States and for holding the Constitution in contempt. The president and Congress, she claims, have robbed the governors of their powers to pass laws designed for local problems and issues in their states and regions, an assertion that many militia and Patriot leaders support.

Thompson argues for the rights of the individual as well. The legislative branch of government does not reflect the beliefs and problems of most Americans, and the voting system is "a national sham and disgrace." It allows only those of great wealth and connections to enter national politics, she says, thus preventing the common man from participating as a candidate and rendering the individual's vote meaningless. Giving further examples of a political system that benefits only insiders, she points to the federal judiciary, selected at the whim of the executive branch and a Congress "inattentive to anything but their own special interests and the will and money of lobbying groups."

Thompson spins the yarn of the right-wing conspiracy theorists. She cites the federal government's role in undermining the domestic economy. She spews the rhetoric of the Posse Comitatus and other antitax protest groups who subscribe to a theory in which federal and private economic institutions conspire to create a world socialist economy controlled by a small international elite. Included in the conspiracy is the Federal Reserve and private banking interests, whom Thompson condemns:

> For imposing taxes on us without our Consent; for failing to publicly acknowledge more than 60 years ago that the federal government was in fact, bankrupt, but instead, concealing these facts from the people and entering into a fraudulent agreement to finance the bankruptcy by creating and perpetuating a fraudulent monetary system, to the enrichment of private bankers, insurance companies, and their stockholders, called the "federal reserve system."

The current monetary system is extortionist, she says, and "a fraudulent, coercive, unjust and unlawful tax scheme foisted upon the people without their knowledge or consent." The oppression is enforced by brutal law enforcement agents acting on the orders of an unrestrained government that seizes property and imprisons those who do not voluntarily submit to its demands. Thompson argues that the federal government ultimately seeks to criminalize the free exercise of our most basic constitutional rights, including the rights of free speech, freedom of the press, freedom of worship, freedom of assembly, and the right to keep and bear arms.

In an interesting allusion to the plagues of tribulation in Revelation, Thompson writes, "The Federal government has erected a Multitude of new Offices, and sent hither Swarms of Officers to harass Our People, and eat out their Substance." Regarding Ruby Ridge and Waco, Thompson argues that, through unlawfully constructed law enforcement agencies like the ATF, the government has "repeatedly murdered or incarcerated those who opposed with manly firmness the Invasions on the Rights of the People." She accuses the government of protecting agents of the federal government and military from trial or punishment for the murder and mayhem they have inflicted on innocent citizens in the abuse of their authority.

She argues that through the seduction and coercion of state legislatures, and through federal tax monies offered in exchange for their cooperation, state governments are relinquishing the sovereignty of the state. Along with state legislatures, and through the same "surreptitious and covert methods," the U.S. military has been given power over civil authorities. Thompson accuses the president, members of the executive branch, and Congress for conspiring to subject Americans to a foreign constitution. She further believes that the federal government is organizing domestic and foreign troops on U.S. soil. The federal government, she writes, "has kept among us, in Times of Peace, Standing Armies, without the consent of our Legislatures":

> The Federal government, at this Time, is transporting large armies of foreign mercenaries to complete the works of Death, Desolation and Tyranny, already begun, often under the color of the laws of the United Nations, and with circumstance of Cruelty and Perfidy, scarcely paralleled in the most barbarous Age, totally unworthy of a civilized Nation.

And the barbarism continues. Thompson believes that the United States government is attempting to depopulate the country by obstructing naturalization laws, refusing to encourage migrations, and buying or stealing large tracts of land for federal management. Even more horribly, the federal government "has waged chemical, biological, and radioactive warfare upon the people, and encouraged and funded abortions and acts of genocide upon large populations of people." At every stage, argues Thompson, the people have sought to redress this oppression, but have been answered by repeated insult and physical attack. She calls Presi-

dent Clinton a "tyrant" and "unfit to be the Ruler of a free People."
She believes it is time for a second American revolution. The
Declaration concludes with an appeal to God:

> We, therefore, the sovereign of the several states of the united states, which
> now form the United States of America, appealing to the Supreme Judge
> of the World for the Rectitude of our Intentions, do, in our own names and
> right and by the authority of God Almighty, solemnly Publish and Declare,
> that each of the sovereign citizens undersigned are, and of a Right ought
> to be, Free and Independent Sovereign Citizens; that they are absolved of
> all Allegiance to the federal government of the United States of America,
> and that all political Connection between them and the federal govern-
> ment of the United States of America, is and ought to be, totally dis-
> solved . . . . And for the support of this Declaration, with a firm Reliance
> on the Protection of divine Providence, we mutually pledge to each other
> our lives, our Fortunes, and our sacred Honor.
>
> Signers, this 18th day of April, in the year 1994, of our Lord.

One hundred individuals signed Thompson's original Declaration of Independence, 1994, which was then sent out over the
Internet, and to like-minded organizations throughout the country,
with a petition to sign to join the second American revolution.[11]
While the Patriot movement and its constitutional purists provide
a secular and political analysis to their call for a revolution, they
continually allude to the sacred stature of the Declaration of Independence, the Constitution, and American destiny. They rarely
miss an opportunity to invoke God or divine providence in support
of their patriotic goals and aspirations. They freely borrow from the
Bible and Revelation and employ apocalyptic symbols and images
in their commentary and predictions regarding the erosion of
American power and influence in the world, the ultimate collapse
of American society, and the emergence of a new world order. Linda
Thompson, the darling of the Patriot and militia movements, is no
exception.

*before a one-world socialist government can be established, the Ameri-*
*can people must be sold on the necessity of globalism as the only salva-*
*tion for "humankind." "Humankind" is a catchphrase often used by*
*the globalists who work to replace Western Christian Civilization with*
*their own secular-humanist new world order.*[12]

In light of these incidents and debates, many old faces on the right reappeared on the national stage as if on cue. G. Gordon Liddy, former Watergate burglar, part-time actor, and host of his own radio talk show, is another American "patriot" who was reading the signs of discontent and anger in American society. Liddy is one of the more well-known spokesmen for the militant right, and he fans the flames of public discontent on his own talk radio program, one of a growing number on the Patriot Network. Liddy rants about government conspiracies and the selling out of American workers by multinational corporations. On one show Liddy advised those who might find themselves under attack by ATF agents to aim for the head as the surest way to terminate the enemy.[13] Liddy has since backed off from those comments, yet how he reconciles them with his past experiences as a member of the federal government is not clear.

Oddly enough, the most moderate voice I heard at the 1995 _Soldier of Fortune_ Convention was Liddy, who was the keynote speaker at the convention's final banquet and awards ceremony. After a run-of-the-mill speech extolling the virtues of traditional American values, including plenty of anecdotes from his own virtuous life, Liddy was asked, in light of Waco and Ruby Ridge, if American citizens and gun owners should begin to actively resist the government and repressive law enforcement agencies, by taking up arms if necessary. Without hesitating, Liddy replied, "No. Armed resistance is not the answer, except as the last resort. That sort of thing will only get you killed. If things need to be changed or set right in this nation, we already posses the best mechanism for doing that—it's called the vote." Perhaps reacting to criticism for his inflammatory remarks about the ATF, or maybe pandering to the "moderates" in the _SOF_ audience, Liddy reflects the fact that not everybody on the far right is calling for armed rebellion. But others in the Patriot movement do.

The USA Patriot Network is a loosely organized group of radio stations, many on shortwave bands linked via satellite to a wider audience, that promote the agenda of the Patriot movement, and has become a beacon to militias, survivalists, and other like-minded individuals and groups. In addition to Linda Thompson, another new star in the Patriot constellation is self-styled militia and Patriot leader Mark Koernke. Questioned by authorities in the aftermath of the Oklahoma City bombing and later released, Koernke now broadcasts on his shortwave radio program, "The Intelligence Report." According to longtime friend and college ROTC buddy Ramon Martinez, Koernke, a literal interpreter of Revelation, believes that we are living in apocalyptic times.[14] Koernke also did a stint in the U.S. Army Reserves, where part of his duty, he now claims, included building "detention centers" for American citizens who might resist a foreign takeover of the United States. Alerted to the dangers of a conspiracy in the American government, Koernke became one of the leading spokesmen of the Patriot movement and has risen in its pantheon of prophets.

Like others in the movement, Koernke has hit the lecture circuit and has produced a series of videos in which he outlines the conspiracy of the new world order. In the video *America in Peril*, Koernke warns Americans to watch for signs of a future invasion force allied to the new world government. He points to unmarked "black helicopters" operating covertly in the United States that serve the interests of the United Nations and forces of the new world order. Koernke's conspiracy theory also holds that over 300,000 foreign troops are already operating on American soil, among them a band of Nepalese Gurkhas in Montana. Their future actions include rounding up Patriots and other resisters of the imposed order and shipping them to detention camps. Many of these have already been built for this purpose by the Federal Emergency Management Agency (FEMA), the agency that organizes the government's response to national emergencies. Koernke believes that FEMA's employees are part of the new world order's secret government.[15]

As he explains in *America in Peril*, the new world government has already accomplished much of its mission. Under pressure from the internationalist conspirators, federal agencies and street gangs have formed an "unholy alliance," he laments, and they have waged a campaign of violence and terror aimed at law-abiding Americans, especially gun owners. Says Koernke, "Once the nation is supine, it will be carved into large regions ruled through terror by new world order proconsuls. Microchips will be implanted in every newborn child, enabling the government to track each move by a new generation of citizens. Americans will live in slavery."[16] He also tells viewers to prepare for the collapse of the present national and international order and advocates resistance to the conspiracy before it disarms the Patriots and all freedom-loving Americans. Koernke predicts a long, violent guerrilla war that will probably end in a nuclear Armageddon.

*Soldier of Fortune* has also welcomed all the attention lavished by the media on the paramilitary and survivalist subcultures, though it has distanced itself from Koernke, Thompson, and other extremist advocates of a new American revolution. However, *SOF* supports the general distrust of government and shares the fear of overzealous law enforcement agents and "gun control liberals." With ongoing coverage of Ruby Ridge, Waco, and other incidents involving federal law enforcement, *SOF* has followed events with biting coverage, especially aimed at the U.S. government, federal law enforcement, and Janet Reno. While paying allegiance to no one group or philosophy, *SOF* attracts those involved in the Patriot and militia movements. Through its coverage of domestic and international military and paramilitary conflict and in its conventions and expositions, *SOF* provides a forum for all manner of antigovernment zealot and new world order conspiracy theorist.

In the past decade the National Rifle Association (NRA) has also seen a shift in its organizational structure and philosophy. In the early 1990s, the 120-year old organization suffered major defeats in Congress, first over the Brady Bill and later with the passage of the assault weapons ban. Adding Ruby Ridge and Waco to the mix of government intrusions on the gun rights of Americans, NRA leadership has increasingly reached out to the far right, a turn that has angered many long-term, moderate members, but has attracted—according to the NRA—far more new members.[17] The turn has been engineered by a new, more strident elite on the 76-member board, an elite led by second vice president Neal Knox and chief lobbyist Tanya Metaksa. On spelling her name, Metaksa helps reporters: "It's 'ak' as in AK-47, and 'sa' as in semiautomatic."[18] The new board has pushed the organization toward what many claim are extremist positions, such as defending the "cop-killer" bullet and resisting identification markers on explosive devices. To many the NRA has become "as inflexible in their interpretation of the Second Amendment as Christian Fundamentalists are in their reading of the Bible."[19]

In a 1995 fund-raising letter the NRA referred to federal agents as jack-booted thugs, a comment that prompted George Bush to resign his lifelong membership in the organization.[20] Many moderate members of the NRA, who personify the more traditional hunting and sporting culture of American gun owners, have also been critical of the NRA's drift into right-wing politics and its association with paramilitary groups like the militias. Still, many NRA members agreed with their leadership and felt betrayed by conservative politicians like George Bush over recent gun legislation. By distancing himself from the NRA, an organization traditionally associated with mainstream American gun owners, the former president became linked to the liberal establishment's program to take guns out of Americans' hands. Those even further to the right demonized him as part of the world government conspiracy to take over America. During the Gulf War, President Bush appropriated the language of the millennial myth, using phrases like "new world order," which, possibly unbeknownst to him, placed him on the side of the evil conspiracy to disarm Americans in preparation for the new world order.

For every prominent figure such as G. Gordon Liddy and Mark Koernke, there are hundreds of local Patriot and militia leaders who dot the canvas of the militant right. They reflect the growing subculture of Americans distrustful of government and law enforcement, many perhaps down on their luck, falling out of the middle class (or unable to reach it), and blaming government for their problems. Many have lost their jobs or feel threatened by unemployment and corporate "restructuring" and "downsizing." They blame affirmative action laws, which give too much to women and minorities at the expense of white American men, who are becoming the new "minority" group. They also feel that the federal government has sold out their factory jobs and manufacturing industries by embracing NAFTA, GATT, and other trade policies that favor foreign countries and multinational corporations over America's interests.

The movement also reflects the values of patriotic Americans who have served or whose loved ones have served their country in times of need. They fear the rapid social and economic changes that are affecting their way of life, and they feel increasingly disenfranchised. America is losing its predominance in the world and is becoming a "second-rate" country. Looking for the cause of their problems, they found it in their own government and its hidden agenda, and in the oppressive agents of law enforcement who carry out its dirty work. But they still sought leaders and prophets who would help them read the signs, support their views, and provide them with guidance. They became survivalists or joined organizations like the Patriot movement, a local militia, or any of dozens of similar organizations operating on a fear of change and a paranoia that a conspiracy is underway that will wrest control from individuals and erode the sovereignty of the American nation. They also demonize various federal and international organizations and minority groups to bolster their apocalyptic beliefs.

In Revelation, the victim of the dragon's attack, the woman who gives birth to a male child destined to rule "all nations," apparently represents heavenly Israel—the "church" and its "chosen" people the Dragon tries to destroy (Rev. 12:5). Many of those who belive in a conspiracy of evildoers bent on destroying American culture and imposing an atheistic, socialist government on the United States and the world see themselves as the chosen people and the crusading soldiers of Christ. Patriots and militias play upon the fear of a tyrannical government, a godless secular humanism, and an oppressive new world order to legitimate the religious and nationalist passions of their own patriotic version of the American millennial myth. More recently, environmentalists, multinationals, government, law enforcement, and international organizations have all become targets of derision for the Patriot and militia movements. These groups have also become targets of the Unabomber, the Oklahoma City bombers, and those individuals and groups responsible for the Amtrak train derailments: the first near Hyder, Arizona, on October 11, 1995, and the second on February 10, 1996. In the melding of an apocalyptic mentality with the fear and paranoia of government tyranny and international conspiracy, the dragons and beasts of Revelation rear their demonic heads.

# Chapter 5

# Antichrist

# The Myth of the Jewish World Conspiracy

*I know thy works, and tribulation, and poverty, but thou art rich; and I know the blasphemy of them that say they are Jews, and are not, but are synagogue of Satan.*

REV. 3:9, KJV

*Are there any Nazis out there . . . I'm a Jew and I'd like to talk to them.*

DENVER TALK SHOW HOST ALAN BERG[1]

Alan Berg was a talk radio personality in Denver in the early 1980s who, like many professionals of the art of talk, could get his audience going. Thin, bearded, and graying, the chain-smoking Berg talked fast, loved to push his callers' buttons, and thrived on controversy. Both popular and despised, Berg was always controversial, especially among the right-wingers in his audience—neo-Nazis, white supremacists, John Birchers, and survivalists. They loved to hate this pushy, loud-mouthed Jew from New York City, and Berg loved to hate them back.

Berg baited the many right-wing zealots among his listeners; they became his stock and trade. "Any Nazis out there?" he'd ask. He would then give phone number of station KOA.

And they would call at every opportunity to rant about government-funded abortions and homosexual rights. They would ridicule "women's libbers" like Jane Fonda and "liberal pansies" like Ted Kennedy. They argued against immigration and for "Americans first." They were Christian and patriotic and many were antigovernment.[2]

More than few were so filled with hatred for minorities and others different from themselves that it even surprised Berg on occasion. Some callers put an apocalyptic spin to their arguments and said they belonged to organizations like the Aryan Nations or the Covenant, Sword and Arm of the Lord, or dozens of other amorphous and shadowy groups with few members and little influence. More often than not, a single individual with a mimeograph machine would call himself an "organization" or "publishing house." Berg took them all on. Their sparring over the airwaves, which often sank into racist and vulgar diatribe, usually ended when Berg pulled the plug. People loved it; it was a great act, making Berg a local celebrity.

Among the right-wing zealots, however, were those who took the taunts seriously and wanted to do more than just argue with these "loud-mouthed Jews" who, supposedly, ran the media, the schools, and the unions, and had their pals in politics. Their interpretation of current events ran deeper. It was a complex bigotry with a long history and roots in millennial Christianity. They blamed the economic downturn in America on a Jewish-led conspiracy to undermine democracy and capitalism and create a communist and Jewish-run world government. "Jew bankers" like the Rothschilds and the "Zionist Occupation Government" (ZOG) in Israel were examples of the evil conspiracy to undermine Western Christian civilization, including the United States, and usher in a tyrannical new world order run by and for the Jews.

Callers would also argue that the Jewish Holocaust was a hoax perpetrated by the Jews in an effort to gain sympathy for their Zionist cause and to discredit the supremacy of the Germans and the larger white race. People like Robert Jay Matthews believed it. In 1983, Matthews, at 31, founded a group called *Bruder Schweigen*, or the Silent Brotherhood, a racist hate group who planned criminal activities to raise money to help build and maintain their organization. Other alleged members and co-conspirators included David Lane, Bruce Pierce, Richard Scutari, and Jean Craig. The Silent Brotherhood planned to assassinate Alan Berg.

On the night of June 18, 1984, Berg was returning home from dinner with his ex-wife, Judith. After picking up some groceries at a 7-Eleven store, Berg headed home. It was a cloudy evening as he pulled his black Volkswagen Beetle into the lighted driveway in front of his apartment. Berg picked up his grocery bag and stepped from his car. At that moment a car pulled up alongside Berg's driveway and an explosion of shots rang out. Thirteen bullets from an automatic MAC-10 pistol hit Berg, who dropped instantly, dead or dying in a pool of blood, his right leg still in the car, his hand still gripping the 7-Eleven bag. One of his killers later joked about how hard Berg hit the pavement.[3]

The Silent Brotherhood planned the killing of Berg out of hatred for Jews and a right-wing-inspired paranoia of world domination by the Jews and minority "mud peoples"—blacks, Latinos, Asians, and the entire "polyglot" cesspool that choked America. Such beliefs run deep in our culture and form the nucleus of a white supremacist Christian survivalism—the most fanatic and vitriolic of the right wing. Those who have used the rhetoric of the millennium for personal or political gain often tend to demonize other peoples, even committing genocide in the name of religion and ideology.

We have seen this throughout history—in the Crusades, in the Inquisition, in the American westward expansion, in Nazi Germany, and, more recently, in the Balkans. In U.S. history since the Civil War, the demonizing of blacks, Jews, and other minorities has appeared in the violent bigotry of the Ku Klux Klan and the fascism of American Nazis beginning in the 1930s. More recently this demonology can be discerned in the rise of the survivalist right, where survivalism becomes a religious practice endowed with a racist and anti-Semitic theology that becomes a holy shield for white supremacy.

For 2,000 years various peoples and individuals have been identified as the evil demons of Revelation—the dragons and beasts that perform the work assigned to them by Satan. Survivalists ascribe their secular counterparts to American government and its agencies of law enforcement, especially the ATF and the FBI, and to the "agents" of the new world order. There is one other demon presence described in Revelation that commands particular attention. Alternately called the dragon or the beast and identified with the other demons, the Antichrist is the inspiration for all evil. The Antichrist denies or opposes Christ and is the master antagonist who unleashes the other beasts and dragons in order to fill the world with wickedness. The Antichrist sets himself up as the Lord and savior, but he is a pretender—the false Christ. The Antichrist rises in the world to deceive the nations. During the Middle Ages various popes—often the more tyrannical—were commonly seen as the Antichrist by those who felt oppressed or betrayed by the church. The need to scapegoat other people or groups to create an outgroup that will in turn galvanize one's own group is common to many societies. Demonizing others has also been used by groups, including state powers, to make legitimate their own political aspirations.

Throughout the world the Jews have been commonly demonized in the apocalyptic fashion of Revelation. Hostility toward the Jews ranging from mild antipathy to genocidal mania has appeared wherever Jews have settled in the Diaspora—the centuries-long scattering of the Jews outside of Palestine and the holy land. In the classical world religious differences were the primary reason for anti-Semitism. The Jews rejected idol worship and refused to worship the emperor, demonstrating a lack of allegiance to the Roman Empire. From the second to the fourth centuries conflicts often broke out between Christian and Jewish authorities over competition for converts. Their detractors have always labeled the Jews as "Christ killers" for the part the Sanhedrin—the Jewish religious and civil authority in Judea—played in turning Jesus over to the Roman procurator, Pontius Pilate. Jesus had been accused of blasphemy by "proclaiming himself the Messiah" and the "king of the Jews." However, since he was from Galilee, the Sanhedrin had no judicial authority over him. So they turned his case over to Pilate, who tried and executed Jesus. The allegation that the Jews were the "crucifiers of Christ" has been the justification for anti-Semitism for centuries.

It was Saint Augustine of Hippo (354–430), regarded as one of the greatest and most influential Christian thinkers of his time, who described the Jews as the favored sons of God. But in refusing to recognize the New Covenant brought by Jesus, they had lost that favor. "I know the blasphemy of them that say they are Jews, and are not, but are a synagogue of Satan" John of Patmos writes in Revelation 3:9. The "synagogue of Satan" was the synagogue of the Antichrist. The idea that the Antichrist would be a Jew and that the "mysterious" Jews were his followers has been a consistent belief in Christianity, though marginal to mainstream theology, for centuries.

In the rich mix of Christian symbols and pagan traditions held by many common folk of the Middle Ages, the Jews were often seen as having mysterious ways. They looked and acted strangly, kept to themselves, and practiced odd rituals. Some came to believe the Jews had supernatural powers and planned evil deeds. An allegation originating in the twelfth century stated that the Jews practiced human sacrifice and stole Christian children during Passover for sacrifice to their God. Norman Cohn writes in *Warrant for Genocide*: "Seven or eight centuries later, in the most militant period in the history of the Roman Catholic Church, these ancient fantasies were revived and integrated into a whole new demonology."[4] Throughout the history of the Crusades, beginning in the 11th century, the Jews were associated with the underworld, especially the Antichrist. They were frequent targets of pillage and war, wherever millitant crusaders crossed their paths en route to recapture the Holy Land. In the minds of many Christians the synagogue of Satan remained a potent metaphor for the Jews as Christianity expanded in Europe.

The legends of Jewish evil and conspiracy survived, appearing in eastern Europe and Poland in the eighteenth and ninteenth centuries and in Nazi Germany in the 1930s. To some apocalyptically minded groups the Jews have been seen as servants of Satan and depicted as "Heaven stormers," destined to be destroyed and cast into the fiery pit of hell by the conquering Messiah. The Jews have always maintained an uneasy relationship with Christendom. While Jesus was a Jew and the historical and biblical history of Christianity is tied to Judaism, it is the Jews who have been blamed for killing Jesus and failing to see Him as the Messiah. To those who subscribe to these myths, the Jews are still persecuting Christians and remain the evil incarnation of Satan on earth. They are the antagonists of Christ and Christianity and, by extension, American sovereignty, democracy, and all of Western civilization.

*It is contended that nations can rise in arms against us if our plans are discovered prematurely; but in anticipation of this we [the Elders of Zion] can rely upon throwing into action such a formidable force as will make even the bravest of men shudder. By then metropolitan railways and underground passages will be constructed in all cities . . . [and] subterranean places [where] we will explode all the cities of the world, together with their institutions and documents.* (NINTH "PROTOCOL" OF THE PROTOCOLS OF THE LEARNED ELDERS OF ZION) [5]

*The goyim are a flock of sheep, and we are their wolves. And you know what happens when the wolves get hold of the flock? (THE PROTOCOLS OF THE LEARNED ELDERS OF ZION)*

Perhaps the most notorious example the myth of the Jewish world conspiracy is *The Protocols of the Learned Elders of Zion*, a tract that circulated throughout the world in the 1920s and the 1930s. Among the many fabrications and forgeries concerning world conspiracy reaching back almost to the French Revolution, *The Protocols* is the most persistent and influential.[6] Created by the secret police of the Russian czars at the start of the Bolshevik Revolution, *The Protocols of the Learned Elders of Zion* is supposed to be a secret plan devised by an ultrasecret council of Jewish elders to seize world power.

Supposedly written in the hands of the Jewish "elders," the document purports to be a record of a series of 24 (in other versions, 27) meetings held at Basel, Switzerland, in 1897, at the time of the first Zionist Congress. At the meeting Jews and Freemasons (a secret fraternal society) collaborated on a plan to undermine Christian civilization and erect a world government under their direction. Liberalism and socialism were to be the means of subverting Christendom. If subversion failed or the plan was discovered beforehand, then all the capitols of Europe were to be blown up. In 1903 *The Protocols* was published in the Russian newspaper *Znamia*

(*Banner*), in abbreviated form; and then again in 1905 as an addendum to a religious tract by Sergey Nilus, a czarist civil servant. Eventually, it was translated into German, French, English, and other languages of the Western world. It soon came to be regarded as a classic of anti-Semitism, widely circulated and often copied or reinterpreted.

According to *The Protocols*, through their cabal of internationalist bankers, politicians, and media elite, the supporters of the conspiracy seek world domination. Through a worldwide network of camouflaged agencies and organizations, the secret Jewish government controls political parties and governments, the press and public opinion, banks and economic development. The secret world government is supposed to be doing this in pursuance of an age-old plan of achieving Jewish dominion over the entire world.[7] It also is generally believed today by some anti-Semites that the conspiracy is close to achieving its aim.

In the 1930s the so-called Jewish world conspiracy and its millennial overtones were trumpeted by Adolf Hitler and his supporters in Nazi Germany. In parts of *Mein Kampf,* Hitler speaks of the overthrow of the "world-Jewry" with a truly apocalyptic fervor. Although he opposed Christianity and used the National Socialist program to arrest those clergy who resisted fascism or criticized the Nazi worldview, Hitler could speak with perverse elegance of the Jewish Antichrist and his final destruction. "The Jew goes his fateful way," wrote Hitler, "until the day when another power stands up against him and in a mighty struggle casts him, the heaven-stormer, back to Lucifer."[8] Hitler's expansionist foreign policy and "new order" for Europe, which called for the extermination of whole peoples (European Jews being the most numerous victims), led to World War II. In one way, the myth of the Jewish world conspiracy was used by the Nazis as propaganda, a way to galvanize popular support for Hitler and the National Socialist Party and program. At other times the Nazis and their supporters seemed to believe that before any "Aryan nation" or German millennium could begin the Jews would have to be exterminated.[9]

Some historians now believe that American industrialist Henry Ford was a firm believer in the authenticity of *The Protocols*. Henry Ford's private newspaper, *The Dearborn Independent*, often cited *The Protocols* as evidence of a Jewish threat to America. In 1920 a series about *The Protocols* ran in *The Independent*, entitled "The International Jew: The World's Foremost Problem." The series was distributed not just in Michigan but in every Ford dealership across the country. Ford supported President Woodrow Wilson's efforts to create a League of Nations, but later "discovered" that Jewish bankers, whom he considered to be behind his own business troubles, were also behind the League of Nations and other international political efforts. Ford concluded that the Jewish world conspiracy was about to plunge the world into economic and political chaos and war. He encouraged some confidants to read and ponder *The Protocols*.[10]

Ford further committed himself publicly on the subject of the Jewish world conspiracy in two books published in 1922—*The Amazing Story of Henry Ford* (especially Part II, "The 'New Era Philosophy'"), by James Miller, and *My Life and Work*, by Henry Ford in collaboration with S. Crowther. Historians now believe that Ford knew *The Protocols* quite well and, in fact, did much to promote them. In many ways, Henry Ford despised the modern world. He pioneered the mass production of automobiles, but in his heart still pined for an America of farms and small towns. He hated big cities, New York most of all, and felt strongly that the real Americans were Christians, living in simple style in the Midwest. Ford believed that Jews, by contrast, had flocked to New York and other big cities, and from there had begun to control large sectors of business, government, and international politics. In doing so, they had destroyed the past.[11]

The fraudulent nature of *The Protocols* was first pointed out in 1921 by Philip Graves of the *London Times*. Graves demonstrated the obvious similarities between *The Protocols* and a satire by a French lawyer, Maurice Joly, on Napoleon III. Published in 1864, the satire was entitled *Dialogue aux Enfers entre Machiavel et Montesquieu* (*Dialogue in Hell between Machiavelli and Montesquieu*). Later, Russian historian Vladimir Burtserv revealed that *The Protocols* were forgeries based on the the Joly satire concocted by officials of the Russian secret police.[12]

While deemed fraudulent by historians, *The Protocols* have continued to serve as a pretext and rationale for racist and anti-Semitic philosophy and practice. In the face of a libel suit that could have ruined him, Ford made a public apology in 1927, acknowledging that *The Protocols* were a forgery. However, most of Ford's biographers believe that the industrialist went to his death holding firmly to the authenticity of the Jewish world conspiracy to destroy Western Christendom and the imminent collapse of civilization as prophesied in Revelation.

*The myth of the Jewish world-conspiracy proved most attractive to people who were attached to the traditional ways and values of the countryside and deeply disoriented by modern civilization. . . . The Protocols are indeed all things to all men. As interpreted . . . for the American public . . . the most horrible thing (about the world conspiracy) is that it undermines Puritan morality.*[13]

*These enemies of Christ have taken their Jewish Communist manifesto and incorporated it into the statutory Laws of our country and thrown our Constitution and our Christian Common Law (which is nothing other than the Laws of God as set forth in the scriptures) into the garbage can.* (GORDON KAHL OF THE POSSE COMITATUS)[14]

In the 1970s and 1980s the myth of the Jewish-led conspiracy, and copies of *The Protocols* themselves, resurfaced in the literature of the survivalist right. Driven by the farm crisis, unemployment, a declining standard of living, and fears of declining American hegemony in the world, right-wing Christian survivalist groups and communities began to develop across the agrarian and rural areas of the country. Spewing the rhetoric of the Jewish world conspiracy as the root cause of farmers' and America's problems, some of these groups became linked to paramilitary and survival training centers and to vigilantes, mercenaries, and the Ku Klux Klan. With the rise of the survivalist right, the 1980s saw the rekindling of a dormant white supremacist subculture in the

United States and a further fracturing of the American millennial myth.

One group that took advantage of the economic downturn in the 1970s to spread its "religion"-inspired racist philosophy was the infamous Posse Comitatus. Perhaps the single most investigated organization of the survivalist right, the Posse Comitatus is an American form of Nazism. In the late 1960s the Posse emerged—evolving out of a neo-Nazi group called the "Silver Shirts" that was formed in the United States following the rise of Hitler in Germany on the eve of World War II. The group takes their name and derives much of its philosophy from the congressional Posse Comitatus Act, passed in the wake of the Civil War and specifically designed to prevent the federal military from intervening in local police matters or enforcing domestic laws. The Posse holds that no American is bound to the legal authority of anyone higher than a county sheriff. Many refuse to pay federal taxes, purchase an automobile license, or vote in nationalist elections. The Montana Freemen held to the Posse Comitatus Act.

The Posse believe in a literal interpretation of the Constitution, which they claim was given to our nation's founding fathers by God himself; however, they do not place absolute faith in it. Some Posse theorists claim that all amendments enacted after the Bill of Rights are unconstitutional because they were endorsed by illegal bodies doing the bidding of the Jewish-led conspiracy. For example, the Sixteenth Amendment, which allows the national government to tax personal income, is particularly odious to Posse members because it plays into the hands of the conspirators by paying for and justifying their control.

In 1975 the Posse were linked to an alleged assassination attempt on then Vice President Nelson Rockefeller. Powerful and wealthy families such as the Rockefellers are viewed by Posse members and sympathizers as "money czars"—the major financiers of the new government. One of the more spectacular incidents involving the Posse occurred more than 10 years later during the manhunt for Posse member Gordon Kahl, who killed two Medina, North Dakota, police officers in December 1986. Kahl, a North

Dakota tax protester, became a martyr for the Posse and others on the survivalist right by his imprisonment for failure to file his federal income tax and his efforts to promote tax resistance. Upon release, Kahl vowed never to allow himself to be arrested again and continued to refuse paying his taxes or cooperating with the government during his parole.

In February 1983, six U.S. marshals attempted to arrest Kahl near his hometown of Medina, North Dakota, on the misdemeanor of failing to meet his parole officer. In attempting to serve the warrant a shoot-out erupted and two U.S. marshals were shot and killed. Kahl escaped and led federal law enforcers on a massive manhunt.

During the manhunt, Kahl sent letters to the newspaper defending his actions and explaining his position. In the first letter Kahl blamed Jews for his personal troubles and feared for his life. He said that since he was an enemy of the "Jewish-Masonic-Communist Synagogue of Satan" he would be killed.[15] In a second letter Kahl divulged more of his apocalyptic thinking when he wrote,

> We are a conquered and occupied nation, conquered and occupied by the Jews . . . [who] have two objectives in their goal of ruling the world, destroy Christianity and the white race. . . . We are engaged in a struggle to the death between the people of the Kingdom of God, and the Kingdom of Satan.[16]

On June 3, 1983, federal agents tracked Kahl to a house in Smithville, Arkansas. A local sheriff named Gene Mathews tried to enter the house and was shot by Kahl. He died shortly after. A gunfight ensued between Kahl and the local police and U.S. marshals. After a time, members of a SWAT team poured diesel fuel into an air vent on the roof. The house caught fire and burned for over two hours while the gunfight continued. As the house burned so did Gorden Kahl; his charred remains were found later inside the house.

The farm crisis of the early 1980s undermined the faith and financial stability of many American farmers and fueled the evolution of the survivalist right. Throughout the American heartland, desperation, mistrust, anger, and fear had been nurtured by low crop prices, high interest rates, foreclosures, and bankruptcies that were beginning to unsettle the region and threaten a way of life as early as the mid-1970s. "Land is a farmer's identity," writes James Corcoran in *Bitter Harvest*, "It is his connection to God; it is his religion, his nationality, his family's heritage, and his legacy to his children. . . . Land is a farmer's way of life and throughout the 1980s he was losing it."[17]

The farmer became a modern exile in the aftermath of the Industrial Revolution and the modernization of the twentieth century. Forced to migrate to strange cities and states in search of a new life, many farmers found help in the company of similarly affected individuals and groups—factory workers, small businessmen, common folk like themselves—who were also losing their jobs, homes, and faith in their leaders. With Posse members and other conspiracy mongers on hand working the crowds, handing out pamphlets, and forecasting impending doom, many downtrodden middle Americans were exposed to the philosophy of the survivalist right.

Other groups offered companionship to America's disaffected and saw an opportunity to promote the ideas of white supremacy and anti-Semitism. In Washington, D.C., Willis Carto saw the opportunity to form a new political party that would champion the cause and ideals of the Liberty Lobby, an organization he founded in 1957. In *The Spotlight*, the lobby's weekly newspaper sent to more than 100,000 subscribers, stories about the plight of the farmers are featured alongside articles that promote "the formation of a new Populist Party that will end U.S. foreign aid to Israel, repeal the income tax, abolish the Federal Reserve system, and uncover the Holocaust for what it supposedly was—a hoax."[18]

Many of the racist and anti-Semitic organizations that emerged in the 1970s and 1980s held to extreme religious and apocalyptic beliefs, engaging in survivalism as both a "practical" and spiritual pursuit. "Christian survivalists" were often members of the Covenant, Sword and Arm of the Lord (CSA), who believed that they were participating in the supernaturally-inspired events leading to the end of the world. As the Battle of Armageddon approached, CSA members were preparing to fight and survive a third world war, marked by a full-scale nuclear war and a race war. CSA members were planning to fight as soldiers at the side of the conquering Messiah as he destroyed Babylon and Satan and instituted his "white" Christian kingdom of the millennium.[19]

"Christian survivalism" is an important term because it demonstrates how the secular elements of disaster preparedness can be combined with the apocalyptic beliefs of the Christian fundamentalist. Racist organizations such as the CSA believe that world events are spinning out of control, that civil and global war are erupting, and that the economy and the environment are moribund. Survival training—including living in isolated and independent communities or "compounds"—is the "practical thing" to do for anyone planning to survive the coming devastation. Survivalism becomes "Christian" when believers attach apocalyptic meaning or "Christian truths," to the impending destruction. In the case of the CSA and other Christian survivalists, there are the additional racist and anti-Semitic beliefs, which are easily adapted to the secular and apocalyptic scripts.

For example, Richard G. Butler, pastor of the Christian Identity Church of Jesus Christ and founder of the Aryan Nations, could view the racial tensions and farm foreclosures of the 1970s as the results of the Jewish "Antichrist's" manipulation of American government and the onset of the Apocalypse. Writing in the *Aryan Newsletter*, Butler said:

> The farmers were the first victims of the Revolution of 1776, as they are the first victims of this revolution. He's been dispossessed of his land, he's been used and abused. . . . He's going to get a lot more angry, and eventually he'll see that the only way to turn things around is to fight to win his country back for white Christians.[20]

Traditional hate groups also seized the opportunity to drive up membership. The Ku Klux Klan, forgoing white sheets for military camouflage, was eager to recruit the newly disenfranchised Americans and, indeed, as Morris Dees of the Southern Poverty Law Center's Klan Watch Project has reported, Klan membership nearly doubled in the 1980s.[21] Writing in *The White Patriot* (February 1987), Thom Robb, chaplain of the Knights of the Ku Klux Klan and leader of the Arkansas-based White People's Committee to Restore God's Law, has warned farmers that it's the same Jewish-led conspiracy that forged the Holocaust hoax that is planning to steal American farmers' land. Organizations such as the Southern Poverty Law Center estimate that there are hundreds of extremist and violent groups and "cells" in the United States today, harboring racist, apocalyptic, and revolutionary beliefs. While they are mostly small groups of fewer than a dozen members and relatively little power, their organizations and "chapters" number in the thousands.[22] Until recently, many of the groups on the survivalist right were, in general, independent of one another, in spite of the self-promotional and organizational abilities of Richard Butler and the Aryan Nations. However, access to cheaper and more powerful computer technology and software, including the rapidly evolving Internet, have increased the reach and networking capabilities of these groups. Computers, fax machines, and e-mail have increased the reach of the extreme right, forging "virtual communities" of like-minded Christian survivalists and "informing" those ignorant to the situation. New forms of mass communication have also increased the international community of like-minded believers, furthering the globalization of the millennium rage.

Some of the more militant and "fundamentalist" groups are less interested in forming allegiances with others, joining social movements, or forming political parties. They promote independence and secession and violently resist abuse of their God-given rights. They prefer to hide their identities and conceal their practices and plans. Others resist "inclusion" or the development of a mass following. They see themselves as the "chosen ones"—the "true believers" who are ready to fight and die for the cause of racial purity and Christian heritage. Writing in the *Inter-Klan and Survival Newsletter,* Louis Beam, leader of the Texas Klan, said, "It is pure fantasy to imagine the Klan as a broad-based movement that will effect peaceful change. There should be no doubt that all means short of armed conflict have been exhausted."[23]

The infamous *Turner Diaries,* written in 1978 by William Pierce (under the pseudonym Andrew McDonald), serves as a guide for understanding the apocalyptic scenario the survival right have in mind for America's immediate future. *The Turner Diaries* have become as popular with contemporary American racists and Christian survivalists as *The Protocols of the Learned Elders of Zion* was for anti-Semites in the 1930s and 1940s. The fictional story begins in 1991 when the great war begins between the Zionist Occupation Government (ZOG), which now rules in Washington, and white guerrilla warriors on the Christian survivalist right. Once engaged in civil war, racist revolutionaries attack the dragons of ZOG, including politicians, state and federal authorities, and Jews. They bomb federal buildings and disrupt public utilities, ultimately bringing down ZOG and exterminating all minorities and their sympathizers. Christians who married Jews or blacks are draped with signs saying "they defiled their race." In the end, Israel is destroyed by nuclear bombs.[24] Federal authorities believe that *The Turner Diaries* may, in part, have provided both motive and method in the bombing of the federal building in Oklahoma City. The incident bears a striking resemblance to a part of the storyline where separatists bomb a federal building.

At the 1990 *Soldier of Fortune* Convention, I met with a representative of the National Alliance, publishers of National Vanguard Books, which includes *The Turner Diaries* among its catalog's listing. On the inside cover of the catalog is written, "National Vanguard Books . . . providers of knowledge and inspiration for the survival of the White race."[25] The representative, who refused to give his name, was selling books and recruiting members at the convention. Speaking to two Vietnam veterans and myself, he said he was looking for people like us "who really know what's going on in the world." He went on to describe the disenfranchisement of white Americans and the need for a "white man's political action committee to lobby Washington politicians on our issues."

Upon solicitation of information from National Vanguard Books, I received a 1990 book catalog, information on the National Alliance, and a bumper sticker that reads, "Earth's Most Endangered Species: The White Race. Help Preserve It." The National Vanguard Books catalog (1990) is especially interesting for the diversity of its titles. Ranging from European prehistory, archaeology, and religion to issues of race, war, and international politics, it can be read as a fragmented example of millennialism. Titles include many you might find in a local bookstore, such as Charles Darwin's *On the Origin of Species*, Bulfinch's *Mythology*, Gerald Hawkins' *Stonehenge Decoded*, and Hjalmar Holland's *Norse Discoveries and Explorations in America*. But there are many titles you would not find, such as *White Power*, *Race and Reality* and *The Armageddon Network*, and numerous titles on the Jewish world conspiracy, such as *The Zionist Connection, Thirteenth Tribe*, and *The World Conquerors*.[26]

There is even a children's section in the catalog, with books "chosen to serve a racially constructive purpose by providing White role models, instilling White values, [and] building a sense of White identity through the teaching of White history and legend."[27] Some children's book titles include Montgomery's *Anne of Green Gables* ("portrays White life at its best"), *Aesop's Fables* ("1912 edition has escaped 'sanitizing' by racial equalizers"), and Tolkien's *Lord of the Rings* ("draws heavily on pre-Christian White legend and mythology").[28]

Christian Identity, a quasi-religious movement and philosophy, conceived by Wesley Smith in 1946, now provides the most unifying theology for the diverse groups that compose the militant and survivalist right, including the Aryan Nations, the Ku Klux Klan, and many in the militia movement, such as the Montana Freemen.[29] Through its literature, audiotapes and videotapes, and conventions and Internet home pages (such as Christian Identity OnLine with the Rev. Ronald C. Schoedel III), Christian Identity is reaching a wider audience than ever before, and providing a common religion for survivalists, neo-Nazis, and anti-government zealots, thereby fusing religion with hate, guns, and an apocalyptic fear of the future.

The roots of Christian Identity can be found in "British Israelism," a belief system whose origins can be traced to the book *Our Israelitish Origins*, written in 1840 by a Scotsman named John Wilson. Wilson's ideas were further elaborated by Edward Hines, an Englishman and the author of *Identification of the British Nation with Lost Israel*, first published in 1871. According to Hines, the essence of British Israelism is that the true Jews and "chosen people," who descended from Abraham, Moses, and Jesus, are actually the people of the British Isles. Those who call themselves Jews today, and have for the past 2,000 years, are really a race of Mongolian-Turkish "Khazars." Presumedly, Khazars derives from "Ashkenazim," one of the two major religious and cultural divisions among Jews, and refers to eastern European, Yiddish-speaking Jews. The Sephardim are Occidental or western European Jews—those who settled in Spain and Portugal and later, according to British Israelism, in Britain and America.[30]

In the Garden of Eden, according to Hines, Eve was impregnated by the devil, whose seed survived alongside that of Adam. Adam and Eve's two sons, Cain and Abel, were really half brothers. Cain killed Abel, and his descendants remained in the Middle East, where they erected their demonic Temple, killed Jesus, and became the world Jewry and eventually the state of Israel. The true Jews of the "Lost Tribes," who are descended from Abraham's son Isaac, supposedly split from the Davidic state around 1,000 B.C. and migrated through the centuries to the west and north. Isaac's sons, or "Saxons," finally crossed the Caucasus Mountains (today the Caucasians) that divide the Black and Caspian seas. Eventually they settled in northern Europe, founding the "British Israel" in the British Isles. The northern Europeans were, therefore, God's chosen people and (North) America, which was colonized by the Europeans, was blessed too.[31]

The late Herbert Armstrong, founder of the Worldwide Church of God, helped popularize British Israelism among the millions of Americans who read his books, attended his lectures, and listened to his radio broadcasts in the 1950s and 1960s. Armstrong held out hope for the Jews and believed that they were entitled to forgiveness and salvation. But Wesley Swift and the racist right have given British Israelism a stronger "identity," centered on the preservation of the white race and resistance to the alleged Jewish world conspiracy. Swift taught that the Jews were the impure and evil Mongolian Khazars, bent on destroying Christianity and enslaving the white race. Blacks, Hispanics, and other minorities—the Jew's henchmen—he called "mud people," the false starts before God made the perfect (white) Adam and Eve. Swift also insisted on the authenticity of *The Protocols,* and he taught that the Bible demanded racial and religious segregation and that marriages and cooperation between the races and between Jews and Christians were sins.[32]

In addition to its religious, racist, and anti-Semitic beliefs, Christian Identity espouses a vehement anti-government attitude. Believing that the United States is a Christian nation whose law derives from Christian "common law," many adherents to Christian Identity refuse to pay taxes, purchase automobile licenses or insurance, or abide by other state and federal laws. It was this line of reasoning that prompted the spring 1996 stand-off between the Montana Freemen and federal agents. Several members were staunch Identity Christians who, when faced with foreclosure of their farms and other properties, refused to abide by the law. Instead, they took the law into their own hands, creating their own township and courts, threatening a local judge, and refusing to vacate their foreclosed and auctioned farm. Their resistance to the government led to the stand-off, which ultimately ended peacefully. Christian Identity holds that the U.S. Government is unconstitutional, a puppet regime doing the bidding of the one world Jewish governemnt. The conspiracy's aim is nothing short of world domination, the destruction of American and Christian heritage, and the enslavement of the white race.[33]

*The old ways are over. It's open season on niggers, cops and capitalists—kill 'em all and let the devil sort 'em out. (*TOM METZGER,*WHITE ARYAN RESISTANCE,* THE NEWSPAPER OF THE INTERNATIONAL WHITE RACIST*)

With the loss of America's major demon in the world, the communist Soviet Union, the myth of the Jewish world conspiracy has once again become revitalized, this time in the survivalist right. In addition, the Jews' stereotypical connection to banking (money lenders), business, and education has linked them to the new world order of bankers, corporations, and "internationalists." For the survivalist right, this new world order is Babylon—the center of Satan's worldly power. Godless (or at least not primarily Christian), increasingly multicultural, and controlled by Jews and internationalist-leaning bankers and businessmen, the new world order is a sinful, deceitful world that has fallen away from the "laws of God." The demonization of Jews and others is most pronounced in the racist theology of white supremacists of the past like the Ku Klux Klan, but it has resurfaced in the survivalist right in groups like the Aryan Nations.

There are other groups, however, that downplay their racist, anti-Semitic roots and apocalyptic views. Groups such as the Liberty Lobby, the National Agricultural Press Association (NAPA), the Iowa Society for Educated Citizens, segments of the Posse, and a host of other organizations that refer to themselves as "Christian patriots" may seek to build a bridge between their terrorist brethren and mainstream America. Instead of sheets and swastikas, they drape themselves in the American flag. They avoid blatant racist and anti-Semitic slogans, using code terms such as "racialist," "eastern and international bankers," "white civil rights," and "new world order." Instead of violence, they advocate the election of people who would dismantle the Federal Reserve system, abolish the income tax, and root out the conspirators who use their government positions to undermine the country's Christian ideals.

Whatever their differences, the groups are loosely bound by ideological and theological threads that, in time, could be woven into a unified political and social movement. The most common of these threads is a right-wing millennial belief that a Jewish-led conspiracy is poised to take over the country and ultimately the world and that there will be a massive class and race war, possibly nuclear war, where Christian patriots will be the last survivors to rebuild the Aryan nation.

As the farm crisis faded from the headlines at the end of the 1980s, American farmers continued to lose their land and their livelihood. A minority of them continue to attend Posse meetings and read the literature of Christian Identity. The FBI and other law enforcement agencies, along with organizations that monitor hate groups, have maintained a close watch on the survivalist right. Groups like the Posse Comitatus have launched spectacular commando raids against armored cars on the West Coast. Many have died in shoot-outs with police, and groups such as the Order, the CSA, and the Aryan Nations have established heavily armed communes in the mountains of Idaho, South Dakota, and throughout the West.

More recently, skinheads and neo-Nazis have been added to the mix. Generally young, white, uneducated, and jobless males, skinheads are, in part, violent and racist knockoffs of the 1980s American punk movement. Blaming their problems on affirmative action and immigration, skinheads have been involved in numerous violent attacks on blacks, foreigners, gays, and other minorities in the United States and Europe in the past decade. The activities of skinheads and other violent racist individuals and groups, such as the Ku Klux Klan and the American Nazi Party, have stimulated an interest in "hate crimes"—violence directed at individuals or groups because of their religion, race, gender, ethnicity, politics, or sexual orientation.[34] Skinheads have found sympathy, philosophy, and support from segments of the white racist subculture, who have adopted them into their fold and see them as the vanguard and future of the Christian Identity movement.

In addition to an economic downturn for many working-class Americans, fears are numerous and growing: a multicultural America, the problem of uncontained immigration, and the loss of American jobs to Third World countries. It might also be seen as a backlash to reforms of the 1960s and 1970s, such as affirmative action, which to some degree have benefited blacks, women, and other minorities. The demonology has extended from the Jews to the American government and to organizations connected with the international order. Increasingly under attack are the justice system and law enforcement agencies, from the federal agencies of the FBI and the ATF to state and local police and even to National Parks officers.

That America can be seen as the center of Babylon, if not Babylon itself, is a further transformation of the millennial myth. The survivalist right is a seedbed for the fascist millennial dreams of a new Christian white supremacy. In Ruby Ridge, Waco, and Oklahoma City, we have seen a crystallization of the apocalyptic fears of the survivalist right translated into acts of resistance and defiance and attacks on the mythical Antichrist and its Babylonian new world order in the form of ZOG.

# Chapter 6

# "Babylon Is Fallen"

## America at Century's End

*And upon her forehead was a name written, MYSTERY, BABYLON THE GREAT, MOTHER OF HARLOTS AND ABOMINATIONS OF THE EARTH.*

REV. 17:5, KJV

*Flee from the midst of Babylon, let every man save his life! Be not cut off in her punishment, for this is the time of the Lord's vengeance, the requital he is rendering her.*

JER. 51.6, RSV

Fifty miles south of Baghdad, Iraq, on a site now occupied by the town of Hillah, lie the ruins of Babylon, one of the oldest and most famous cities of antiquity and the ancient capital of southern Mesopotamia (Babylonia) from the early second millennium B.C. to the early first millennium B.C. During the Persian Gulf War with Iraq, U.S. bombers flew over this site en route to Baghdad. Much to the horror of archaeologists, some areas of the ancient site were damaged by United States and multinational bombs. Still, it was fitting that the great battle to help build the new world order was fought on the site of ancient Babylon. The metaphor of Babylon for Iraq was not lost on one enterprising seller of bumper stickers and T-shirts at the 1990 *Soldier of Fortune* Convention in Las Vegas: A T-shirt depicted a tank rolling over a map of Iraq and had the caption "Babylon or Bust."

Whether knowingly or not, George Bush employed a mythology that rendered Saddam Hussein and Iraq as symbols of the decaying old world order, a Babylonian world of vicious, greedy, and dangerous tyrants that must be restrained or destroyed in the pursuit of a glorious new world order on the horizon. In his State of the Union Address (January 24, 1991) Bush said, "This we do know: Our cause is just. Our cause is moral. Our cause is right."[1] The battle to liberate Kuwait from Iraq was a "just cause," according to the president, and the punishment inflicted on Iraq equally just. Because of his unbridled rape and pillage of the Kuwaiti people, not to mention the gassing of Iraq's own Kurdish people, Saddam was defined as "tyrant," and his nation as "outcast" among the family of nations. While many innocents might die in a multinational attack on the war machine of Iraq, that was Saddam's fault and his responsibility. The legitimacy of such logic was evident in the way Saddam and Iraq were demonized by Bush and many media analysts in the United States. Bush equated Saddam Hussein with Hitler, and Arab experts spoke of "the Arab mentality" or the Arab soldier who is ready and willing to "die for Allah."

Such "political" analysis served to demonize Saddam Hussein and the Iraqi people, and it became a common way to garner support for going to war in the Persian Gulf. It also served to make legitimate the massive bombing campaign and to reduce sympathy for the enemy and its people. Iraq became the symbol of the "old order," a deceived people fallen from the grace of the new international order and thus doomed to be destroyed by the powers of righteousness. Like Muammar Gadhafi, Fidel Castro, Daniel Ortega, and other "petty" dictators and internationalist terrorists masquerading as national leaders and who never missed a chance to thumb their noses at the United States, Saddam was an old-fashioned "tyrant," who had to be brushed aside to build and preserve the new world order.

Even in light of the tired, dirty, and half-starved Iraqi soldiers who surrendered by the thousands after the second week of the war, many of them kissing the cheeks of their captors, the Bush administration sustained the image of the demonic Arab stereotype through the caricature of Saddam and the Iraqi Babylon.

Unfortunately, all Iraqis came to be viewed as expendable in the fall of Babylon, even those minorities who had resisted Saddam and supported the United States and the multilateral force. This fact may have played into the slow response by the Bush administration to the Shiite uprising in southern Iraq and its brutal put-down by forces loyal to Saddam, and later to the Kurdish revolt and its put-down, which resulted in a refugee nightmare. At the start of the war, Bush had encouraged the Iraqi people to resist Saddam's orders and overthrow his regime. If they did, he suggested, the United States would help. As the Kurds were routed from their homes and villages and forced to migrate to the mountains on the verge of winter, the only humanitarian aid that came were Red Cross packages dropped from cargo planes. The Kurds are there still, living in long-term, makeshift villages, while Iraq continues to border on economic collapse and Saddam continues to rule.

In any event, the end justified the means. As the president said at the end of his State of the Union Address to Congress and the nation, "This is the burden of leadership—and the strength that has made America the beacon of freedom in a searching world. . . . Any cost in lives is beyond our power to measure. But the cost of closing our eyes to aggression is beyond mankind's power to imagine."[2] "The burden of leadership," "the beacon of freedom"—this is the language of American manifest destiny and millennial dreams. It is a language employed by American leaders in the past and it continues to be used as a device to interpret and manipulate events to garner public support; Bush plugged into the rhetoric of the American millennial myth to frame our nation's goals and actions in the Gulf War. To George Bush and to many Americans, Saddam Hussein and Iraq had become symbols of old world ignorance and decay and a metaphor for "Babylon the Great," the "Mother of Harlots," who had sold out God to the worldly power of Satan, the deceiver of souls.

The demons of Revelation—the Dragons, the Beast, and the Antichrist—represent the archetypes and architects of evil who have deceived the world. In Revelation, the seat of the devil's realm on earth is often referred to as Babylon. Historically, Babylon was an ancient city on the middle Euphrates River that was the capital of both the old Babylonian empire (1000–2000 B.C.) and the neo-Babylonian empire in the seventh and sixth centuries B.C. Babylon has a long and spectacular history as a rich, cosmopolitan city continually rising to tremendous power and influence and then falling to utter ruins, often because its wealth and prestige made it a target for foreign conquerors. Under Nebuchadnezzar II (reigned 605–562 B.C.), who joined forces with the Medes to defeat Egypt at the Battle of Charchemish (605 B.C.) and create the Second Babylonian Empire, Babylon destroyed Jerusalem and its Temple (587 B.C.). Later, in 539 B.C., Babylon fell to the Persians. Alexander the Great's plans to rebuild the old sanctuaries of Babylon ended with his death in 323 B.C, and the city never regained its former glory.

Theologians, however, are more interested in the metaphor of Babylon as the rich, cosmopolitan, and powerful city that had become sinful and had fallen away from the moral and spiritual guidelines set down by God. Even in Revelation, John uses Babylon and its history of great power and final destruction as a metaphor for Rome. As time went on, the early church continued to use Babylon as a symbol for Rome and the Roman emperor as the symbol for the Antichrist.

In Revelation, Babylon also takes the form of the harlot: "a great whore . . . with whom the kings of the earth have committed fornication, and the inhabitants of the earth were made drunk with the wine of her fornication" (Rev. 17:2). Arrayed in purple and scarlet colors and decked with gold and precious stones and pearls, Babylon sits upon a "scarlet colored beast, full of names of blasphemy, having seven heads and ten horns (Rev. 17:3). She is "drunken with the blood of the saints, and with the blood of the martyrs of Jesus" (17:6). Babylon prostitutes her body and soul and deceives the multitudes with her earthy pleasures. The kings of the world's nations fall under her spell: "These have one mind and shall give their power and strength to the beast" (Rev. 17:13).

John is told by the angel showing him these signs that "the woman which thou sawest is that great city, which reigneth over the kings of the earth" (Rev. 17:18). Babylon and her followers eventually go to "make war with the Lamb" and his "chosen" and "faithful" followers, who destroy Babylon and her deceived people as a punishment for their wicked ways and in preparation for the millennium. While Rome, primarily, has been identified with Babylon by the early Christians, millenarian movements throughout history, including secular ones, have linked the metaphor of Babylon to their oppressors.

*Thy pomp is brought down to the grave, and the noise of thy viols: the worm is spread under thee, and the worms cover thee.* (ISA. 14:11, KJV).

*The Industrial Revolution and its consequences have been a disaster for the human race.* (UNABOMBER'S MANIFESTO, 1995)[3]

So begins the Unabomber's manifesto—a most intriguing piece of the apocalyptic puzzle. The manifesto is a 35,000-word analysis and explanation of the state and fate of the modern world, as interpreted by the mysterious and deadly prophet of the secular apocalypse, now identified by federal authorities as Theodore Kaczynski. The Unabomber does not include a great deal of discussion of Christianity, religion, or other supernatural elements in his vision of the decay of Western society. Instead, throughout the infamous "jeremiad," he delivers a highly detailed and sociological analysis of the causes and events leading to the collapse of modern civilization—a secular version of the millennial myth. The apocalyptic metaphor for Babylon can be seen in the modern industrial and technological society "which has led to wide-spread psychological suffering," "inflicted severe damage on the natural world," and "will probably lead to greater social disruption, and psychological suffering . . . even in 'advanced' countries" (para. 1).

In June of 1995, the Unabomber's manifesto was sent to *The New York Times* and *The Washington Post* to be published; if not published, the Unabomer threatened to continue to kill with his patented letter and package bombs that had already killed three people and injured 23 others over the course of 18 years. FBI agents in charge of the investigation later said that along with the manifesto the Unabomber included a list of potential bombing targets. "Whether you like it or not, we're turning our pages over to a man who has murdered people," said *New York Times* publisher Arthur Sulzberger.[4] On the advice of the FBI, who had sought the Unabomber since 1979, *The Washington Post* printed the manifesto, with technical support from *The New York Times* (it can also be found on the Internet), in the hope that it might turn up some leads. While many criticized the *Times*, the *Post*, and the FBI for "giving in" to terrorism, the decision to publish the manifesto in September, 1995, appears to be a key event that led to Kaczynski's arrest. Reading the manifesto caused Kaczynski's brother David to link it to writings attributed to Ted that had been discovered by the family at their Lombard, Illinois, home in January, 1996. He then alerted the FBI.

The Unabomber first became known to the public on May 25, 1978, after a package was found in the engineering department parking lot at the Chicago Circle Campus of the University of Illinois. Addressed to an engineering professor at Rensselaer Polytechnic Institute in Troy, New York, the package had the return address of a professor at Northwestern's Technological Institute. The package was returned to the Northwestern professor, who became suspicious and alerted the police that he had not sent the package, his name had been forged, and he had no idea what was inside. On May 26, 1978, the parcel was opened by a police officer who suffered minor injuries when the bomb detonated.

From then on, until Kaczynski's arrest at Stemple Pass, Montana, on April 10, 1996, a series of bombings occurred across the United States. The bombs were sent to eight states from California to Connecticut. Three individuals were killed, and 23 others were injured, some severely. According to the FBI, between 1987 and the beginning of 1993 there were no bombings associated with the Unabomber. Then, in June of 1993, a famous geneticist living in California and a well-respected computer executive were both severely injured when they opened packages addressed to them. A year later, in June of 1994, an advertising executive was killed by a bomb, and almost a year after that, on April 24, 1995, five days after the Oklahoma City bombing, a bomb attributed to the Unabomber killed a timber industry lobbyist in Sacramento, California.[5] Each bomb was delivered to a well-known scientist or corporate executive for their supposed role in helping to advance the modern world, with its massive industrial and technological establishment. According to the Unabomber, it is the current industrial and technological system that poses the world's primary danger. It is the "system" that the Unabomber rails against, and it is the system that is his secular Babylon. In this regard, the Unabomber's manifesto can be read as an apocalyptic text. Though not overtly religious in nature, it prophecies the imminent mass destruction of society and the necessity of social and global collapse, in order to cleanse the earth and humanity and prepare to enter a new and better state of existence—a millennial view that closely resembles that of the survivalists.

Among the many abnormal conditions caused by the modern industrial society, the Unabomber lists isolation of man from nature, excessive density of the world's population, serious damage to the environment, and rapid and widespread social changes that are breaking down small-scale communities such as the extended family, the village, and the tribe. All of these, he concludes, are consequences of technological progress and modernization. "The conservatives are fools," he says, because "they whine about the decay of traditional values, yet they enthusiastically support technological progress and economic growth" (para. 50). Pointing to the inevitable, the Unabomber writes: "There is no way of reforming or modifying the system so as to prevent it from depriving people of dignity and autonomy . . . so if it [the system] is to break down it had best break down sooner rather than later" (para. 2–3). Such language is apocalyptic and similar to both classical and secular millennialism in that it sees as inevitable, if not imminent, the collapse of society. The Unabomber feels that there is nothing one can or should do to preserve the current order. In fact, it would be better to hasten its demise and then rebuild from there.

Throughout the manifesto, the Unabomber refers to himself as "we" to suggest that there are followers or a group of like-minded revolutionaries with him. However, federal authorities now believe Kaczynski alone is responsible for the Unabomber's crimes, though copycat crimes may have been inspired by him. In his manifesto the Unabomber calls for a revolution against the industrial system and outlines the ways to do it. He emphasizes that the revolution is not a "political" revolution: "Its object will be to overthrow not governments but the economic and technological basis of the present society" (para. 4). Still, he employs apocalyptic language when he speaks of the collapse of society, and he creates evil and demonic characters out of the scientists, "technophiles," bureaucrats, and other technological and philosophical elites who perpetuate technological progress and the "psychology of leftism" and who most benefit from the existing social order.

That which he calls the "psychology of modern leftism" is what most plagues our society. Created in the universities, it gained power and influence during and after the 1960s. As a young Berkeley math professor from 1967 to 1969, Kaczynski witnessed the rise of the New Left counterculture and its "psychology of leftism" and the tumultuous events of the late sixties that rocked the California campus and the nation. Apparently, he was not a sympathizer. According to the Unabomber, the psychology of leftism reflects the values and authority of socialists, collectivists, "politically correct" types, feminists, gay and disability activists, animal rights activists, and other "craziness." For example, he cites

> Leftist anthropologists [who] go to great lengths to avoid saying anything about primitive peoples that could conceivably be interpreted as negative. They want to replace the word "primitive" by "nonliterate." They seem almost paranoid about anything that might suggest that any primitive culture is inferior to our own.

In parentheses the Unabomber writes, "We do not mean to imply that primitive cultures ARE inferior to ours. We merely point out the hypersensitivity of leftish anthropologists." Interestingly, at the same time that he's criticizing political correctness and its promoters, the Unabomber uses a politically correct qualification, or defense, as he tiptoes around the land mines of the politically correct war. Throughout the text the Unabomber uses similar qualifications when he speaks of minorities, Native Americans, or religious groups, though not for homosexuals.

Throughout the manifesto the Unabomber identifies the "university system" and university professors as a primary site of leftist psychology and political correctness. Leftist ideology and beliefs emanate from our universities, are taught in our schools, and are promoted by the mass media, as is the ideology that supports technological progress, industrialization, and mass culture. He states that "Many leftists have an intense identification with the problems of groups that have an image of being weak (women), defeated (American Indians), repellent (homosexuals), or otherwise inferior" (para. 13). Because leftists have an inferiority complex they identify with these groups, which they themselves see as inferior. The Unabomber speaks at great length about the perils of leftist thought, so much so that the FBI had suspected early on that he might be a graduate student or even a disgruntled university professor, perhaps a failed one or one burned by the politically correct conflicts that permeated American higher education following the 1960s. In retrospect the FBI was quite correct. In his manifesto the Unabomber wrote:

> Leftists tend to hate anything that has an image of being strong, good and successful. They hate America, they hate Western civilization, they hate white males, they hate rationality. . . . They SAY they hate the West because it is warlike, imperialistic, sexist, ethnocentric and so forth, but where these same faults appear in socialist countries or in primitive cultures, the leftist finds excuses for them. . . .
>
> Words like "self-confidence," "self-reliance," "initiative," "enterprise," "optimism," etc. play little role in the liberal and leftist vocabulary. (paras. 15 and 16)

According to the Unabomber most leftists dismiss reason, science, and objective reality when it comes to human social behavior and insist that everything is culturally relative. He challenges the liberal excesses as seen in affirmative action and political correctness and links them to the pervasive influence that leftist psychology has accrued in America's major institutions, particularly in education. Leftists are a main component of the Unabomber's pantheon of evildoers because they represent the most educated and influential class in American society and also its most left-wing. He berates leftists who believe that the duty of the individual is to serve society and the duty of the society is to take care of the individual. These values are deeply rooted in our society (at least in its middle and upper classes), but the Unabomber sees them as "contemptible."

For different reasons the Unabomber has gone after the scientists and technologists whom he believes have helped engineer the mass technological and industrial Babylon that has so ruined the world. Scientists, engineers, and "technocrats" are singled out because they create the evil industrial and technological demons that serve to control almost every aspect of people's lives. He believes that, ultimately, science, technology, and industry strangle the individuality of people and the autonomy of small groups and communities.

The Unabomber feels that our modern fascination with longevity and physical attraction well into adulthood is a sign of the uselessness and decadence of modern science and its technological application. Not only is it expensive and wasteful, but it also gives the false idea that we can fight or improve upon nature or God. (This use of "God" is the common way in which the Unabomber refers to religion.) We keep fatally ill people alive long past the time that nature would claim them, argues the Unabomber, so that fearful people can hang on a few more days or weeks and a huge medical industry can feed off the dying carcass.

"To many of us, freedom and dignity are more important than a long life or avoidance of physical pain" he writes. "Besides we all have to die sometime, and it may be better to die fighting for survival, or for a cause, than to live a long but empty and purposeless life" (para. 168). Through the production of ever new technologies and applications for mostly mundane useless commodities and technologies, the individual and small groups become more dependent on the system. In other words, he suggests that the system makes it impossible for people or small groups to live independent lives, survive by their own devices, or die of their own accord.

So the Unabomber has attacked those in the fields of medical science, genetic engineering, and biotechnology. He also attacks computers, mass communications, government and corporate bureaucracies, complex social structures, and all of the modern scientific and technological culture that entraps people and keeps them from having control over their own lives. The activities of scientists and technologists, such as the university professor, he calls "surrogate" activities, work with no meaningful purpose or value engaged in for the "personal" fulfillment the scientist or engineer gets out of the work. The "benefit to humanity" explanation, the Unabomber says, does not hold water, because the only benefit scientists get out of their work is in seeing their theories put into practice. He questions the "humanity" of those who created the atomic bomb. These weren't people interested in saving humanity; they were "nerds" who wanted to see if they could blow up the world—and they could. The difference between he and they, apparently, is motivation. By throwing his own bombs at the system, the Unabomber hoped to save humanity from a conspiracy of evildoers.

Like those who subscribe to a conspiracy of communists or Jews who are hell-bent on gaining control over the world through the creation of a slavelike new world order, the Unabomber paints a picture of technocrats, scientists, and leftists conspiring to push forward the destructive forces of modernization, development, and political correctness. Also like those who fear the demonic elements of secular humanism and modernization, the Unabomber rejects the notion that modern technology represents "progress." Like the Luddites of the early nineteenth century, a movement of English craftsmen who rioted against and destroyed the new machinery of the Industrial Revolution that was replacing them, the Unabomber rails against modern society and the institutions of science and technology that are replacing an older and better way of life.

The Unabomber argues for a return to a more peaceful, less hurried, community-oriented past, where all people knew one another and people lived in tightly knit, self-contained, and autonomous communities. Ironically, Ted Kaczynski had become so "autonomous" as to be a socially introverted and survival-oriented hermit. The Unabomber is hostile to the fast pace of everyday life and what many observers consider an overly rational mass society. He rails against a society that has become self-centered, materialistic, and so dependent on technology. He glorifies the cultures of the preindustrial world, the primitive peoples who lived as a part of nature, not in control of it or destroying it.

> Primitive man, threatened by a fierce animal or by hunger, can fight in self-defense or travel in search of food. He has no certainty of success in these efforts, but he is by no means helpless against the things that threaten him. The modern individual on the other hand is threatened by many things against which he is helpless; nuclear accidents, carcinogens in food, environmental pollution, war, increasing taxes, invasion of his privacy by large organizations, nation-wide social or economic phenomena that may disrupt his way of life. (para. 68)

Much like the rural survivalist, the Unabomber idolizes nature and living interdependently with it, rather than living in a complex industrial society that exploits and attempts to control nature. He also believes that individualism, autonomy, and developing the abilities to survive by one's own wits are the "right" way to live, rather than working as a cog in the machine run by the power elite's system. The Unabomber calls for a return to nature and a more natural way of life. "Nature takes care of itself," he says, suggesting that in the end Nature will get her way. Nature was a "spontaneous" creation, says the Unabomber, and it existed long before any human society. When humans finally evolved, many different kinds of human societies coexisted with nature for centuries without doing it much harm. But with the Industrial Revolution the effect of human society on nature was devastating.

Hoping to avoid a nasty backlash from nature that might destroy many forms of life on earth, including humans, the Unabomber suggests that it is not necessary to create a special kind of social system; it is only necessary to get rid of the old industrial one. The Unabomber is not too concerned about what happens after the collapse of the industrial system. Most people will live close to nature, of course, since without advanced technology there will be no other way to live. To survive, people will have to become peasants, herdsmen, fishermen, or hunters. At this most basic level, says the Unabomber, local autonomy and independence will increase. In the absence of advanced technology and rapid communications, the capacity of governments or other large organizations to control local communities will be severely limited.

In his manifesto the Unabomber outlines the strategy to accomplish the collapse of modern society. He says that revolutionaries should work to increase the stress within the social system so that it will break down or be sufficiently weakened in order for revolution against it to become possible. It will be necessary, he suggests, to develop and propagate an ideology that opposes technology and the industrial society so that when the system is teetering on the brink, many will herald its ultimate collapse. Hence, the letter and package bombs, which the Unabomber believed would further add to the chaos of a civilization on the eve of destruction. Whatever one can do, however small, to give a little push, one should. In the end, the collapse of civilization will be a good thing, and we will all be cleansed by the experience, at least those who survive.

The Unabomber argues that revolutionaries will be unable to bring the system down unless it is already in deep trouble, which he believes it is. There's a good chance that it will collapse anyway—sooner or later. He reasons, however, that the bigger the system grows the harder it falls, and the more disastrous it will be for the planet's ecosystem and the survival of the human race. "So," he concludes, "it may be that revolutionaries, by hastening the onset of the breakdown, will be reducing the extent of the disaster" (para. 167).

The Unabomber makes an interesting and pointed argument about the state of modern society regarding the effects of rapid social change and the transformation and fragmentation that advanced industrial society seems to be creating or contributing to. But why does he kill? Quite simply, to be heard. Through large and complex political and economic organizations, the mass media and "information industry" are under the control of the system, says the Unabomber. They will never hand over control to the people. While anyone with a little money can have something printed or can distribute it on the Internet, which will be swamped by the volume of material already there and multiplying hourly. Most

Americans aren't even paying attention, he laments, mesmerized by TV, materialism, and a decadent way of life created by a mass entertainment culture. Revolution is easier than reform, argues the Unabomber, but "in order to get our message before the public with some chance of making a lasting impression, we've had to kill people" (para. 96). The only way out is by a revolution, says the Unabomber, though not necessarily an armed uprising. The radical and fundamental change in the nature of society will come about with the collapse of the industrial–technological system. Hopefully, with the arrest of Theodore Kaczynski, the active participation of the Unabomber in bringing on the technological apocalypse is over. But the manifesto lives on, ironically, through the technological wonder popularly known as the Internet, where it is easily accessed by potential "revolutionaries" and other apocalypticists.

The Unabomber sees parallels between the Babylon of Revelation and so many other civilizations in history that have collapsed during the advanced stages of their development: "History shows that leisured aristocracies tend to become decadent ... aristocracies that have no need to exert themselves usually become bored, hedonistic and demoralized, even though they have power" (para. 34). The Unabomber is quite explicit about the problems caused by the mass media and popular culture and their propagandistic and manipulative functions:

> To start with, there are the techniques of surveillance. Hidden video cameras are now used in most stores and in many other places, computers are used to collect and process vast amounts of information about individuals. Information so obtained greatly increases the effectiveness of physical coercion (i.e., law enforcement). Then there are the methods of propaganda, for which the mass communication media provide effective vehicles. Efficient techniques have been developed for winning elections, selling products, influencing public opinion. The entertainment industry serves as an important psychological tool of the system, possibly even when it is dishing out large amounts of sex and violence. Entertainment provides modern man with an essential means of escape. While absorbed in television, videos, etc., he can forget stress, anxiety, frustration, dissatisfaction. Many primitive peoples, when they don't have work to do, are quite content to sit for hours at a time doing nothing at all, because they are at peace with themselves and their world. But most modern people must be constantly occupied or entertained, otherwise they get "bored."...
> (para. 147)

Throughout the manifesto the Unabomber employs a form of social and cultural criticism, referred to in sociology as the mass culture critique. It is an argument that has been made by many critics of modernization in the past. The mass culture critique also transcends specific ideologies, whether conservative, liberal, radical, fascist, socialist, or Marxist, and becomes, like the millennial myth, imbued with tremendous explanatory power. It permeates the philosophies and literature of numerous great thinkers and writers through the ages.[6] In fact, since the Industrial Revolution, the argument against the tyrannical "mass society" or "mass culture" has been made by those the Unabomber would call "leftist."

The mass culture argument's most sustained theory and research came in the work of the Frankfurt School, a group of Marxist intellectuals who left Europe during the rise of Hitler and the Nazis and came to the United States, where their experiences in Europe and then in the United States infused much of their work.[7] The Frankfurt School viewed the mass media and culture industry pessimistically and saw them as political weapons in the hands of the ruling elite. Its critique was a sharper and more radical one than that which had preceded it—the predominantly Protestant middle-class attack on the decline of values and cultural tastes contained in the tradition of the American jeremiad (see Chapter 2). In this regard the Frankfurt School can be credited for moving the debate on mass culture away from the lament over declining standards and morals in society to questions concerning new technologies of communications and how these represented the interests of those in power.

Throughout the work of the Frankfurt School genuine artistic expression, or "high" culture, is contrasted with a commodified and fetishized mass culture, devoid of any true "aura," critical potential, or other redeeming social value. The Frankfurt School identified the "culture industry" as the crucial point for the reproduction of capitalist economic control. Here, in the structure and content of the mass media and mass culture, could be found the key elements in the manufacturing of "mass consent" to the systems of domination. This raised important issues concerning the relationship between the ideology of the powerful classes and the consciousness of all those who made up the "masses." The new media and technologies of mass information production and communication, such as radio, television and satellites, could be used, believed the Frankfurt theorists, for the ideological control of the masses.

In *The Authoritarian Personality* (1950), Theodore Adorno pointed to the problems of modern capitalism, burdened as it was by overproduction, "commodity fetishism," and the fragmentation and alienation of people from public life.[8] Only by "creating needs" could markets be stimulated, Adorno suggested. The culture industry became the central agency in contemporary capitalism for the production and satisfaction of these "false needs." By controlling and reproducing the content of mass communication in the form of news, entertainment and education, the culture industry suppresses critical thought and manipulates the masses through a propagandistic and ideological indoctrination. *The Authoritarian Personality* held that the consumer had become an automaton paying blind allegiance to authority and feeling blind hatred toward outsiders, a personality who "surrenders to conventional values," is "anti-introspective" and rigidly stereotypical, and has a "penchant for superstition." The rise of fascism most definitely gave rise to the authoritarian personality in the writings of Adorno and others of the Frankfurt school.

Today the mass culture critique persists in our society and takes different forms. On the one hand, as its critics charge, mass culture is designed to appeal to the "lowest common denominator" (the mass public) and is produced by cynical business interests solely for profit. On the other hand, mass culture serves the interests of the ruling political elite, who maintain control over media industries through laws and regulations, but who also employ its manipulative techniques to their own political advantage. In both cases mass media and mass culture have harmful effects on individuals and society. Ultimately, mass culture serves the interests of the ruling class as a kind of propaganda that creates a passive audience responsive to techniques of mass persuasion and indifferent to totalitarianism. Little hope was seen for modern humanity to escape the grip of mass cultural totalitarianism. At these moments the Frankfurt School theories are cynical and pessimistic, paralyzed by their own visions of doom.

The mass culture critique has focused on mass culture as a combination of elements corroding the cultural diversity essential to a pluralistic society. Mass (and popular) culture is seen as a form of social decay, the "bread and circuses" of a culture in decline. The mass culture critique can be viewed as an apocalyptic idea that continues to inform theories about our modern society and its way of life. In his book *Bread and Circuses: Mass Culture as Social Decay* (1983), Patrick Brantlinger traced the history and persistence of cultural criticism regarding mass culture and showed that this form of "negative classicism"—the idea that watered-down culture for the masses leads to the decay of civilization—is both apocalyptic mythology and political ideology.[9] It is an apocalyptic philosophy that pervades all levels of public consciousness today, from scholarly and intellectual writing to the mass media itself. Mass culture is a metaphor for Babylon, and behind it lies a concern for the preservation of civilization as a whole.

While Rome, the Catholic Church, and Western civilization in general have been past symbols of Babylon, America as a metaphor for Babylon has been a common idea both here and around the world for much of the past "American century." Today, the United States is increasingly becoming an information and service economy centered on entertainment. In fact, we are the world's entertainer. The United States produces and sends around the world more popular culture than any other nation. Disney, Hollywood movies, rock 'n roll, Coca Cola, Calvin Klein, and McDonalds are the images and products that make America so familiar across the globe.

Popular examples of American Babylon have included Hollywood and Los Angeles, with their fast cars, fast deals, and fast lifestyle—a persona created by Hollywood itself and reproduced around the world. The moniker "La La Land" attests to this land of false consciousness. More recently Hollywood and Los Angeles have been all over the news and entertainment media of our mass culture. From the Rodney King beating and riot to the Menendez trials to the O. J. Simpson case—broadcast around the world for almost a year in a most bizarre case of real life becoming entertainment—LA looks more and more like the decadent Babylon of Revelation. For critics of American culture, these are further examples of the "bread and circuses" of a civilization in decline.

Other American cities have also been seen as the locus of Babylon. For many, "Fun City," Las Vegas, is another of those icons of pleasure and perversion, where legalized gambling and prostitution (outside Las Vegas) become the major draw. Ironically, Las Vegas has become a kind of "pleasure dome" for those attracted to the survivalist philosophies of *Soldier of Fortune* magazine, which for the past several years has held its annual convention in Las Vegas (see Chapters 1 and 8). New York City and Disney World are other examples of American Babylons—places that represent American materialist and entertainment values at their extremes.

The fragmentation of American culture at the end of the twentieth century is due in large part to the proliferation of more and newer information and information systems, the expansion of the global economy, and the continually evolving forms of mass and popular culture. Because it so distorts its symbols and meanings, the mass culture may serve to render the millennial myth a powerless and empty worldview with little power to explain or persuade. Apocalyptic symbols and images in the popular culture, in film and popular music, for example, become background noise, shrill and sensational "style," the latest "noir" fad, of little greater consequence to society. It may be that the opposite is true. Perhaps the myth is empowered by the modern mass media and revitalized by popular cultural trends. All of the destructive images we see on TV and in the news, including those of messianic cults and bomb-throwing "patriots," may convince some people that bad times are coming, that maybe there's something to this apocalyptic stuff. The multiple and conflicting expressions of the millennial myth are reflective of the postmodern nature of American culture, one that is fragmented and rapidly changing, its already shallow roots and traditions threatened by change.

To many of those on the far right, Americans are a decadent people, deceived by a mass culture and mass media that serve up madness and mayhem as entertainment hourly in TV programs, films, and popular music. From Oprah, Phil, and Sally Jesse to Stallone, Schwarzenegger, and Seagal, to convicted rapper Snoop Doggy Dog, to O. J. Simpson and Rodney King, we are a violent and sinful society. Still, we seem to love the whole "doom and destruction" thing—at least the entertainment version of it served up by our popular culture.

The United States also makes a good candidate for Babylon to those on the survivalist right. The American government had sold out the United States to the new world order by joining and promoting sinister internationalist organizations like the United Nations and its multilateral forces. As usual, it was America who was being used and abused by the demonic conspirators of the new world order, a code word for Babylon. The notion that the world is becoming controlled by a small, elite group of "internationalists" who plan to enslave all nations, including America, is prominent in the philosophy of the survivalist right. Alternately seen as either the Federal Reserve, the United Nations, the World Bank, multinationals, the modern technological and industrial system, or a combination of them all, the new world order for many represents a global Babylon.

As American popular culture spreads around the world via mass communications and global capitalism, its products and philosophies also spread. With them spread the popular cultural images and values of America and the West, with America as the center of the world, its way of life the most copied and sought after. Other images of America also spread—those of greed and hedonism, ethnocentrism and nationalism, cultural imperialism and American millennialism. To many on the right, and for many around the world, America is a sinful and perverted place—a Babylonian empire just before the fall. And it must fall in order to make way for the millennium and the new (old) world to come. For those of the survivalist right, it is America and the new world order that have become the primary symbols of Babylon. So when George

Bush trumpeted the "new world order" as the clarion call to arms to turn back the tyranny of Saddam Hussein, those on the right heard "Babylon," those on the left heard American "manifest destiny," and those in the media went in search of apocalyptic story angles.

*Nostradamus, Hal Lindsey, and Jeanne Dixon are all selling briskly.* (PETER JENNINGS, ABC NEWS REPORT ON THE EFFECTS OF THE GULF WAR, JANUARY 23, 1990)

It was curious that, although the war with Iraq was hailed as the most televised war, it was also a war where little live action or depictions of death were actually seen by viewers. Aside from the barrage of military and Middle Eastern experts, charts, file footage, and pictures of the military buildup, the kind of raw footage commonly seen by Americans during the Vietnam War was largely absent. The only real "combat" televised were jets taking off and returning, battleships firing their cannons, and the much quoted "Nintendo pictures" of jet aircraft dropping their bombs and recording their hits in the tiny circles of smoke that would arise from their impact. Reporters' hands were tied when they were confined to "media pools" and warned that what they broadcast could endanger U.S. efforts and the lives of Americans. Media coverage of the war was highly sanitized, coordinated by the government with an overwhelmingly supportive American people (so it seemed) and an easy victory (so it also seemed).

A large part of this support was gained through the production and dissemination of the symbols, images, and messages of the American millennial myth throughout the popular culture. Even the Gulf War became a kind of "bread and circuses" for the masses, who have become inured yet drawn to the spectacle of war that permeated the mass media. This was seen clearly throughout the first week of TV coverage of the "War in the Gulf," as Ted Turner's CNN captioned it. On the night of the American-led air attack on Baghdad, while Israelis waited terrified by the threat of scud missile attacks by Saddam Hussein, who had threatened to burn half of Israel, CNN ran a story about a group of Israeli college students celebrating an "Apocalypse party."

Midway through the second week of the war (Jan. 23), ABC News reported that American bookstores were experiencing a run on books about prophecy and the end of the world. At the end of the second week (Jan. 25), CNN polled American viewers on the question: "Do you think the Gulf War is the beginning of Armageddon?" Fourteen percent said yes while 8 percent "didn't know."[10] On CBS Sunday Morning (Jan. 27), a correspondent reported from the plains of Armageddon in northern Israel, less than 15 miles from Nazareth, a site where many great battles of the past were fought. In Revelation 16:16, Armageddon is the place where the final battle between the forces of Christ and those of Satan occur. The reporter interviewed Jews and Arabs living in the vicinity, all of whom knew of the ancient stories and drew their own parallels between Armageddon and the current Persian Gulf crisis.

In addition to the bits and pieces of millennial images that appeared in the media, such as Babylon, the new world order, and Armageddon, the attachment to the symbols of the war was most clearly seen in the patriotic phenomenon of the yellow ribbons. No matter what one thought of the war, its supporters argued, one could not be against the soldiers. That was the message of the yellow ribbons and that was the lesson learned from Vietnam that seemed to stick the best. But once one accepted the yellow ribbon philosophy, it became difficult to criticize the war and question whether or not American soldiers should be there in the first place. Certainly the wearers of yellow ribbons rarely did. The yellow ribbons were about patriotism, and the patriotism unleashed by the yellow ribbon syndrome was enormous. Many of the wearers of yellow ribbons tended to ignore or obscure the deeper politics of the war and thus blunt any sustained criticism of it.[11]

The spectacle continued on Saturday, June 8—"National Victory Day." In Washington, D.C., the largest military parade since the end of World War II marched down Constitution Avenue—a 100-minute ($12 million) parade to celebrate a 100-hour war that pushed Iraq out of Kuwait in February. More than 200,000 people turned out. President Bush, Mrs. Bush, and the entire first family reviewed the parade from a tall, prefabricated steel and bullet-proof glass box. In the stands, Secretary of State James Baker, Defense Secretary Richard Cheney, and Chairman of the Joint Chiefs of Staff Colin Powell mingled with the dozens of other political luminaries.

Painted across a long wall erected along the parade route and at the base of the viewing area, a yellow ribbon greeted the passing parade of soldiers and artillery led by the newest American folk hero, Desert Storm Commander, General "Stormin' Norman" Schwarzkopf. Following the general were almost 9,000 of the American troops who fought in Operation Desert Storm. The infantries and artillery divisions were escorted by military bands, M-I Abrams and Howitzer tanks, and Patriot missiles, as jet fighters, bombers, helicopters, and cargo jets flew overhead.[12] Out of no-where a black F-117A stealth bomber slashed through the air. Dozens of other planes and jets followed in formation. This was the spectacle of the just war and the return of its victorious warriors who had helped to rebuild the "new world order" and quash the old one.

The yellow ribbon phenomenon is a good example of what William Kornhauser has called the tendency for people to form "hyperattachments" to symbols and meanings in mass society.[13] Rapid social change causes disruption in the current social order, resulting in strong feelings of alienation and anxiety among those hurt by the changes. Confused by events they can neither understand nor change, some people become susceptible to symbols and "spectacles" that provide a simple solution to their problems. They may form hyperattachments to these symbols in order to escape from their fears and tensions. In a postmodern culture like our own, where images and symbols are produced and reproduced at increasingly high rates of speed and in greater numbers, hyperattachment to powerful and familiar symbols increases.

The "War in the Gulf" was in part a gigantic spectacle designed by the government to hide certain facts and engender support from Americans through the ideological manipulation of images and meanings, including those of the millennial myth. Indeed, the war did produce many distinct spectacles, such as the yellow ribbons and the numerous television specials that honored and saluted "our men and women in the Gulf." These spectacles provided illusory unification and meaning, distracting attention from the deeper problems inherent in society and the world, such as dwindling natural resources, environmental degradation, increasing cultural conflict, and eroding ways of life.

# Chapter 7

# Messiah

## "Many Will Say They Are Me"

*I am He that Liveth, and was dead; and behold, I am alive for evermore, Amen; and have the keys of Hell and of Death.*

REV. 1:18, KJV

*But now, he that has a purse let him take it, and likewise his money, and he that has no sword, let him sell his garment and buy one.*

LUKE 22:36, RSV

David Koresh, the 33-year-old self-proclaimed "messiah" of the Branch Davidian Church—a separativist Adventist sect—believed that he was an "anointed" messenger from God, chosen and inspired to reveal to his followers and to the world the meaning of Revelation and 2,500 years of Jewish and Christian apocalyptic prophecy. He also believed that it was his job, as the slain Lamb and thus the interpreter of the seven seals of Revelation, to reveal the time and manner in which the end of the world would occur. Koresh and his followers fervently believed that they were living in, indeed, helping to usher in, the biblically prophesied millennial age.

Given these beliefs, and the federal authorities' ignorance of them, the tragedy outside of Waco, Texas, was bound to happen, and it serves as an example of self-fulfilling apocalyptic prophecy. David Koresh—the messianic identity of Vernon

Howell—and the Branch Davidians burst into the American consciousness shortly after 9:00 am, Sunday morning, February 28,
1993. Television cameras, reporters, and police were swarming
over a community just west of Waco, Texas, called Mount Carmel,
where there had been a deadly shoot-out between a messianic cult
called the Branch Davidians and federal agents of the ATF.

During an aborted attempt to serve a warrant to the cult's
leader, David Koresh, for the illegal purchase and accumulation of
firearms, explosives, and other weaponry, four ATF agents were
killed by members of Koresh's small church. Twenty other federal
agents were also injured during what looked on TV like a raid by
ATF agents, fully outfitted in paramilitary fashion, on the sect's
main building. Television viewers were shown the violent and
bloody pictures of ATF agents huddled by a window and under
gunfire by heavily armed Davidians, as one of their comrades lay
wounded and dying by their sides. During the shoot-out six Branch
Davidians were also killed, while four others, including Koresh,
who was shot in the shoulder, were wounded. The Waco incident
became one of the largest disasters and, ultimately, the most tragic
in the history of federal law enforcement in the United States.

The spectacular shoot-out between members of the messianic
cult and 75 armed paramilitary ATF forces—broadcast shortly after
around the country and the world—shocked viewers. But it should
not have shocked them, since it wasn't the first time that someone
calling himself the messiah had appeared in the United States and
on American television in connection with some sensational, often
deadly encounter with the law. Jim Jones and members of the
People's Temple, who committed mass suicide in Guyana in 1978,
quickly come to mind. Still, the "Waco Apocalypse," as the news
media later dubbed it, turned out to have a more immediate effect
in comparison, if only because of the live television coverage and
the drawn-out siege that the media and the public followed inces-
santly. (Of course, the tape recording of the shrieks and screams in
Guyana were shocking enough.)

The case for the raid on the Davidian compound was based on
evidence compiled by the ATF showing that the Branch Davidians
were stockpiling illegal weapons. According to documents later

released by the ATF, David Koresh and his church had spent nearly $200,000 on weapons and ammunition, and they possessed illegal firearms materials and were converting AR-15 semiautomatic rifles into machine guns. According to federal authorities, the arsenal already built by the Davidians included 123 M-16 rifles and possibly hand grenades and other explosives. In the months leading up to the siege, federal authorities had been tipped off by a UPS delivery man, who had told of dropping off two cases of hand grenades and black gunpowder.[1]

The ATF affidavits also stated that the Davidians appeared to be "arming for Armageddon" and thus they should be considered dangerous. They described the Davidian residence as a "compound," implying a military fortress or training facility. Reports claimed that there were bomb shelters on the compound and that the Davidians stockpiled food and water, fuel, and other equipment, as well as guns, in the fashion of survivalists in preparation for social collapse. The Davidian complex, which included a gymnasium and indoor pool, also included a school bus with its seats removed that had been sunken underground to be used as a bunker or bomb shelter. There was also a concrete bunker beneath the main building's watchtower, and reports state that the cult had amassed a two-year supply of military food rations.[2]

Federal authorities also claimed that the Davidians were stockpiling weapons in preparation for armed rebellion or insurrection, and that shoot-outs such as this were more likely to happen. They claimed that Koresh was militantly antigovernment and saw government, law enforcement, and the entire American society as the corrupt Babylon. For months the ATF was planning a "search and arrest" assault on the group based on allegations and precautions. These were reasons enough, they said, for using force in the service of the arrest warrants. The media came to dub the Davidian community "Ranch Apocalypse." Here was a somewhat new twist on an old theme: the messiah figure—a classic apocalyptic symbol—who also practiced a modern or secular version of doomsday prophecy called survivalism. The entire event was quickly interpreted and reproduced in the media as an apocalyptic event. The appearance of violent and murderous messiahs such as Jim Jones and Charles Manson had come before in American society, but a "crazed" messiah and apocalyptic cult that stockpiled military-style weapons, practiced survivalism, and had built a "paramilitary survival compound" had a new ring to many Americans, though not to those on the survivalist right.

Why would an apocalyptic cult be concerned with weapons and survivalism, especially if they believed the end of the world was imminent? The answer lies in the group's defensive and anti-government orientation and in the "premillennialism" of the Branch Davidians and their forebears the Adventists, who believed that the Messiah would return before the final battle of Armageddon had begun. Koresh and other Davidians claimed that dealing in guns was a legitimate business operation the group engaged in to raise funds for their communal lifestyle.

Like millions of Americans, Koresh cherished the right to own weapons and the right to use them in self-defense, even against law enforcement. However, Koresh also believed that while Jesus had come in meekness and humility, prepared to sacrifice Himself for the sins of the world without resistance, the Second Coming of the Messiah would involve violent confrontation with the forces of evil. The Davidians were not pacifists, but expected a great war to occur in Palestine, in which they would fight side by side with the Israelis against the invading forces of the United Nations. Koresh taught his followers not to actively initiate violence until the final confrontation, but if attacked, they were instructed to forcefully resist.[3]

To Koresh—who saw himself as a second messiah, if not the returning first—the events set forth in the seven seals of Revelation, which unleash the terrible plagues of destruction and war upon the earth, were underway. Thus, to police and to the public as interpreted by the mass media, David Koresh and the Branch Davidians were a dangerous apocalyptic cult stockpiling weapons and food who practiced survivalism in the isolated Ranch Apocalypse outside Waco, Texas, in preparation for the imminent war with the forces of evil and in anticipation of the battle of Armageddon. In the case of David Koresh and the Branch Davidians, the messiah and his followers blended classical elements of the millennial myth with current events and trends such as the fear of government intrusion into their lives, concerns over the right to bear arms, and survivalist preparations.

The Branch Davidians are only the latest in a long line of messianic sects or "cults" that center around a person who claims to be, or whom others claim to be, a messiah, one imbued with supernatural powers channeled through God. Such religious groups tend to branch off from larger, more mainstream churches, the break—a culmination of a severe departure from the practices of the parent church—often involving apocalyptic and millennial aspirations. However, the Branch Davidians also reflected a further evolution of the messianic cult and millenarian movement, in which the classical elements of the myth merge with contemporary elements. Koresh was dedicated to his cause and was prepared to use those weapons somewhere and at some time to realize his imagined Armageddon. Unwittingly, perhaps, federal authorities helped him fulfill those prophecies. But they also badly misjudged David Koresh and the Davidians, and the complexities of an apocalyptic worldview that authorities could have better understood and, perhaps, better handled.

Many questions remain, however, regarding the strategies employed by federal law enforcement supervisors in the confrontational serving of the warrants by ATF agents and the fateful decision by the FBI to inject CS tear gas canisters into the compound's main building, which somehow triggered the inferno consuming most of those within. It was later discovered that a church member outside the compound had learned of the impending attack that morning and had alerted Koresh and those inside the compound. The ATF had also discovered the breach in security but decided to go ahead with the plan anyway, even though the element of surprise had been lost. Some critics asked why such a force would be used in the first place, with the presence of so many women, children, and other passive members. Were the dangers posed to innocent people justified by such overwhelming force and the potential for violence? Why was there no alternative and more peaceable strategy developed for serving the warrant?

Koresh was, in fact, known to leave Mount Carmel on occasion, even after his run-ins with the law. Could he have been arrested away from the compound? Koresh had cooperated with federal authorities earlier and had even volunteered documents pertaining to the purchase of his weapons. He had even invited federal agents inside the compound to see for themselves. Was all that government confrontation really justified? Once again, images of "Ruby Ridge" and "liberal gun control" became the rallying cries of the right. Waco was another example of overzealous law enforcement agencies abusing the basic rights of legitimate gun owners and small American churches, even if they were led by a misguided messiah. Was this how far the government was willing to go in the effort to take guns away from Americans?

*Why do the heathen rage, and the people imagine a vain thing? The kings of the earth set themselves, and the rulers take counsel together, against the Lord, and against his Anointed, saying, Let us break their bands asunder, and cast away their cords from us. (PS. 2: 1–3, KJV)*

*Thus saith the Lord to his anointed, to Cyrus, whose right hand I have holden, to subdue nations before him; and I will loose the loins of kings, to open before him the two-leaved gates, and the gates shall not be shut. (ISA. 45:1, KJV)*

Much was made of Koresh and the seven seals of Revelation. During much of the standoff, Koresh had said that he could not act until he had received a sign. That sign turned out to be the revelation from God that he was to unlock the secrets of the seven seals of Revelation and interpret its contents to his followers and to the world. Once he had done this, he said, he would give himself up to authorities and let the courts and world judge his sins. In Revelation it is "a Lamb as it had been slain, having seven horns and seven eyes" that opens the seals of tribulation, beginning with the Four Horsemen of the Apocalypse. Koresh had long been impressed by the seven seals and had built much of his sect's theology upon the images and meanings of the Four Horseman and the vials of sorrow and destruction. He believed that the entire Bible could be interpreted from the seven seals alone.[4] As Koresh read from the seven seals and fashioned his own interpretation of the events to unfold before the world, he saw himself as the Lamb, though not yet slain.

The Messiah, or Christ figure, takes several different forms in the Bible. While Christians generally assume all the messiah figures in Revelation to be Jesus Christ, others, like David Koresh, see different messiahs, of which Jesus is only one. In Revelation, Christ, or the messiah figure, appears early as an angel "as to the son of man" who appears to John at Patmos and reveals to him the apocalyptic events to occur. Shortly thereafter, the messiah is the slain Lamb that stands in the midst of the Elders as John enters through the door to Heaven. At Revelation 5:6, the Lamb opens the seven seals for John. Still later the messiah is transformed into the rider on the white horse, the "Second Coming" of Christ, who arrives just as Satan and his army are about to annihilate the world. Leading his crusaders in the final Battle of Armageddon, the conquering messiah destroys the Antichrist and the devil, throwing them into the pit for 1,000 years. Following the millennium, he brings redemption for the chosen and damnation for the wicked and restores the earth's former beauty, with the descent from the heavens of the "New Jerusalem." This messiah figure is also very unlike that of Jesus Christ in the Gospels of Matthew, Mark, and John, and more like the God of Genesis in his severity and unforgiving nature. He is both savior and executioner as he lays out the rules for final judgment.

Early in Revelation, John of Patmos sees "a book . . . sealed with seven seals" in the right hand "of him that sat on the throne" (5:1). In a loud voice a "strong angel" raises the question, "Who is worthy to open this sealed book?" (5:2). The only one worthy to unlock the seals and reveal the contents of the book, which unleashes the events it foretells, is the slain Lamb. In the Lamb Christians see Jesus. David Koresh believed, however, that the Lamb was not Jesus, but a second messiah, who Koresh claimed to be. He did not see himself as the Second Coming of Jesus Christ. Instead, he was a second messiah, or a second Christ, sent by God to fulfill Scripture by interpreting the seven seals of Revelation, which would ultimately bring on the events prophesied in Revelation. Koresh saw himself as God's anointed prophet and Messiah—the slain Lamb. How prophetic that identity would be.

To his followers and to Christians since, it was Jesus Christ who was the Messiah. However, in Jewish tradition, the word "messiah" has a more varied meaning. In Hebrew messiah means the "anointed one," appointed and empowered by God through the impartation of His own spirit to become the savior of his people. While many Jews have hoped for the supernatural appearance of one special savior and continue to wait for him, in ancient Israel the messiah could take a human form (as Jesus had), as a king, for example, who would lead his people, often in political and military ways, to the holy land in this world.

Hebrew kings were consecrated by having their heads smeared with holy oil, marking them as set apart for a special role as messiah. King David (1010–970 B.C.), second king of Israel and architect of the united kingdom with Jerusalem as its capital, is the model of Yahweh, the Hebrew God's messiah—a savior figure who was the symbol of the bond between God and his people. Among Christians King David is revered as the esteemed ancestor of Jesus. All of King David's descendants who ruled over Judah were Yahweh's messiahs as well.[5] After the end of the Davidic monarchy, various Hebrew prophets applied the promises made to the Davidic dynasty to a future heir who would eventually restore the kingdom of David.

This appearance of the messiah has been prophesied in many passages throughout the Hebrew Bible, or "Old Testament," particularly in Psalms and Isaiah, where he is called Koresh, the Hebrew name for Cyrus, the ancient king of Persia who conquered Babylon. Vernon Howell changed his name to David Koresh because this is who he claimed to be: the messiah Koresh, who had come to interpret the apocalyptic prophecies of the Bible, particularly the seven seals of Revelation. Just as Koresh saw himself as the chosen one, so were his followers chosen. He was less interested in showing the entire world the way than in organizing and preparing a "select" group—the 144,000—revealed to him by God. Koresh believed that he was living in and helping to direct the end of history, and he interpreted the events of the world and those that unfolded around him as supernaturally charged and in some way reflecting apocalyptic Scripture. Had the ATF and FBI authorities known how firmly Koresh believed these things—and they had access to scholars and researchers in a position to know—they might have better appreciated the entire situation from the viewpoint of Koresh and the Branch Davidians.

*Thou art worthy to take the book, and to open the seals thereof: for thou wast slain, and hast redeemed us to God by thy blood out of every kindred, and tongue, and people, and nation.* (REV. 5:9, KJV).

Messianism, or the belief in the coming of a messiah, and millenarian movements associated with the Messiah have appeared throughout the history of Western civilization since the death of Christ, including in the United States, as we saw in Chapter 2. The nineteenth century in America is regarded by historians as a period of tremendous millennial activity, and the period saw the development of numerous social movements aimed at social, political, moral, and spiritual reform. The so-called Age of Reform (1800–1830) saw the origin or revitalization of many millenarian movements. These included the Shakers, the Oneida, and the Church of Christ Scientist, popularly known today as Christian Science.

Other millenarian groups that began in the period and are familiar to many Americans today include the Church of Jesus Christ of Latter-day Saints, or the Mormons, who also advocate survivalist practices such as disaster preparedness and the stockpiling of foodstuffs in preparation for "lean times" (see Chapter 9). Other millennial movements followed, including the Jehovah's Witnesses, founded by Charles Taze Russell in the early 1870s, which, along with the Sacred Name groups and Seventh Day Church of God, are part of the "Adventist family." Americans are very familiar with the ubiquitous Jehovah's Witness, who leaves copies of *The Watchtower* and *Awake* magazines in their mailbox one week, returning the next with a sales promotion that is the envy of many door-to-door salesmen. Should you read their magazines or indulge their evangelizing, they will tell you that the end of the world is coming, and that they alone will survive the coming Armageddon. But you can survive, too, if you read the signs of the times and heed the word of God. Animated by the urgent need to warn mankind of the coming Battle of Armageddon, the Witnesses have brought their message to over 400 countries around the world. The Watchtower Bible and Tract Society, their legal agency and publishing company, proclaims the truth of the Bible against the demonic triumvirate of organized religion, the business world, and the state. Close to 16 million copies of *The Watchtower* magazine have been published in more than 100 languages.

Generally polite, Witnesses express contempt for the religious beliefs of others, particularly those of Catholics, whom, in their reverence for symbols, rituals, the Holy Trinity, and the Pope, Witnesses accuse of idol worship, paganism, and heresy. Most people turn the Witnesses away and either chuckle at their sincerity or sneer at their naïveté. But if we stopped to listen to them, we would better understand their enthusiasm for Jehovah and the messianic appeal of the Second Coming. The Witnesses believe that God's kingdom is an actual government now ruling in Heaven and that God will soon restore the earth to its original paradisiacal condition. They also expect an end to the present world system in a "great tribulation" that will rid the earth of wickedness and suffering. Following Armageddon will come a millennial reign of Jesus over the earth.

For the Witnesses the gaining of eternal life depends on complete obedience to Jehovah God and faith in the provision of Jesus Christ's ransom sacrifice. Because of their neutrality as to affairs of secular government, their refusal to salute any flag, and their rejection of the practice of blood transfusion (which they believe is forbidden by the Bible), the Witnesses have been the subject of controversy over defiance of the state. Interest in the Jehovah's

Witness movement has steadily increased over the years, and today there are more than four million Witnesses worldwide in 400 countries, with the single largest group—close to one million—living in the United States.[6]

The Jehovah's Witnesses are also concerned with "survival." In one of their biblical tracts, the author writes,

> Survival has become a major concern in our times.... what confronts mankind is far more awesome than a nuclear war. It is an accounting with the Creator himself. Astounding Bible prophecies show clearly that there will be survivors and that grand prospects await them right on this earth.

This quote, from the Jehovah's Witness tract *Survival into a New Earth*, defines salvation in terms of "survival" through faith in Jehovah. While the Witnesses do not advocate survivalism as a means toward salvation (as some millennial religious groups do), the survivalist analogy they draw is purposeful. The book speaks of paramilitary survivalism and its relationship to the nuclear age, but says that real survival can only come through Jehovah: "The Armageddon that the Bible speaks of is not something that can be avoided by a nuclear freeze. International negotiations will not head it off." The text informs us that "the countdown nears its zero hour!" and that we cannot stop "Nuclear Armageddon."[7]

*Emancipate yourselves from inner slavery. None but ourselves can free our minds. Have no fear of atomic energy. 'Cause none of them can stop the tide. How long shall they kill our prophets, while we stand aside and look? Some say its just a part of it. We've got to fulfill the book. Won't you help to sing these songs of freedom. Is all I ever have. Redemption songs. (BOB MARLEY, "REDEMPTION SONG")*

Blacks, too, have looked for the return of the Messiah to deliver them from the chains of their oppressors. In the 1920s, under the leadership of Marcus Garvey, who inspired the "Back to Africa" movement, black populations of America, Jamaica, and Africa began to show political consciousness and assertiveness, oftentimes inspired by millennial expectations. Marcus Mosiah Garvey, one of the world's most renowned black leaders, was born in Jamaica in 1887, when repression of blacks was at its highest under British colonialism. Garvey came to see the plight of the black Jamaican, indeed, of all blacks in the world, as oppressed people, and he saw it as his life's mission to deliver his people out of their bondage. In 1914 he organized the Universal Negro Improvement Association (UNIA) in Kingston, which was to change the image of blacks around the world. The goals of the UNIA were to promote pride among blacks, to help them to acquire economic power, and to build in Africa a black-governed Negro Nation. Garvey's middle name, Mosiah (Moses), was an apt and prophetic appellation, as he tried to free his people from the yoke of colonialism and lead them into the ancient promised land of Africa.

When he failed to attract a following in Jamaica, Garvey left for the United States (1916) and set up branches of the UNIA in Harlem and in the ghettos of the north. Through the movement's main newspaper, *Negro World*, the movement championed the history and culture of blacks through stories of black heroes and their exploits, of the great African civilizations of Ethiopia and Egypt, and of the great black culture of the present. In time Garvey became a "messiah" for many blacks in Jamaica, the United States, Africa, and throughout the world. By 1919 the "black Moses" claimed a following of two million and established one of the largest mass movements of blacks in American history (1919–1926). In 1921 Garvey proclaimed himself president of the "empire of Africa" and united numerous black organizations under his Back to Africa movement.[8]

Troubles would eventually undermine the black prophet and his movement. Slipshod business deals, a black separatism that approved of the separativist philosophies of the Ku Klux Klan and that angered more moderate, integrationist blacks, and the indictment of Garvey and other members of his organization of mail fraud in 1922 undermined Garvey's influence. But his nationalist black movement would inspire similar political and millenarian movements among blacks in the United States: for example, the messianic Father Divine Movement of the 1930s and 1940s; black separatists such as the Nation of Islam, Malcolm X, and the Black Panthers in the 1950s and 1960s; and the black nationalism of Louis Farrakhan in the 1990s.

Another well-known example of a messianic movement begun by blacks with a global and popular cultural appeal is Rastafarianism. Drawing much of its original inspiration from Marcus Garvey and the Back to Africa movement, Rastafarianism developed in Jamaica in the 1930s and adopted a theology of conscious rejection of modernity and liberation from the Jamaican and Western dominant culture, or "Babylon." In Haile Selassie, who ascended to the throne of Ethiopia in 1930, the Rastafarians saw the "black messiah," or Ras Tafari. Almost explicitly apocalyptic in its message and meaning, Rastafarianism prophesies the fall of Babylon and the arrival of the black messiah, who will destroy the evils of Babylon (Western civilization) and bring redemption and restoration of the Rastafarians and other African peoples to their rightful homeland in Africa. While Rastafarians never sought to reconcile their beliefs with those of whites or other peoples of color, their hope of salvation from poverty and oppression and their dreams of a black identity and a homeland have inspired nationalist movements worldwide.

Bob Marley, a reggae musician who rose to worldwide fame and fortune, is regarded by most fans as a kind of prophet of the music of Rastafarianism and its message. In 1986 Bob Marley died at the age of 36 of a brain tumor, further strengthening his position as a prophet for the millennium. Ten years after his death, he remains the most famous representative to the world of the Rastafarian movement. Considered the music of Third World consciousness, today reggae is perhaps the most recognized and performed music around the world. Rastafarianism, like so many millenarian movements, is the religion of an oppressed people. Messianic movements such as Rastafarianism reflect the desires of those who want either to separate from the dominant culture or to be more fully included in it. Marley called the Rastafarians "soul rebels."[9]

In the United States today, the appeal of the messiah and the hope for the Second Coming of Christ is a central feature of Christian Fundamentalism. Since the 1970s Christian Fundamentalism has increased in the United States and has contributed to a conservative trend that grips America, especially in Washington. This is reflected in the political assertiveness of the Christian right in American politics and culture. Indeed, many factors, including church membership, the rise in sectarian activity (especially since the 1960s), and the emergence of many nondenominational churches, point to the revitalization of new religious movements and that "old time religion" with its Bible-thumping evangelists and "Christ-is-coming-soon" eschatology. Not all of these new religions are focused on the Second Coming of Christ or another individual, but many do focus explicitly of the return of Christ or are awaiting the onset of the Apocalypse.

While fundamentalists have learned not to choose particular dates for the return (though many in the past have made such predictions), most are sure that it will happen soon, and they don't hide their excitement about the imminent Apocalypse. For they believe the Apocalypse is the crucible we must pass through to get to the other side—the millennium. In fact, they say it's really something to look forward to. Popular Christian fundamentalist Pat Robertson, host of the Christian television show the *700 Club* and CEO of the Christian Broadcast Network, commonly includes apocalyptic discussion in his programs. Robertson is an example of the "Christ-is-coming-soon" set. The *700 Club* is one of the many talk shows that announce that the end of the world is near. Robertson and guests review current events after "news" segments, and then comment on the biblical veracity of the current events, pinning them to biblical verses like those in Revelation. Robertson, who ran for U.S. president in 1984, continues to play politics as he helps build the Christian right and its conservative and fundamentalist agenda, which includes prayer in the schools, the repeal of abortion rights laws, and returning America to its Christian heritage.

It is not uncommon to hear fundamentalist ministers speak of nuclear Armageddon. If God chooses to destroy the world with nuclear weapons, a third world war, or a flood brought on by the greenhouse effect and melting ice caps, then He can do it. Indeed, it seems most likely to them that He will. This puts an interesting twist on the conservative Christian right's support of a strong military and a pronuclear position throughout the 1980s. As Grace

Halsell has pointed out in *Prophecy and Politics*, this was in fact the agenda of the Christian right in the era of Reagan. Halsell points to Ronald Reagan's firmly held beliefs that the end times were near. It has been reported that Reagan kept a copy of Hal Lindsey's bestseller *The Late Great Planet Earth* on his nightstand while he was in the White House.[10]

Two of the more millennial of fundamentalist churches or movements include Evangelical Christianity and the Assemblies of God, large umbrella organizations, both of whom report increasing attendance and membership since the 1970s. The Assemblies of God has been listed as the fastest-growing Protestant church in the United States, and also one of the most apocalyptic. This is the church that produced televangelists Jimmy Swaggart and Jim Bakker, both of whom faced highly publicized falls from grace as they were seduced by power, money, and sex. While the world of "televangelism" and mass media apocalyptic prophecy took a terrible hit during the scandalous 1980s, it is now back as strong as ever, with cable, satellite, and Internet access increasing the reach and numbers of small, loosely organized fundamentalist groups and individuals.

Recent interest in angels, extraterrestrials, and "channeling" supernatural spirits reflects further, though more distant, expressions of the messianic hope. Such "cosmic messiahs" reflect the beliefs of the more extreme segment of the New Age movement, where all manner of supernatural occurrences are signaling a "new age" on the horizon (see Chapter 9). Organizations that track paranormal activity, such as the appearance of ghosts or aliens and other odd occurrences, have been reporting steady increases in paranormal phenomena in the final decades of the twentieth century. Alien abductions, for example, have become a booming industry for UFOlogists, psychotherapists, and the popular culture and media.

Sci-fi literature, television shows like *The X-Files*, and films such as *Independence Day* and *Communion*, based on the bestselling book by Whitley Strieber, all tell tales of alien visitors who are watching us and preparing for an invasion or transformation of the earth. Strieber claims to have been abducted by aliens, and to this day he contends that he is regularly visited by extraterrestrials, whom he believes are planning the supernatural transformation of our world. Strieber has become a hot item on the lecture circuit and appears regularly on TV shows and at the growing number of UFO and alien abductee seminars and conventions.

There are many forms that the "messiah" figure can take. While angels and aliens may not appear to be explicitly apocalyptic, to many people their elements and meanings have apocalyptic significance. In Revelation, the Four Horsemen of the Apocalypse are angels unleashed by the Lamb, and Scripture tells of the great wonders and heavenly events, including the appearance of angels, that will accompany the end times. The Virgin Mary has been making many appearances of late, particularly in Yugoslavia, where she has been seen regularly since just before 1990 and in Betania, Venezuela since the early 1980s. Some who claimed they spoke with her reported that she predicted the collapse of the Soviet Union and the civil war in Bosnia, as well as other calamities that must come to pass before the return of Christ. Extraterrestrials can also be seen in a messianic light, as supernatural forces that are coming to this world in order to bring about some kind of transformation. But whether they bring destruction or redemption depends on who you read or listen to. Visitors from other planets or times, and angels or "spirit guides," indicate a further fragmenting of the millennial myth and the messianic and demonic beings of Revelation.

*For there shall arise false Christs, and false prophets, and shall show great signs, and wonders . . . they shall deceive the very elect.* (MATT. 24:24, KJV)

Over the past few decades Americans have witnessed their share of "second comings" and would-be messiahs, from Charles Manson to Jim Jones to Sun Myung Moon. Our understanding of the groups themselves and their experiences have for the most part been negative. We have come to view such groups as deluded "cults," their charismatic leaders as manipulative, their methods and motives demented, dangerous, or just plain criminal. Some point back to the countercultural 1960s as the seedbed for much of the subsequent evolution of cults. The year at the heart of the "Aquarian Age," 1968, was a fateful year for the United States and the counterculture itself. That year saw Martin Luther King and Robert Kennedy assassinated, a riot erupt between police and youth protesters at the Democratic National Convention in Chicago, and the Vietnam War escalate both in Indochina and at home on American college campuses and on inner-city streets.

While Americans debated the issues raised by civil rights leaders, student radicals, and antiwar demonstrators, they were really shocked by Charles Manson. Controlled by a master maniac and messiah of the twentieth century, and in a drug-induced haze, the Manson "family" brutally murdered several wealthy Beverly Hills residents, including Hollywood actress Sharon Tate, wife of film director Roman Polanski. Two young Manson followers even slit open the abdomen of the pregnant Sharon Tate to gaze upon the fetus. When later arrested and taken to trial, Manson appeared to be a classic sociopath, deluded as to his own grandeur, but with a power of control and manipulation that startled most of those who caught his gaze.

Deemed by conservatives as the logical extension of the hippie counterculture, Manson followed a long line of prophets and messiahs to take root on American soil, though most were not as violently destructive as he. In addition to its countercultural politics and its drug and "acid rock"-infused psychedelic culture, the 1960s also experienced a renaissance in eastern religions, such as Zen Buddhism, Confucianism, and yoga, and their New Age spinoffs in EST, Transcendental Meditation (TM), Silva Mind Control, and the Hare Krishna. Would-be messiahs also continued to appear on a fairly regular basis.

During the 1960s the Reverend Sun Myung Moon, a North Korean Christian evangelist and leader of the Unification Church, whose followers were popularly known as "Moonies," moved his evangelical and millennial church to the United States and began to make converts. Perhaps lost among the new spiritual and religious explosion of the 1960s, the Moonies didn't make national headlines until the mid-1970s because of bizarre practices—some continuing to this day—such as mass weddings and communal living conditions, in which members gave all of their wealth and belongings, including bank accounts, to Moon and the Unification Church.

The South Korean evangelist, who claims he is the Christian messiah returned to create the millennial utopia right here on earth, has parlayed his church into a multimillion-dollar operation with worldwide religious and business interests. Moon has not escaped the turmoil of claiming to be the messiah, however. Convicted of tax evasion by U.S. courts in 1987, he spent three years in jail. Now he is back in charge of his vast economic holdings, which include a newspaper business, satellite television network, and a political action committee. Moon also represents the global nature of the millennial myth, since he is also revered as the messiah by many in South Korea, his country of origin.

The Reverend Jim Jones, minister and messiah of the People's Temple, is another messiah figure very familiar to Americans. The Reverend Jones unleashed a scene of horrific carnage in the mass "suicide" of members of his People's Temple in Guyana in December, 1978, when 900 members drank Kool-Aid laced with poison at the jungle commune they called their Temple. Those who didn't drink were shot point blank.

In America, we have had our fair share of messiahs, and while this brief sampling of the some of the more recent and spectacular messiahs and millennial groups could render all new religious movements as dangerous and deluded "cults," many scholars challenge the popular meaning and use of the term "cult." They point out how it demonizes a wide range of new religious movements appearing in our culture, most of which are nonviolent and reflect a long tradition of religious change and experimentation on American soil. Branding all new or small religious groups as bizarre, deluded, or violent makes it impossible to perceive objectively this country's vast array of religious beliefs and communitarian practices.

Based on a few spectacular events, and fueled by a popular culture that loves the grotesque, we are alternately repulsed and fascinated by the bizarre beliefs and practices of cults and their leaders. However, we are seeing only a very small piece of the picture and may be falling prey to our own delusions of demons in the night. Perhaps we need to examine the actions of law enforcement agencies and their strategies at Waco and elsewhere in light of this tendency to demonize. The term "cult" has also been misused by some Christian fundamentalist groups, who try to pass themselves off as "cult experts" and act as consultants or "deprogrammers," presenting "cult seminars" for police departments. By the definition of these "experts," early Christianity would have been called a cult, too. Today, scholars and theologians are cautious to use the term cult because they recognize the bias the term now commands in the culture.

Generally, cults are small, loosely organized groups, often founded by and focusing on a charismatic leader who plays a central role in interpreting the meaning and destiny of his or her people and attracting new members. Cults often dissolve when their leader dies, which is why they don't last long enough to become more organized sects or larger established religions. Some do survive and may grow into major religious traditions such as Christianity or Buddhism. Because cults are organized around new and unconventional beliefs and practices, outsiders may come to view them as deviant or dangerous. However, the degree of control exercised by leaders over followers and the level of commitment of members to the leader or cult may vary considerably. Cults may be so loosely based that they meet only occasionally during meetings or conventions, as do some survivalists, extraterrestrial encounter groups, and witch covens. Others may join cults for companionship, as a relief from suffering, or as a search for enlightenment. On the other hand, cult leaders may require members to break all ties with family and friends and to give all of their money, property, and energies over to the cult.

The term "sect" more concretely defines small communities of believers with little formal authority or official governing body overseeing their activities. Typically composed or led by people who have come to view the parent church as corrupt, sects tend to form by splintering off from the church in an attempt to preserve the essence of the religion and its original believers. Often, however, sects may unknowingly create something new. The roots of sectarian churches are not unique to Christianity, either in Europe or in their transplantation to America, beginning with Puritanism. The sectarian nature of Christianity continues in American society as new churches continually arise and fall, reflecting the dynamic nature that social and cultural changes can have on groups who interpret their lives and experiences through an apocalyptic lens. Messianic groups like the Branch Davidians are a part of that tradition, and they point to the importance the messiah figure plays in religion and its adaptation to social and cultural change. In the case of David Koresh and the Branch Davidians, elements from both the cult, in the form of a charismatic leader, and the sect, in the splitting of the Davidians from the parent Adventist Church, were present.

*I saw in the night visions, and, behold, one like the Son of man came with the clouds of heaven, and came to the Ancient of days . . . (Daniel 7:13, KJV)*

*Darkness in the night. Frantically watching the night. The end has come. Riding on white horses through the night. (DAVID KORESH, "DARKNESS IN THE NIGHT")*[11]

The apocalyptic beliefs of David Koresh and the Branch Davidians can be found in the history and teachings of the messianic Seventh-Day Adventists, another of the millenarian movements to arise during the Age of Reform. The Adventists were a group of Protestant Christian churches that evolved from the teachings of William Miller (1782–1849). The largest body to arise from this movement is the Seventh-Day Adventist Church, which today includes more than 3,000 congregations and nearly eight million members worldwide, some 750,000 members in the United States.[12] The Adventists always placed emphasis on the anticipated Second Coming of Christ and on the Last Judgment, at which time Christ would separate the saints from the wicked and inaugurate the millennial kingdom.

Rooted in Hebrew and Christian prophecy and millennial expectations recorded in the Bible, Adventism has always contained a strong Jewish component. Adventism has been an important part of Jewish expectations about the future. Orthodox Jews have looked for the coming of the Messiah, have harbored messianic hopes, and have longed for their return to Israel and the restoration of the Temple in Jerusalem. Christians have maintained that Jesus is the Messiah, and in the early church they anticipated that he would return again soon after his death. They interpreted these expectations in terms of the prophecies found in the Book of Daniel and in Revelation. Since the Jews do not believe that Jesus was the Messiah, they continue to await His first advent or, in the more reformed sects, a messianic age. The Jews, however, have no special relationship with the Seventh-Day Aventists.

Adventism emerged in Europe during and after the Reformation, which saw the ultimate rejection of the Catholic Church and the establishment of the Protestant churches. It first arose among the radical movement known as the Reformers (c. 1534), but its real impact would not be felt in the United States until almost 200 years later, during the late eighteenth and early nineteenth centuries, when excitement arose among Christians of many denominations that a messianic age was at hand. Historically, this was a time of rapid and far-reaching social changes brought about by the Enlightenment and the emerging Industrial Revolution. Using the current period and events as their inspiration, millennialists combed their Bibles for clues to events that had happened and were to come, thereby fulfilling the prophecies made in Revelation. The millennium, they believed, was near at hand.

Many believed that the American and French revolutions and the great social, political, and economic changes of the Industrial Revolution were signs that the end was near. The Enlightenment reflected the beginning of a new age of justice in which the whole world would be gradually converted to Adventist Christianity. These Christians believed that Christ will return only after 1,000 years. This expectancy was represented in the communitarian experiments of the Shakers, who believed that in Ann Lee

(1736–1784), the founder of the Shakers, was revealed the female incarnation of Jesus, who would help establish the earthly paradise with her followers. Postmillennialism is also seen in the Mormons, whose prophet Joseph Smith (1805–1844), to whom God and Jesus Christ had revealed themselves, told followers that he would build an earthly Zion, or "promised land," in advance of Christ's Second Coming.

In this atmosphere, William Miller (1782–1849), a founder of the Adventists, began to preach. While an officer in the U.S. Army, Miller had become a skeptic. After a conversion he began to study the books of Daniel and Revelation. He concluded that Christ would return on March 24, 1844. Miller was encouraged in his views by other clergymen and soon by 100,000 followers, according to some estimates. Miller also stressed the return of Christ in a fiery conflagration. When Christ did not return on the date fixed by Miller, he set a second date on October 22, 1844. This date also came and went without the Messiah, and so did many of his followers, who found it hard to reconcile the two mistakes with their faith in Miller. Others however, returned to their Bibles and reasoned that Miller had miscalculated and so the date was yet to come, which hardened their resolve to continue on and reshape the Adventists' mission.

Another seminal leader of the Adventists was Victor Houteff, who founded the Davidian Adventists, distinct from the Branch Davidians, who came later. Born in Bulgaria in 1886, Houteff came to the United States in 1907. Settling in Los Angeles sometime after 1918, he became a Seventh-Day Adventist. Studying biblical prophecy, Houteff came to believe that he was divinely inspired to "purify" the church and to gather together the 144,000 servants of God mentioned in Revelation. According to Revelation 7:4, this select number is "sealed" by an angel from the east shortly before the final plagues of the Seven Seals are unleashed upon the world at the climax of the Apocalypse.[13]

Houteff also came to see the parent church as flaccid and lazy. It had fallen to "worldly" pursuits and pleasures, he preached. An enthusiastic evangelist for his beliefs and in his criticism of the Adventists, of which he was a member, he was forced out by church leaders in 1934. After his ejection from the parent church, Houteff took the name Davidian Seventh-Day Adventists. The name "Davidian" referred to the new sect's teachings that the ancient messianic Davidic kingdom in Palestine was about to be restored. Houteff saw his main goal, at that point, to gather up the "remnant" true church in preparation for the return of the Messiah.

Houteff and his group purchased a remote 189-acre parcel of land outside Waco that they named Mount Carmel and moved to Texas in May 1935. Starting with just 12 followers, by the end of the year the group numbered 27. Within the year they expected Christ to return, at which time they would gather the 144,000 and move to Palestine. When Christ failed to appear at the appointed time, the exodus to Palestine never occurred. The new church, however, carried on evangelical work into the 1940s with tremendous success. Their church membership, properties, publishing company, and missions expanded throughout the United States and Canada, and they sent representatives to England, India, the West Indies, and Australia. Victor Houteff died in 1955 at the age of 69. After a period of infighting, Houteff's wife, Florence, gained control of the church. She consolidated the church's holdings, selling off properties, paying off debts, and selling the Mount Carmel property for $700,000, and purchased new property nearby, consisting of 941 acres. This was the property that David Koresh and the Branch Davidians would later occupy.[14]

Sometime around early 1959, Florence Houteff became convinced that the world would end during Passover season. The call went out to Davidians across the country and the world to gather at Mount Carmel in anticipation of the end of the world and before the migration to Palestine to witness the Second Coming of Christ and the birth of the millennium paradise. Around 900 Davidians gathered at Mount Carmel with Mrs. Houteff, many having quit their jobs and sold their homes and personal belongings to be with the chosen remnant. Like Adventists and messianic leaders of the past, David Koresh would herald this same call 30 years later. When the day came and passed, expectations fell, people left, and the sect found itself in disarray. Mrs. Houteff moved to California to spend her declining years in solitude. Opposing factions alternately took control of the church's operational functions, but membership dwindled, as did church property, as acreage and buildings were sold off to pay outstanding debts. By the mid-1960s only 77 acres remained of the Adventist sect called the Davidian Seventh-Day Adventists.[15]

On August 17, 1959, the year when Florence Houteff and the Davidian Adventists eagerly awaited the end times, Vernon Howell, later called David Koresh, was born. By the 1970s the Davidian sect at Mount Carmel began to settle down to some semblance of order. In 1977 a member by the name of Lois Roden had a revelation concerning the Holy Spirit as a feminine figure. She began to emphasize the feminine nature of God and the Messiah, or "New Adam," and she began to talk about the female aspects of divinity. Roden was a prolific writer and speaker and became a living prophet and leader within the Mount Carmel church.[16]

In 1981, Vernon Howell joined the sect. Two years before, he had been baptized by the mainstream Adventist Church, and was staunchly loyal to that church. But he came to Mount Carmel to hear the resident prophet, Lois Roden. Howell embraced Roden's teaching; she admired his faith and command of Scripture. Roden's son, George, bristled at his mother's close friendship with Vernon Howell, and accused the two of being lovers. George Roden feared that Howell would supplant him as a leader. Lois Roden was 67 years old then, but was probably, indeed, having sex with Vernon Howell. Some followers even believe that Howell and Roden were married in a secret ceremony.

By 1983, Lois Roden openly favored Howell over her son, and Howell himself began to speak of having revelations, particularly one concerning the "seventh angel's message": "But in the days of the voice of the seventh angel, when he shall begin to sound, the mystery of God should be finished, as he hath declared to his servants, the prophets" (Rev. 10:7). In 1984 Howell married a 14-year-old daughter of another sect member. This so upset Lois Roden that some claim she suffered a near breakdown.

She died in 1986.[18] The animosity George Roden held for Howell grew keener. He began wearing a .357 Magnum to Bible meetings and allegedly threatened Howell and those who supported him. The group began to fracture even more. In January 1985, Howell and his wife, Rachel, now pregnant with their first son, Cyrus, went to Israel and the "promised land," the trip in which Vernon Howell had the revelation that he was the messiah figure "Cyrus" of Davidic lore and the "slain Lamb" who must reveal and release the horrors of the seven seals.[19]

While Howell was in Israel, George Roden conspired to expel all of Howell's followers and take control of the church, which he renamed Rodenville. Howell's followers resettled on a scrap of land in the aptly named town of Palestine, Texas. When Howell returned, he took up residence with the group in Palestine and rebuilt his church, which experienced tremendous growth at the time. It was also at this time that Howell announced that he would require more than one wife, since this was a part of his revelations as he interpreted them. By 1987, Howell had taken at least six wives, five whom were 17 years of age or younger.[20]

The story took a grotesque turn in November 1987. Anna Hughes, a former Davidian, had died back in 1967. George Roden now dug up her body, placed it in the Mount Carmel chapel, and dared Howell to restore it to life. Howell called the sheriff to report a corpse violation, and to prove it, he and seven followers, toting guns and wearing fatigues, slipped onto the ranch to photograph the corpse. Roden and his followers fired on Howell and his men, who returned fire. Howell faced a charge of attempted murder but his jury split, and the judge called a mistrial. In a separate case six months later, George Roden was charged with murder. He was ruled insane and sent to a state hospital. Howell, meanwhile, was able to pay off the taxes and debts of the Mount Carmel Ranch that Roden had so badly managed. Under the secure leadership of Vernon Howell, the Branch Davidians joyfully reclaimed Mount Carmel. In August 1990, at 31 years of age, Vernon Howell changed his name to David Koresh, the messiah of the Branch Davidians.[21]

*Thou art worthy to take the book, and to open the seals thereof: for thou wast slain, and hast redeemed us to God by thy blood out of every kindred, and tongue, and people, and nation.* (REV. 5:9, KJV)

The personality of David Koresh reflected many of the qualities psychologists and sociologists associate with religious leaders. He was intelligent and well studied in his religious beliefs, and he demonstrated a charismatic personality.[22] Koresh also tried to build a religious commune, as have many sects of the past, based in shared values, work, and rewards. While many were critical of the way members were "relieved of their bank accounts," the socialist nature of communitarian groups, very often apocalyptic in nature, is common throughout the history of American millennialism and other social reform movements. Unfortunately, this taking of followers' possessions and bank accounts is commonly done by so-called religious leaders.

The "Branches," as the Davidians now called called themselves, were a sect in the mold of the early Adventist Church. In fact, this is what Koresh saw as his main goal—to bring the modern Adventist Church back to its apocalyptic and sectarian roots. Like so many sects of the past, Koresh thought that the modern church was in league with the "churches of Babylon"—the mainstream Christian churches that were now formal religious "institutions"—rather than the true church of the select, who would ultimately serve at the right hand of God. Koresh came to see himself as the messiah of Revelation, symbolized as the slain Lamb, the only one who is worthy to open the seven seals and interpret its contents to his followers and the world. Koresh understood the sealed book to be the entire Bible, particularly the prophetic writings. Accordingly, to open the book is not only to explain it, but also to orchestrate the events it sets forth, leading to the climax of history, the end of the world.

During the 51-day standoff between the Branch Davidians and federal law enforcers, Koresh claimed he was waiting for a sign from God before he would give up. Eventually, he claimed that he received that sign from a radio broadcast of Paul Harvey, in which the radio personality spoke of a "guitar-shaped nebula" in the evening sky, which Koresh and the Davidians took to be a "sign" from God pointing to Koresh, who played guitar. Next to the Bible, playing the electric guitar in his rock band was Koresh's other consuming interest. Koresh believed the sign meant that he was now to interpret the seven seals to the world, after which he would give himself up to his persecutors.[23]

Thus for Koresh, this did not mean that the end was immediately going to occur. Koresh based his interpretations of the seven seals on the events occurring around him. To the extent that these events were flexible or controllable by the government negotiators, the end of the siege did not necessarily mean the end of the lives of so many Davidians. Had the FBI appreciated Koresh's interpretation of the Bible and the events that were going on around him, they would have been better able to predict and maybe peacefully control events. Evidence suggests that, in fact, Koresh was searching for a way out that would result in no more bloodshed. He continually said he needed to wait for a sign from God, something that would supernaturally reveal to him what course to take.[24]

There is little doubt that Koresh had a Machiavellian streak. He was manipulative with members of his sect and with outsiders. His "secret marriage" with the 67-year-old prophetess Lois Roden has the ring of seduction and manipulation. He allegedly had sex with and married girls who were minors. During the siege he backed out of deadlines he himself had set, and he continually annoyed his antagonists with his long biblical expositions. Still, he was always friendly and willing to talk, especially about religion; he was knowledgeable and highly skilled in the interpretation, or "exegesis," of the Bible. Discussing the Bible was one of the things that Koresh cherished most, because for him Scripture was alive, not the dead literature and history of ancient times. According to James Tabor and Eugene Gallagher, authors of *Why Waco?*, this theological opening to Koresh was always there for federal authorities, not just as a reason to talk, but as a method to find a way out. Even Koresh did not claim absolute authority in all biblical interpretation. On occasion, members of his Bible study classes would challenge his interpretations and he would argue and sometimes concede, since he believed that Scripture provides inspiration and reveals its meaning to many.[25]

After the initial shootout at Mount Carmel, a 51-day siege ensued in which the ATF tried to negotiate a peaceful settlement with Koresh and his church. The ATF tried to take as much time as possible to reach a settlement. Seven adults and ten children left of their own accord, signaling progress in the impasse. The rest remained with their leader. Koresh kept saying that he needed more time to wait for a sign before coming out. He spoke on Dallas radio stations KRLD and KGBS and tried to impress upon the talk radio hosts and their listeners the biblical significance of the events.

When the FBI took over control of the operation from the ATF, they instituted a different approach. They would be less indulgent with Koresh and more demanding for a solution to the standoff. They severed water and electricity lines from the compound and became more hard-nosed in their discussions with Koresh. He had refused to come out at other times, saying simply that he had to wait. The FBI refused to listen to Koresh's "Bible babble," as they called it. They brought in loud speakers and began blaring loud music at the building, including songs by Nancy Sinatra, Tibetan chants, heavy metal music, and even recordings of rabbits being slaughtered. They flashed high-wattage beams at the compound in an attempt to so irritate the inhabitants that they would eventually give up. The attitude toward Koresh by the FBI was one of ridicule. The FBI chief in charge of the operation in Waco called Koresh a "con man" and a petty, self-deluded psychopath. In short, they refused to take Koresh seriously in his delusion of messianic grandeur and decided to put an end to the standoff.

Referring to his young wives, they accused him of molesting of children. The Davidians were stockpiling weapons and had fired on and killed federal agents. The federal authorities felt that they had negotiated in earnest, patiently waiting it out for more than a month. Polls reported that most Americans saw Koresh as the villain, just as the FBI saw him. This was also the picture that FBI authorities in Washington painted for the new attorney general, Janet Reno. Their answers to her cautions and her desire to find a nonviolent solution were answered with claims that all attempts had failed, that Koresh was continuing to abuse children, and that Koresh had gone back on his words so many times that the only hope for an end to the stalemate was to inject CS teargas into the building, which would force them out. It was relatively safe, they said, and the strategy would lead to a nonviolent conclusion.

The announcement blared over the loud speakers just before daybreak on April 19: "This is not an assault! Do not fire! Come out now and you will not be harmed," the FBI agent warned those inside the compound, who were by now awakened or had been reading their Bibles in the early morning hours. The FBI was in full force with all 170 agents on hand in Waco. M-60 tanks reconfigured into combat engineering vehicles (CEVs) were brought in. Attached to the front of two of the CEVs were large booms. The plan was to punch holes into the building on the far left and right hand sides, and then pump the CS gas into the upper and lower levels of the compound, which would drive members out into the front yard.

As the operation commenced, the wind at Mount Carmel began to gust as it always did around Waco, sending clouds of dirt and dust into the air around the compound. The FBI waited for the gusts to settle since they felt the gas might dissipate too rapidly before it could be effective. By 5:55 am the FBI called into the building, both by telephone and loud speaker, and basically told the Davidians the plan, but emphasized it was not an attack, just an end to the standoff. Church members donned their gas masks, children included, who had wet towels stuffed around them to make them fit.

The FBI continued the gassing strategy into the late morning, willing to wait 48 hours for all Davidians to come out. The final round of gas was injected into the building at 11:50 am. By 12:05, smoke was seen fanning out of the right front corner of the compound. At that time an FBI helicopter overhead reported as many as four separate fires burning around the building. The fires spread quickly, fanned by the gusting winds, and in short order much of the building was in flames. Several Davidians began to leave the building, some being grabbed by federal agents and dragged away from the burning building. For the rest, however, it was too late. A large explosion, presumably of a weapons or ammunition cache, sent up a huge ball of flame. The building burned to the ground in the next few hours, with no hope for any other survivors. Of the 123 Branch Davidians present on the Davidian Mount Carmel Ranch that first morning of the siege, including 43 children, 74 adults and 21 children under the age of 14 died in the Branch Davidian apocalypse on Monday, April 19. Ten children and seven adults had voluntarily left earlier, and there were 17 survivors of the fire.

What or who started the fire is a contentious issue. Federal authorities have claimed it was started by the Davidians in a final act of resistance through mass suicide. Surviving Davidians and their lawyers, however, contend that either the CS gas accidentally ignited the fire, or federal agents purposely set the fire to hasten the eviction of the Davidians or to destroy evidence of their own misdeeds.[26] Authorities claim that several Davidians appeared to have been shot in the head, perhaps to prevent them from leaving—a tactic carried out by Jim Jones during the mass suicide in Guyana in 1978. These contentions have been challenged, since the remains of the dead were so badly charred and disfigured that such evidence was inconclusive.

*Then the kings of the earth and the great men and the generals and the rich and the strong, and every one, slave and free, hid in caves and among rocks in the mountains, calling to the mountains and rocks, "Fall on us and hide us from the face of him who is seated on the throne, and from the wrath of the Lamb; for the great day of their wrath has come, and who can stand before it." (REV. 6:15–17, RSV)*

In that mix of right-wing politics and fundamentalist lore, there was bound to arise among the survivalists a savior, or at least someone who claimed to be. Among Christian fundamentalist churches the expectation for Christ's Second Coming is still an expectation. However, for others steeped in right-wing Christianity and the survivalist right, a prophet had come, and he was David

Koresh. To them, Koresh was crucified for his beliefs, and he has become a martyr for the cause of government-fearing militias, Patriots, and white supremacists.

Koresh and his church's view of a larger world rested on classical pillars of the millennial myth, which provided not only a frame of reference for current events but also a guide for members' behavior. For example, the FBI, ATF, and the aggregate of American government were seen by Koresh and the Branch Davidians as symbols of Babylon. This is much the same view, though in a more secular fashion, of many on the survivalist right. Even while many on the right saw Koresh as deluded, he still was the head of a church in America whose rights were violated. Yet because his church was different from others—they were Christian survivalists who stock-piled food and weapons, presumably in anticipation of Armaged-don—they lost their church and their lives because of government intrusion on their rights. Most important, Koresh became a full-fledged martyr for antigovernment individuals and groups throughout the country.

How could federal authorities so badly misjudge and mis-handle the Davidian's intentions? To suggest, as federal authori-ties have, that they did not believe the Davidians would commit suicide is foolish. There was enough reason for federal authorities to consider suicide from the Jonestown mass suicide of 1978, which the media constantly compared to Waco. As the slain Lamb who unlocks the secrets of the seven seals, Koresh was convinced of the certainty of his death at some future time during a bloody confrontation with the forces of Babylon. Martyrdom is a compel-ling message to the truth of a religion. In any event, Koresh believed there was apocalyptic significance to the situation at Mount Carmel and he acted on those beliefs. Unfortunately, federal authorities failed to understand the depth and complexity of the Branch Davidians' beliefs, as well as the personality of David Koresh, who was both deluded messiah and manipulative con man.

Some members on the right reflected on the ways the Branch Davidian apocalypse resembled the Jewish defenders at Masada in A.D. 71, who committed mass suicide rather than surrender to the Romans by executing women and children and then killing themselves. This has happened in other times as well and was common among the early Christian martyrs, who willingly chose death rather than capitulate to their persecutors. In the case of the Branch Davidians, whether they committed mass suicide or whether some were killed to give that impression may never be known. But the results did reflect a phenomenon of millennial history, as well as the apocalyptic fears of Americans on the militant right.

In this way David Koresh has become a martyr for the right, whose rights were violated by a vicious militarist government and its goon squad FBI and ATF. The survivalist right has consciously used the images of American religious freedom, Koresh as a legitimate minister and the violent confrontation at Waco as a rallying cry—"Remember Waco." In the aftermath of the tragedy, the federal government, the ATF, and the FBI took a lot of heat. ATF director Steven Higgins and five other top-ranking officials resigned from the agency. Many Americans not connected to the militant right or to Christian fundamentalism began to take a second look at the actions of their government and wondered if there wasn't something to the far right's paranoia.

On April 19, 1995, exactly two years from the day when the Branch Davidian church at Mount Carmel went up in flames, the federal building in Oklahoma City was bombed. A note recovered at the scene pointed to the Waco tragedy and the conspiracy of the federal government to destroy the Davidians as the reason for the bombing of the office building in downtown Oklahoma City that morning—an explosion that killed 169 people.

Although there are many examples of millennial Christian symbolism in the subculture of survivalism, the notion of a messianic savior who holds salvation for the true believer does not consume many on the survivalist right. In its place, however, is a more secular version of salvation—the notion of "self-salvation" or survivalism. David Koresh may not have been the Messiah as prophesied in the Bible, but he has become the icon of a more secular apocalypse, in which the federal government stands for an American Babylon. In survivalist ideology, salvation comes to the

individual through personal defense and the practice of survivalism. The otherworldly savior has been transformed into a this-
worldly survivor.

# Chapter 8

# Armageddon

## "Kill Them All, Let God Sort Them Out"

*Then war broke out in Heaven. Michael and his angels battled with the dragon. The dragon and his angels fought back, but they did not prevail and they were expelled from Heaven. So the huge dragon, the serpent of ancient times, who is called the devil and Satan, the deceiver of all the whole world, was hurled down upon the earth, and his angels were hurled down upon him.*

REV. 12:7–9, RSV

*And he gathered them together into a place called in the Hebrew tongue Armageddon.*

REV. 16:16, KJV

In Revelation 16:16, Armageddon is the name of the place where the kings of the earth are to be gathered together by the dragon, the beast, and the false prophet (Antichrist) to make war upon God at the end of world history. A Greek translation of the Hebrew Har Megiddon, or "Mountain of Megiddo," refers to a famous battlefield in the Plain of Jezreel in Palestine, where many battles of the past were fought. Megiddo is a city in what is now northeastern Israel, southwest of Nazareth. In Revelation, the city of Megiddo was probably used as a symbol for the Battle of Armageddon because of its strategic importance in the history of Palestine and Israel. By controlling a pass that cut through the Mt. Carmel ridge from the coastal plain of Sharon into Esdraelon, Megiddo commanded the road leading from Egypt and the coastal plain of Palestine to Galilee, Syria, and Mesopotamia.

While the most generally accepted location of Armageddon is in Israel, another explanation finds in the word a survival of the name of the place in which the gods of ancient Babylon defeated the dragon Tiamat. Like Babylon, the physical site of Armageddon is less important than the metaphor for Armageddon as the "spiritual battlefield" and the place of the final showdown between the armies of the Messiah and those of Satan—the forces of light and the forces of darkness. More generally, Armageddon refers to the conflict itself, both the military and ideological battles that mark the end times.

In survivalism, Armageddon is reflected in military conflict, terrorism, and war between the forces of good and evil. It is a moral war and a cosmic war. In *Soldier of Fortune* magazine the Battle of Armageddon has been commonly expressed in the symbolism of crusades and holy wars. *Soldier of Fortune* magazine is a major site in the survivalist subculture where Armageddon, a key element in Revelation, has its fractured expressions.

For more than 20 years *Soldier of Fortune* magazine has provided reports and analyses of military and paramilitary conflicts from around the world, including the United States. While vehemently antiliberal and ultraconservative in its editorials, especially concerning issues of American military policy, gun laws, and self-reliance, *SOF* has often been critical of the white supremacist, anti-Semitic, and conspiracy theorist philosophies of the far right. At the same time, its focus on survivalism and international military conflict has done much to endear *SOF* to these groups and individuals. From the start *SOF* was "pro-American" and "anticommunist." Its analyses of the political and military conflicts around the world were framed by its patriotism and American cultural values. It was also framed by the American millennial myth, which saw America as the world's primary defender of freedom and democracy in the world.

International military conflict was easily defined by *SOF* as a simple philosophical dualism that marked the forces of good from the forces of evil—the secular equivalents of the "forces of light" and the "forces of darkness," the opposing armies at the cosmic Battle of Armageddon. In the pages of *SOF* the United States and its Western allies, with their values of democracy, individualism, and free market capitalism, were the forces of good in the world. Communists, dictators, terrorists, and tyrants represented the evil forces in the world, and *SOF* could easily tell the difference. *SOF*'s version of the American millennial myth, complete with apocalyptic symbols, images, and language, was most obvious during the magazine's Cold War years (1975–1989), when the Soviet Union was the evil empire and America was the world's only hope for salvation from the communist monolith.

A *Soldier of Fortune* subscription advertisement from September 1985 commands the reader to "Join the Crusade . . . Subscribe to *SOF*. . . . *SOF* survives—and gets better—because our subscribers give us the support to continue our . . . crusade against worldwide communism and our struggle to alert Americans for a strong national defense." The advertisement goes on to lay out what *SOF* stands for and what *SOF* subscribers "know":

> *SOF* subscribers know they are strong planks in our platform supporting the cause of freedom worldwide. *SOF* subscribers know their subscriptions are votes of confidence in all the things we stand for. An *SOF* subscriber is anti-communist, pro-military and pro-veteran. . . . In short, an *SOF* subscriber stands four-square behind traditional American values and a point of view that proclaims—loud and clear—that America is the world's primary defender of peace and freedom . . . and he's proud of it.[1]

For *Soldier of Fortune* the forces of evil in the world can be lumped under the umbrella heading "tyranny." The *SOF* motto is "Death to Tyrants." "International terrorists," "cartel drug lords," "tinhorn dictators," and the "communist monolith" are the tyrannical representatives of evil that America and her allies must resist and destroy in the coming battles. It was, of course, the Soviet evil empire that (until recently) has been the leading force of tyranny that irritated the world, according to *Soldier of Fortune*. The apocalyptic rhetoric in *SOF* was especially sharp throughout the 1980s, when Ronald Reagan sat in the White House and American covert military actions, such as those exposed in the Iran-Contra affair, became familiar occurrences in the American battle against world communism.

An article from the mid-1980s entitled "The Evil Empire Eyes the Big Enchilada" was a common example of the tyrannical threat posed by the Soviet Union. The article reports on the destabilizing political and economic situation in Mexico and its potential effects on the 2,000-mile border between the United States and Mexico. The reporter, Colonel Rex Applegate, warns that:

> As long as the Soviets and Cubans continue to influence and instigate events in Mexico, civil war or a gradual political and economic dissolution is a very real possibility. As demonstrated in Cuba, Nicaragua, and other areas within our hemisphere, this creates a fertile ground for planting permanent communist influence . . . the internal situation south of our borders. . . could lead to a communist take-over in Mexico. [2]

For most of *SOF*'s history the "Battle of Armageddon" was generally defined in terms of an American–Soviet showdown. This final battle is depicted in the film *Red Dawn* (1984), reviewed in *SOF* under the title "Apocalypse in America."[3] Written and produced by John Milius (author of *Apocalypse Now* ), *Red Dawn* is about the takeover of America by the Soviet Union and the resistance posed by a ragtag group of American guerrillas who attempt to overcome impossible odds and turn back the tide of history. The magazine's reviewer gave the film an enthusiastic "thumbs up." The same theme is expressed in an advertisement for the Conservative Book Club, in a free offer available to all new subscribers, "the one book every American should read, *"What to Do When the Russians Come: A Survivors Guide.*[4] The Soviet communist threat and American resolve is further expressed in editorials and letters to the editor and in cartoons, poster art, and T-shirts. A familiar T-shirt shows an MX missile exploding over downtown Moscow while a mushroom cloud forms. The caption reads, "And Now It's Miller Time." Another reads simply, "Russia Sucks."[5]

Conservative columnist William F. Buckley, Jr., has been a regular contributor to *Soldier of Fortune* over the years. In an article about American military involvement in Central America during the 1980s, Buckley drew the analogy between America, communism, and the millennial myth. Under the title "Death Squads and U.S. Policy," Buckley writes, "We are in El Salvador because its government, with all its impurities, is geopolitically allied with us in the great cosmic effort, however disheveled, to give freedom and democracy and decency a chance against the communist monolith."[6] Such metaphors as "freedom fighter," "spiritual allies," "communist monolith," and "great cosmic effort" frequently appear in discussions of international conflict and political ideology in *SOF*. They demonstrate the ways in which apocalyptic symbolism regarding the Battle of Armageddon is redefined through the millennial script of *Soldier of Fortune*.

Into the 1990s the communist monolith and the "domino effect" has continued to be a plank in *SOF* ideology. "And these battles will continue," warns *SOF*, until the world is made safe for democracy. In light of the revolutionary changes that continue to sweep through Eastern Europe, *SOF* has had to look elsewhere for the sources of evil in the world. Fortunately, there is no shortage of tyrants in the world, and *SOF* maintains a long and ever-changing list of them. SOF also defines the roles played by other militant groups, including vigilantes, youth gangs, and leftist radicals, as they battle it out on the world stage that *SOF* and other mass media provide.

Not all who claim to be soldiers of fortune are of that special breed. In *SOF* there is a major distinction made between the mercenary and the soldier of fortune. The notion of the freelance professional soldier serving in the army of a foreign country merely for pay defines the mercenary. Soldiers of fortune, on the other hand, fight the "good fight." This myth is as true for soldiers of fortune as it is for the classic Western gunslinger, who (like the hired gunmen in the 1960 film *The Magnificent Seven*) fights primarily for ideological reasons, with monetary gain almost always secondary. Soldiers of the French Foreign Legion, for example, are Christian soldiers of fortune and not mercenaries. In a review of a book entitled *Mouthful of Rocks: Modern Adventures in the French Foreign Legion*, the reviewer notes that the experience of serving in the Legion requires the legionnaire to "accept the faith . . . because the Legion is held together by faith . . . [and] through its officers, noncoms, and large doses of collective ritual, the faith is maintained."[7]

Although mercenaries are often written about in *Soldier of Fortune*, and their military and survival skills displayed and admired, they are often criticized for their ideological neutrality and lack of moral character. In an article entitled "No Honor among Mercs," reporter Peter Douglas discusses the presence of British mercenaries in the guerrilla conflict in Suriname. Among mercenaries, says Douglas, there is usually a "lack of normal unit discipline and moral code," and mercenaries tend to be "backstabbing," "deceitful," and "treacherous."[8] Mercenaries are, however, important participants in the great cosmic battles that mark today's global conflicts.

Fighting the Battle of Armageddon is also, for the most part, gender specific. "Be a Man among Men" is the slogan of a popular *SOF* T-shirt. In *SOF*, women generally appear as victims of war (along with children, the elderly, and other civilians), as sexual symbols in advertisements (mostly for guns), and as soldiers, spys, or other "dupes" of tyranny. Thus when women soldiers do appear, they are usually fighting on the wrong side—with Sandinista, Cuban, Palestinian, or other terrorist and communist-inspired organizations. While women are encouraged to arm and be able to defend themselves and their families, the magazine discourages them from being frontline soldiers of fortune.

A soldier of fortune is also a "Christian soldier": one who has enlisted in the worldwide fight against the evil of tyranny. "Onward Christian Soldiers" is an article on the Christian Lebanese Forces fighting a long-range battle against "Muslim fanatics in the inferno called Beirut."[9] According to *SOF*, it is Muslim countries like Syria and Iran and Arab dictators like Saddam Hussein and Muammar Gadhafi who represent the primary tyrannical threats to the world in the aftermath of Soviet communism. The front of an *SOF* T-shirt reads, "Visit Lebanon: Help a Syrian meet Allah." On the back it says, "Hey, we just stepped in some Shiite." Another shows a group of dead Arabs lying in a pool of blood surrounded by barrels of oil. A soldier carrying a machine gun looks over the

FIGURE 8.1. "Know Your Enemy Targets," *SOF* Exposition, Las Vegas, 1990.

dead men and says, "What price now Opec!" For target practice you can buy a life-size "commie" or "terrorist" target, which looks strikingly like an Arab (Figure 8.1). However, *Soldier of Fortune* does not paint all Islamic peoples as demons. If they are fighting the same tyrannical foes as the United States, then they are soldiers of fortune.

While America represents the supreme force of good in the world, it has allies in its international fight against tyranny. These allies include all those peoples who comprise "the resistance" and who fight tyranny in the name of freedom and liberty. SOF often refers to "freedom fighters" such as the Nicaraguan Contras, the Afghan Mujahideen, and the Angolan National Liberation Front (FNLA) as America's "spiritual allies." Each issue of SOF commonly carries a battle report on the conflict between a tyrannical force and a freedom-fighting force somewhere in the world. "Inside Nicaragua with Contras and Commies" and "Thais Crush Viet Assault" were *SOF* feature articles detailing the fight against tyranny from the 1980s. In these examples, Thai allies and Contra soldiers of fortune battle the "terrorists" and "communist-inspired" governments of Nicaragua and Vietnam. In the 1990s it's "The Guerrilla

Myth" of the Maoist Shining Path and "Flashpoint Liberia" where the clear lines have been drawn between good and evil in *SOF*.[10]

In an article written by David Mills entitled "Abandoned Angola: FNLA's Uncertain Future," the term freedom fighter is defined in terms of the group's anticommunist and pro-American spirit, its native resistance to foreign invasion, and its religious motivation.[11] Given that their enemy is the Marxist government (the Popular Movement for the Liberation of Angola), the battle lines are clearly drawn. Another article, entitled "Harassing the Bear," written by David Isby during the Russian occupation of Afghanistan, is about the Afghan freedom-fighting Mujahideen. Isby reports that Robert K. Brown and *Soldier of Fortune* are well known among the Mujahideen for their support of the Afghan resistance. Responding to a Mujahideen commander's question as to Brown's whereabouts, Isby says he "is in El Salvador, helping to fight communists there." The commander (wearing a *SOF* T-shirt) asks, "Tell me, the people in El Salvador, not many of them are Moslems are they?" "No, they are mainly Catholics," answers Isby. "Well," says the commander, "if they fight the communists, they are still also Mujahideen."[12]

The notion of religious wars and anticommunist freedom fighters as spiritual allies of the United States is also a theme in an article about the Burmese Shan guerrillas entitled "Burma's Golden Triangle." The author, Sterling Seagrave, calls the opium wars of Burma's Golden Triangle an "old-fashioned battle between good and evil."[13] The forces of good are the Shan, an ancient, religious people from whom the people of Indonesia are descended. The forces of evil are the repressive communist government and their Chinese drug-lord allies. Seagrave suggests that because the free-dom-fighting Shan, Karen, and Kachin peoples are often mistaken for ethnic Chinese opium smugglers, "just as Contras were often mistaken for murderous Sandinista soldiers," they have not right-fully garnered the support of the American government. Seagrave quotes the dismay of one Shan commander: "We have always considered America our spiritual ally. We have tried to remain friends. But with friends like America, who needs enemies?"[14]

Their status as freedom fighters, or as "the resistance," labels soldiers of fortune as a special breed of warrior. Unlike Christian fundamentalism, where the select, or "elect," must be "born again" Christians, in *SOF* religious affiliation is less important than religiosity, or "faith" in a supreme power, with a healthy measure of anticommunist and pro-American sentiment. In *Soldier of Fortune* the "select" cut across cultural and denominational boundaries to become "spiritual allies" in the "great cosmic effort."

*And I saw Heaven opened, and behold a white horse; and he that sat upon him was called Faithful and True, and in riotousness he doth judge and make war. . . . And the armies which were in heaven, followed him upon white horses.* (REV. 19:11, 14, KJV)

During the closing months of the 1980s, millennial fever peaked in the United States and in other parts of the world. For many Americans the breaching of the Berlin wall signaled the end of the Cold War and the collapse of authoritarian communism. For the truly optimistic it heralded the birth of a new age of peace, freedom, and international cooperation. *SOF* also presented these momentous changes in a positive light: as successes of the forces of good in the great cosmic effort. For *SOF*, however, these events did not mean the end of the war or the start of a utopian world order. Thus, in *Soldier of Fortune*, the great cosmic effort is far from over.

Nothing has happened in the closing decade of the twentieth century to sheathe the swords of *Soldier of Fortune* magazine. That much was proved in the bloody turmoil that erupted in places like Bosnia and Chechnya, and in the domestic clashes between antigovernment groups and government law enforcement agencies in the United States. *SOF* has taken a hard line on "government intrusion" into the lives of ordinary citizens, as exemplified at Ruby Ridge and Waco. The magazine has been highly critical of the ATF and the FBI, and was out front in calling for investigations of both Ruby Ridge and Waco.[15] Its unrelenting assault on the government for enacting increasingly stiffer gun legislation has put *SOF* in the camp of the many groups fearful of the government's abuse of its powers.

However, *SOF* has also been critical of racist groups like the Aryan Nations and anti-Semitic newspapers such as *Spotlight*.[16] *SOF* has also taken on the conspiracy crowd, who fear the new world order and its one world government. Both Mark Koernke and Linda Thompson are regularly cut down for their preposterous theories and comments about the imminent takeover of the United States by agents loyal to the new world government.

Challenging the theory that black helicopters are a strike force for the new world order, *SOF* contributing reporter Craig B. Hulet challenges the "crazy, convoluted world of conspiracists" where everything is suspect, "especially those things not understood."[17] In his article "Patriots or Paranoids?" Hulet shows that there *are* black helicopters operating in the United States, but any check with the FBI, the DEA, and the Forest Service will reveal that these organizations routinely use them. "The Mark Koernkes and Linda Thompsons who espouse conspiracist doctrine are dangerous" says Hulet, "because, like much of the militia leadership, theirs is the 'big lie' exactly as Hitler and Goebbels knew it."[18] Hulet goes on to point out that Timothy McVeigh had seen and been impressed by Linda Thompson's 1993 videotape, *Waco: The Big Lie*, in which she spins a yarn of government conspiracy and cover-up in the Waco tragedy. Hulet reports that McVeigh was allegedly a bodyguard for Mark Koernke during a Florida militia gathering. "McVeigh was completely taken in by these two clowns," writes Hulet, ". . . and it is because of those of this ilk, not in spite of them, that this country is at risk."[19]

"It's only appropriate" begins Robert K. Brown, in the twentieth anniversary issue of *Soldier of Fortune*, that "I find myself on the Bosnian border preparing to take an *SOF* team into Sarajevo under the murderous guns of the barbaric Serbs." [20] As he had so often done in the past in the name of "participatory journalism," Brown, editor of *SOF* magazine, was in the midst of a murderous international conflict. Fighting the good fight with the soldiers and citizens of Sarajevo, the mission of Brown and his *SOF* team was "to hump Scott Air-Pacs—breathing gear for firemen—through Serb lines, over Mount Igman, and deliver them to the Sarajevo Fire

Department." Brown continues: "Our current operation sums up much of what *SOF* is and has been about over the past two decades slashing away at tyrants both foreign and domestic and at the same time not ignoring our 'humanitarian' mission to alleviate some of the world's suffering." [21]

Brown goes on to list all those tyrants that *SOF* has "crossed swords" with, from the now defunct "evil empire," to the "politically correct frauds" to the "barbaric Serbs" in the former Yugoslavia. "For the past 20 years we've tromped with the good guys and bad guys," writes Brown, "in our quest to get the story first-hand. . . . We've been fired on and fired back. . . and paid a price" in the deaths to *SOF* comrades serving "the cause of freedom." [22] In a nod to "our loyal readers," Brown concludes with an apocalyptic flourish and a reference to the Battle of Armageddon: "Without your continued support we would not have been able to forge the swords necessary to gut the dragons we've taken on. Stand by us for the next 20 years and we'll continue to march—sword in hand." [23]

As transfigured in *Soldier of Fortune* magazine, Armageddon is represented by the great cosmic battles against the forces of tyranny that threaten America, its spiritual allies, and "our" way of life. For *SOF*, the future hopefully will be a world where peace and democracy and the "American way" thrive, preserved and protected from tyranny by the world's crusaders of light and right—the soldiers of fortune. But *Soldier of Fortune* rarely expresses this millennial world outside of its clarion call for vigilance toward the enemy and its ethic of survival preparation. SOF focuses on those areas of the myth that express a near future of death, war, and survival (Apocalypse, Armageddon, and salvation, respectively). More likely, the *SOF* "millennium" will be a world of domestic and international conflict, where Americans are threatened by foreign and domestic tyrants—"the never-ending battle against tyranny and terrorism." [24]

*War—Mankind's Oldest Contact Sport* (BUMPER STICKER, *SOLDIER OF FORTUNE* CONVENTION, LAS VEGAS, 1995)

The survivalist emphasis on warfare, "cosmic battles" with demonic armies, and the Battle of Armageddon has found a wider acceptance in the United States through its expression and reproduction in the popular culture, including in books, films, television, and even in the toy and game industries. Throughout the 1980s, war toys, also called "action" or "fantasy" figures and toys, consistently made up at least half of the 20 bestselling toys on the market. Laser Tag and Foton and sophisticated-looking "squirt machine guns" allowed American children to indulge their fantasies of war in more realistic fashion than ever before.

The interest in war toys and games is not new. Nor is it limited to children, as evidenced by the long history of "war gaming" for adults.[25] War games are as old as civilization. According to *The Complete Book of Wargames*: "The remains of board games have been found in the ruins of ancient Ur, and there are several versions available today of a game called Senat, or Senet, which was played in the days of the boy-king, Tutankhamen. Pachisi (Parcheesi) may be as old as 'Tables,' a Roman ancestor of backgammon. No one knows how old chess is, but it is thought to have evolved over many centuries from something like a modern simulation: before the process of abstraction went so far that the game became only a pale shadow of real battle, chess pieces probably represented different sorts of troops whose movement and combat capabilities were reflected, more or less realistically, on the board. Chess variations designed to add realism were popular throughout the Middle Ages."[26]

However, the practical beginnings of modern war gaming reach back to the late eighteenth century when European aristocracy participated in elaborate battles with hundreds of miniature soldiers and artillery pieces. In the nineteenth century war gaming took a detour and became less an entertainment for the military-minded and more a training technique for the military. The Prussian Chief of Staff, General Von Muffling, saw the value of war gaming training and ordered the army to adopt popular board games and adapt them to strategic operations. He and a successor, Helmuth Von Moltke, continued to support such training. Despite many changes and advancements that made the games more involved, war gaming became a fixture in the Prussian army. After the Prussians' 1870 victory over the French, other armies adopted the Prussian's accoutrements, hierarchy, and the *Kriegspiel*, "war game."[27]

*The Complete Book of Weapons* reports: "As the war gaming practiced by the military establishments of the world became more strategic and ever more specifically oriented toward real plans and policies, it reappeared on the tactical level as a game and entertainment for civilians after a hiatus of almost a century. On the eve of World War I, H. G. Wells published *Little Wars*, which contained rules for recreating warfare on land using miniatures: carefully made and authentically painted toy soldiers. The book received wide notice and became the foundation for nearly all the miniatures rules in use today." [28]

Recent innovations in technology have seen war games evolve into newer and more realistic formats. In the 1980s the "arms proliferation" in military toys and games was heralded by industry leader Mattel "as a big part of the new interactive toy revolution."[29] *Dungeons and Dragons* and *Crusade in Europe* were early successes in the burgeoning software for computers and war gaming, and interactive toy guns like Laser Tag and Foton quickly found their way from American toy stores to college dormitories, and from there to organized competition and league play. Recent technological innovations and sophisticated marketing strategies have added greater realism to toy weapons and war gaming. These changes, along with a popular culture traditionally receptive to such pursuits, have rekindled the interest in war games for adults.

In the early 1980s, the invention of high-powered "splatball" weapons and games like the *Survival Game* also appeared on the war toys market, but marketed mainly to an adult male audience. The *Survival Game* is a form of mock warfare in which players wear camouflage clothing and carry high-impact, "simulated" weapons that fire dye-filled "splatballs." While its supporters claim the *Survival Game* is, after all, "only a game," some militia and survivalist groups use it as a training strategy and test of basic survival skills and instincts—a training tool for Armageddon.[30] Indeed, the ability to survive against all odds was the idea that sparked the creation of the game in the first place.

The *Survival Game* originated as a means of settling a dispute over whether survival was a basic human instinct, transferable from one environment to another (the belief held by Hayes Noel, game cofounder and New York stockbroker), or "a function of specifically learned behavior, applicable to particular environments" (the belief held by cofounders Charles Gaines, writer and author of *Pumping Iron,* and Robert Gurnsey, a ski shop owner). To settle the dispute a game was designed to test players' basic survival skills.[31]

The first game was played on a Saturday morning in June 1981. Among the 12 original players were a doctor, a venture capitalist, an ocean sailor, a stockbroker, a forester, a movie producer, and several writers. Players were supplied with a "paint gun" (a tree- and animal-marking pistol), protective goggles, a compass, and a map of a 100-acre wooded playing field. At 9:00 am each player was taken to a pre-arranged part of the playing field, alone and out of sight of the other 11 players. None of the players had previously been in the field, which had been divided by judges into four quadrants. At the center of each quadrant—its position indicated on the player's map—was a "flag station" with a color-coded flag hanging on a tree. At 9:30, a horn blast began the game, the point of which was for a player to make his way into each quadrant, capture the flag at each of the four stations, and escape from the playing field to one of the twelve safe zones located at either end of the field, without being shot or otherwise marked with paint by another player.

After two and a half hours the game was won by the professional forester, Ritchie White, who never removed his pistol from its holster and never shot anyone. Instead, he stealthily walked through the woods, avoiding his enemies and collecting all their flags, without once drawing gunfire on himself. There was plenty of exhilarating battle action for the other players, however, and all agreed that the game was a phenomenal success. Charles Gaines later wrote:

> It was everything we hoped it would be—challenging, exhilarating, and fascinatingly reflective both in the various ways it was played, and in the various ways in which the men who played it lived. The careful played

carefully; the shrewd played shrewdly; the aggressive played aggressively.[32]

Although the outdoorsman won it, Gaines believed that he and "the city men had successfully brought to bear on the game, on this mock survival situation in the woods, what we had learned of life and how to survive it on the streets."[33] Writers, Tim Cahill (*Outside*), Tony Atwill (*Sports Afield*), and Robert F. Jones (*Sports Illustrated*), also participated in the first games. Their stories about the *Survival Game* set off a year of publicity and interest in the game. The inventors incorporated in the fall of 1981 as the National Survival Game and established headquarters in New London, New Hampshire, near the site of the first games. The new company started a dealership network throughout the United States, and soon the *Survival Game* became the model for a new leisure industry centered on "paintball games"

The *Survival Game* has won praise in the popular culture, the paramilitary press, and among politically conservative magazines such as *The National Review*, whose reporter D. Keith Mano, in an article entitled "Skirmishing, Part I" seemed to have had a transcendental experience:

> The temptation was to lie still, in a forgetful stupor of one's own lovely, discreet silence . . . in patriotic obedience to an Orange or Yellow nation just formed, . . . Mind becomes all highlight film and no sequence. You imprint on squad-mates in a kind of ecstatic intimacy that will bypass friendship or even decent acquaintance.[34]

In the spring of 1984, the National Survival Game developed the first water-soluble gelatin pellets that would retain form under wet, dirty, or otherwise undesirable conditions. "Splatballs" were a major breakthrough for the game, and they paved the way for the production of numerous specialized weapons. By February of 1985, the company had produced the "Splatmaster"—the first paint-marking pistol designed specifically for the new game. *Survival Game* franchises and spinoffs (e.g. *Skirmish* and *Pursuit*) quickly followed, and by 1988 the National Survival Game had over 400 playing fields in the United States, with hundreds more in Canada,

Europe, and Japan, each with a start-up cost of $4,000. Franchises also have reached into Mexico and South Africa.[35]

Today most North American dealers sponsor both regular and organized league play, and approximately 100,000 Americans play the *Survival Game* each weekend. [36] Since 1986 the North American *Survival Game* Championships have been the most popular, and lucrative (in terms of prize money), of the many national tournaments and competitions. Teams from across the country compete in a variety of games of strategy, marksmanship, and survival. Paintball shoot-outs are a mainstay of *Soldier of Fortune* conventions. The game is especially popular among college students and corporations. Many college fraternities and American companies organize games for members as a means to build camaraderie and team spirit. In San Francisco, IBM, Atari, National Semiconductor, Verbatim, Inc., and the Santa Clara Republican party send out squads to do battle locally. Nationwide, corporate teams compete for General Dynamics, Wang, Digital Equipment, Data General, Metropolitan Life, Westinghouse, Shearson Lehman/American Express, NBC, and CBS. While business executives believe it is a useful way to integrate new members and build the "esprit de corps," the game is also believed to encourage workers' initiative and competitive abilities.[37]

Generally, franchise operators provide for the entire *Survival Game* experience, but splatball weapons can be purchased by individuals or hobbyists from many companies, including some makers of real weapons like Tippman Pneumatics—a former manufacturer of machine guns who in 1987 introduced the SMG-60, an automatic paint gun that fires 600 paintball rounds per minute.[38] Weapons are becoming so advanced that both game purists and critics have bemoaned the "arms race" in survival gaming.

Splat guns and survival gaming equipment are commonly advertised in gun magazines such as *American Hunter, Sports Afield, The American Survival Guide,* and *Soldier of Fortune.* There is also a literature devoted entirely to splatball weapons and survival gaming, including franchise operators' manuals, gaming strategy books, equipment catalogs, and magazines such as *War Games*, *Weekend Warrior*, and *Paint Check*. Many *Survival Game* enthusiasts collect paintball weapons and other equipment and use the guns for marksmanship and self-defense training. Not surprisingly, the American military and numerous law enforcement agencies have adopted and adapted paintball weapons for training purposes.

*The Survival Game is the closest you can get to the military . . . We are a militaristic nation, so this country must have militaristic games. A Survival Game like this undoubtedly supports a military ideology, its structure is so closely related. If this country was not militaristic, then there'd be no use for this game.* (TWENTY-YEAR-OLD BUSINESS ADMINISTRATION STUDENT)[39]

Players queue up at the equipment shed where they collect their weapons, ammunition, $CO_2$ cartridges and goggles. Game officials instruct players in the use of the Splatmaster Marking pistol—the standard *Survival Game* weapon, which fires gelatin-coated paint balls with an accuracy of up to 30 yards. $CO_2$ cartridges are loaded into the base of the gun handle and provide the high velocity and impact force of the weapon. Splatball ammunition cartridges (10 paintballs per cartridge) are loaded into the upper barrel of the gun and must be hand cocked into the trigger mechanism before firing. Goggles are required at all times and heavy clothing advised, given the impact force of the splatballs, which frequently leave "splat welts."

No hand-to-hand combat or sniping from trees is allowed in regular franchise play. However, these, and many other strategies and specialized weapons (e.g., semiautomatics, obstacle courses, "booby splats," and even helicopters), are allowed at advanced levels of play. At one outing I attended, a player arrived with a semiautomatic splatball rifle. He was not allowed to use the weapon during game play, but he did give a demonstration to the crowd of mostly first-time *Survival Game* players. "Splat grenades" (balloons filled with paint), additional ammunition, camouflage clothing, and plastic face masks are available at additional costs.

Each player is handed an arm band, which identifies the player as a soldier of an orange or yellow army. Officials with walkie-talkies stake out the battlefield and flag sites, keeping in contact with the home base. With guns in hand and goggles over eyes, the two teams are led to opposite sides of the field, where each follows a dirt path a quarter of a mile into the woods. Along the way players are instructed on the rules of the game. The basic *Survival Game* format consists of two opposing teams playing Capture the Flag. While strategy and game plan are up to the teams, generally each side designates certain players to defend its flag and elects others to attack or try to capture the opposing team's flag and return it to home base without being splattered.

One dimension of *Survival Game* play that many players remarked on was the déjà vu experience of childhood. "It was just like being a kid again" is the comment of many who played army, cops and robbers, and cowboys and Indians as children. Of course they're adults now, but the feelings are much the same. A 20-year-old business major recalled, "I kept having flashbacks to childhood, and I remembered how much I loved playing army, and it seemed weird that here I was playing army again and still loving it."

Much of the *Survival Game's* success is due to its simulation of warfare. Twenty-five- to fifty-acre wooded playing fields, camouflage clothing, and realistic guns add immensely to the adult experience of the game. Most players equated the game with real warfare. The realism adds to players' fantasies of warfare:

> At one point I was hiding at the bottom of a hill imagining I could blow an opponent's head off because I could get a great shot at it . . . and when I killed someone for the first time I felt excited, very powerful and slightly god-like. With one simple shot I had taken a guy out of the game. One of my teammates gave me high five. (A 19-year-old electrical engineering major)

A business and finance major recalls, "The best part was hunting and shooting down the enemy and scoring kills! On my first kill, I was so excited, I jumped up and immediately got shot. The hit splattered on my back and I felt the sting, then I rolled on the ground to add some theatrics." Said a marketing major, "When you are out in the woods you forget what's going on outside of the woods. You concentrate on the game and release your tension by shooting people . . . When I shot somebody I was psyched and usually just yelled 'yeah.' " "The thing I liked the best about the game," said a criminal justice major, "was the tension and excitement to hunt and kill enemies. . . . The battle action was awesome, real, and the gunfire exchange was great and added to the competition in the game."

When players are shot for the first time—an unpleasant sensation—*Survival Game* surrealism turns to realism, as players are jerked backed to reality and forced to consider their fate:

> The game was very realistic. I was dirty and scraped, a little bit afraid at first, and there was some blood on the welt on my arm. Sometimes I fantasized that I was really in battle and how exciting it would be. And then I got hit and I thought that if this were real war, I would be dead now, with half my head blown off since I had taken a head shot. This scared me for a moment and made me imagine what war must be really like. But I eventually got over it and enjoyed the rest of the day.

"Head shots," a painful and potentially dangerous part of the game, are the principle reason why goggles or face masks are mandatory. Many players received head shots and, apparently, many players purposely delivered them. The average number of head shots made by players who admitted to the practice was a high percentage, especially considering rules that discount them as hits; that is, the splattered player is not "killed" or required to leave the game. At the same time, when asked whether they ever purposely made head shots, all but one player said yes. Among the reasons offered were "for fun," "for revenge," and as "a strategy to flush the enemy out." "And besides," said one player, "in war there's no penalty for playing dirty." Such behavior may suggest that playing the *Survival Game* increases aggression levels in participants, at least in the short term, but more importantly, the game provides motive and opportunity for such behavior, all in the context of fun and games. In fact, more than two-thirds of the players felt that playing the *Survival Game* made them more aggressive during the course of the day. One player noted how the game "forced some timid people out of their shells . . . and that most people who played were aggressive and wanted to kill other people, even if they are the quietest people you know."

Both male and female players agreed that the *Survival Game* was more of a "man's game." A male pharmacy major said, "The game is more attractive to men because men have more of the instinct of survival." Another suggested that, "On the average, men are more attracted to this sort of thing than women . . . men are less able to control a desire to strike out and therefore they take more pleasure in killing." As one female player put it, "I think it's definitely a man's game. Men are better at shooting people and being aggressive and violent." Another woman, a psychology major, agreed:

> The men were much more aggressive and more involved in the game. It is a violent game and you can see their manly, aggressive attitudes come out. There were a few men who could be classified as 'Rambos.' I think it might be too violent for some women.

Still, most players seemed to feel that playing the *Survival Game* was a positive experience and that the aggression—which most believed was present—was a kind of catharsis. "I enjoyed the *Survival Game*," a female major in international business and marketing said, ". . . if someone was frustrated it is a good way to relieve that tension." A male player agreed: "The game stimulates your aggressive energies, but in a positive and harmless direction. At the end I was hurting and exhausted, but I felt great! I'm definitely doing it again."

Most would agree with the player who said, "Sure the *Survival Game* is a stimulant of aggressive energy, but so is Monopoly." What was shown on the field was young adults playing war games and fantasizing about killing and being killed. War fantasies can be further discerned through the language of war that comes naturally to many players: "Charging" or "taking a hill," "taking out snipers," or "cornering an enemy" with "strategic shots" or "positioning," and then "blowing him away." Players also spoke in images of death when celebrating "kills," "annihilating an opponent," "wreaking carnage," and "massacring the enemy."

Some players assumed fictional identities as well. For example, a group of four players conspicuous by their gung ho enthusiasm were referred to by other players, including members of their own team, as the "Rambo Squad." One player who wore a white towel wrapped around his head like a turban was called the "Arab." Another player (of Jamaican descent) was labeled "the Jamaican mercenary," and a player with a hockey mask was dubbed "Jason"—referring the the demonic ghoul of the *Friday the 13th* film series. Verbal abuse among players, such as name-calling, threats, or taunting, frequently occurred during game play as well. For example, some players addressed their opponents in homophobic and racist terms such as "queer," "wimp," "nigger," and "Arab scum."

While most players agreed that the *Survival Game* was "only a game," more than two-thirds of the players felt that there were valuable tools and skills that could be acquired while playing. "You can develop skills of agility and alertness" said a first-time player, "and I felt braver than I thought I would, and feel now that I might be calmer in dealing with critical situations in real life." Similarly, an accounting major wrote, "I think the *Survival Game* sharpens your reaction time and it makes you more aware of your immediate surroundings." Another suggested that, "Powers of concentration and listening skills can be learned in this game . . . and while it's going on, total concentration is required or you risk having your head blown off."

Other "practical" skills players believed could be developed in the *Survival Game* included "reacting to a crisis," "sneaking up on people," "shooting a gun," "combat tactics," "camouflage," "evading fire," "self-protection," "problem solving," "harnessing one's aggression," and "trust." One player who said he was a survivalist also said that he "played the *Survival Game* regularly to practice survival skills like shooting and tracking." A player noted that, "You can see how important trust must be in real war. You have to rely on people you hardly know to protect your ass from being blown off. You become more trusting of your teammates." Another said, "I think learning to be discreet, how to hide well, track people and use camouflage are skills that might be useful in other areas of life."

Some players even said they had developed a better appreciation for guns. "The guns fascinated me the most," said a player, "and I'm less afraid of them than I used to be. I might even consider getting one for self-defense." Another player said, "I own a gun and I can see how these splat guns can be useful for marksmanship, but much safer." Still another said, "the guns surprised me, they were powerful but easy to handle. I'd like to try firing a real one now, to see if I can handle it as well."

Many players suggested that the skills and values of the *Survival Game* could be adapted to everyday life, as shown by the following comment from a business major:

> Playing the Survival Game can make you more aggressive in the real world. You can develop a better sense of individualism and competition, and develop a "killer instinct" which in America is important to business. Today having no mercy for your enemies can be useful in business too.

Although many players felt that such skills might be useful in everyday life, how transferable these are is more difficult to determine. Since the skills are linked to warfare—camouflage, tracking, shooting, and combat strategy—what may be learned are paramilitary or survivalist skills. One player suggested that, "People who play this thing regularly probably do so to improve their weapons and military skills." And another thought that, "the *Survival Game* is a 'war sport' [that] can make those who play the game more knowledgeable of survival in war than others . . . for people who care about such things, this is their game." Another player remarked, "After playing this game I think I'm more attuned to the seriousness of war. If Americans are in trouble they need to band together to survive. After playing the *Survival Game* I think America should give a larger percentage of the budget to the defense department." Other players also made links to the military industrial complex:

> The game supports the military establishment because you come to realize how easy it is to die in warfare. You appreciate the people who actually do serve in the military, and think how brave they must be. Also,

if some people enjoy this type of thing, it may encourage them to enlist in the army.

It may be that the congruence between the general social values and outlooks of players are activated, rather than learned, by playing the *Survival Game*. However, the analysis does demonstrate that some players make the connections between instrumental American values and military ideology.

Today, the popularity of games like the *Survival Game* has renewed debates on the relationship between violence and aggression in war toys, games, and sports. While Laser Tag and Nintendo may impact a greater percentage of America's young, the appearance of new war games and "war sports" for adults like the *Survival Game* is particularly interesting. Games and sports have long been observed by sociologists, psychologists, and historians as symbolic and recreational forms of warfare, where violence is encouraged and often part of the game, but controlled by rules, referees, and sanctions.

In recent years much of the debate concerning warlike or violent sports has centered on whether such phenomena serve to create or reduce aggressive or violent behavior in participants, active spectators, or casual followers. Critics of war games and sports have suggested that their violent nature enhances or causes further violence both on and off the playing fields. Some argue further that nations that promote militaristic games and sports will produce a people who are supportive of military policies and activities. Supporters, on the other hand, argue that contact sports, including war games, serve a cathartic effect and may reduce tension and violence in the real world, at the same time that they teach useful skills.[40]

In either case, to play the *Survival Game* and other war games is to participate in an expression of American popular militarism and survivalism. It is through the symbolic dynamics of the game that the meaning of survivalism is negotiated for the player within a dramatic field of fantasy and play. Exaggerated survivalist tendencies are seen in the aggression that the game arouses in players, especially men. While some women do play the *Survival Game*, and at the competitive levels there are some highly skilled women, the game remains male dominated. Like the paramilitary magazines such as *Soldier of Fortune*, the aggressive and violent nature associated with masculinity is common to the *Survival Game*.

Many players also tended to see the *Survival Game* as more than just recreation. They felt that practical skills—survival skills—are learned during the course of the game. Some felt that skills in firearms, hunting and tracking, camouflage, and combat strategy could be adapted to the struggles of everyday life, especially in business. In addition, many players felt that the *Survival Game* reflected important American values—the instrumental values of individualism, competition, and survival of the fittest. After playing the *Survival Game* for the first time, some players even indicated an increased sense of patriotism and respect for the nation's soldiers.

The relationship between the *Survival Game* and the military-industrial complex has already been noted in the military's use of paintball weapons and equipment. In addition, some defense companies have openly supported the game. Raychem, for example, has important ties to defense contractors such as Lockheed's Naval Ordinance Plant, a research and development site for the Trident 2 missile. The company sees no contradiction in organizing *Survival Games* for its employees.[41]

In certain ways the *Survival Game* expresses an ideological legitimation for the military-industrial complex. That this can be accomplished through toys and games should not surprise us. It was perhaps fitting that many television critics were quick to note the Nintendo version of "Desert Storm" that the American military and mass media so successfully produced, directed, and starred in.

Innovations in technology have seen war games evolve to newer and more realistic formats. In an article entitled "Armageddon under the Christmas Tree," Albert Gross reviews the computer game Nuclear War.[42] Created as a board game in 1965, the game has enjoyed increasing popularity since 1981 with its appearance as a computer game. Gross asks if playing a zero-sum game like Nuclear War may socialize one toward the mature and conscientious consideration of the nuclear debate, or if players may reach a point at which the reality and the imaginary are indistinguishable.

While the *Survival Game* reflects a further fragmenting (perhaps shattering) of the apocalypticism of the millennial myth, most people who play the *Survival Game* play for the fun of it. "Its only a game," they are likely to say at the slightest criticism of the game as militaristic or violent. However, deeper cultural myths are rooted in the objects of play and fantasy in the *Survival Game* that players readily admit to—myths of survival: "kill or be killed," "every man for himself," "peace through superior firepower," "survival of the fittest." The survivalist myths of Armageddon are expressed in the the pages of *Soldier of Fortune* magazine, the *Survival Game*, and other areas of the paramilitary popular culture. Though altered in form and content, they reinforce traditional American values of individualism, as well as the survivalist and militaristic tendencies of the American millennial myth.

# Chapter 9

# Millennium

## New Age Harmony or New World Chaos?

*You must change your hearts and minds—for the Kingdom of Heaven has arrived!*

MATT. 3:1, 4:17, NTME

*And they lived and reigned with Christ for a thousand years. But the rest of the dead lived not again until the thousand years was finished. This is the first resurrection.*

REV. 20:4–5, KJV

The millennium is the final apocalyptic element of Revelation that takes various forms in our modern culture, especially in the subcultures of survivalism, religious fundamentalism, and the "New Age." In Revelation, the millennium refers to the 1,000-year period initiated by Christ on his return, in which he establishes his kingdom on earth. It is only in Revelation that the reference to the millennium can be found. According to the account (Rev. 20:2–7), the dragon (i.e., the Devil) is to be thrown down into a pit for 1,000 years following his defeat at the great Battle of Armageddon, while the martyrs, having been raised from the dead, are to reign with Christ. At the end of the millennium, Satan, prior to his final destruction, is to be released for a time to "deceive the nations" once more, but he is subsequently defeated and "cast into the lake of fire and brimstone, where the beast and the false prophet are, and shall be tormented day and night for ever and ever" (Rev. 20:10). During this "postmillennial" time, all of the dead are raised back to life in a second resurrection and are gathered together for the final judgment, where those who are saved are separated from those who are damned. Shortly thereafter, the Messiah shows John of Patmos the "new Jerusalem" descending from the heavens and he invites all to drink from the eternal waters of life (Rev. 21:2, 22:17).

In the history of Christianity the reference in Revelation to a "new Heaven and a new earth" has often been taken literally to refer to a worldly millennium, where a paradise would appear on earth, just as it had been when God first created humankind. The earth would be transformed into a world free of disease, war, and hatred, but filled with the natural and sacred beauty of God's creations. This blissful view of the millennium is one commonly accepted by Jehovah's Witnesses. The Witnesses also believe that this paradise will be on the earth, transformed by Jehovah back to the original Garden of Eden. It will be a real earthly paradise, not one only of the spirit or in Heaven.

While this reference to the millennium in Revelation is unique to the New Testament, an earlier form of the "eternity" concept can be traced to the literature of Babylonia and Persia. In the Epic of Gilgamesh, for example, the hero, seeking to grasp the real nature of mortality, visits an old man who has earned eternal life, Utnapishtim. This old man tells Gilgamesh that he has received his precious gift in a way we recognize as a source tale for Noah and the great flood. A soulful god named Ea confides in Utnapishtim that the other gods plan to unleash a brutal storm on earth. For seven days, Utnapishtim builds a giant ark. By the seventh day, it has seven decks and a huge coal-burning furnace. As the deluge hits, Utnapishtim, his family, workers, and animals take refuge on the ark. For six terrible days, storms and floods submerge the world, killing all living things outside of the ark. On the seventh day the weather clears and the ark comes to rest atop Mount Nisir. No other land is anywhere to be seen but Utnapishtim leaves his ark, sets loose his animals, and offers a sacrifice to the gods who have let him live.

The gods have had their consciences pricked by Ea's chiding. They give Utnapishtim and his wife the gift of eternal life, and a solid place to live, where two rivers meet.[1] In contrast to the story of Noah, there is no apparent moral reason why the gods decided to destroy the world. The only reason why the hero of the flood and his kin are saved is because Ea favors Utnapishtim and tricks the other gods, including the chief god, by allowing them to survive. In addition, only Utnapishtim and his wife are given immortality, whereas in Revelation, many thousands will be awarded everlasting life during and after the millennium.

A 1,000-year period of spiritual and physical bliss is present in Jewish apocalyptic literature as well. For example, in the Slavonic Book of Enoch (chs. 32 and 33), a noncanonical apocalyptic text, this utopian period is described as following a week and a day, each day being 1,000 years in length. The first six days (i.e., 6,000 years) are said to have elapsed from the time of the Creation to the Judgment, at which time will come a "sabbath of rest" of a thousand years. The eighth day will be timeless. In the Talmud a similar expectation can be found. In rabbinic thinking the establishment of God's kingdom was tied to the Messiah, who was to be a descendant of King David. The Messiah would redeem the Jews from exile and reestablish their independence in Israel, instituting a new age of righteousness and universal peace.

Rabbis referred to this age as "the world to come." They refrained from commenting further about it, saying that human language and fantasy were inadequate to depict its wonders. And unlike both Utnapishtim and the throngs of the saved in Revelation, the notion of eternal life is omitted in the Old Testament, because to the Israelite mind, no man, woman, or child could receive that status. More commonly, the hope for paradise or homeland in "this world" has a deep history in Jewish Scripture. Just as the Messiah took the form of King David, the land and people he ruled in the name of Yahweh was Zion, the ancient name for Jerusalem and the promised land of the Jews.

In the history of the Christian Church the doctrine of a worldly millennium, also called *chialism*, has played a considerable role, though the great theologians from St. Augustine onward have opposed it in favor of a metaphysical millennium based in Heaven or "in the spirit." Others, like Saint Justin the Martyr, an early church father from the second century A.D., regarded the expectation of a worldly paradise as an essential part of Christian faith. Such were also the views of Victor Houteff and later David Koresh and the Branch Davidians, who saw the millennial paradise as something that they could help create right here on earth. It would not be a spiritual Heaven or millennium, but a worldly one, a new Garden of Eden.

Strongly held millennial views are common among apocalyptic groups called premillennialists, who believe that the "Second Coming of Christ" will precede the period of 1,000 years and the establishment of an earthly paradise. Most Christians, on the other hand, believe the theory that the resurrection is to include all Christians, not only the martyrs. Postmillennialists believe that Christianity will eventually be accepted throughout the world, at which time a 1,000-year period of Christian righteousness will prevail and then be climaxed by the return of Christ, the resurrection of the dead, final judgment, and then life everlasting. Among postmillennial Adventists, the crowning event of the Apocalypse will be Christ's "Second Advent" at the close of the millennium.

Other than the author of Revelation, no other New Testament author has given as much prominence to the expectation of spiritual bliss and Edenlike paradise of the millennium. However, the idea has persisted throughout the 2,000-year history of Christianity, breaking out with almost predictable regularity under periods of rapid social change, disaffection, and a declining social and cultural order.

*Yet have I set my King upon my holy hill of Zion.* (Ps. 2:6, KJV)

*And I saw a new heaven and a new earth; for the first heaven and the first earth were passed away; and there was no more sea. And I John*

*saw the holy city, new Jerusalem, coming down from God out of*
*heaven, prepared as a bride adorned for her husband.* (REV. 21:1–2,
KJV)

Zion appears in the Hebrew Bible 152 times, as a reference to
Jerusalem. More than half of these references appear in just two
books, Isaiah and Psalms. The word is primarily a poetic reference
to the holy city Jerusalem, God's chosen home for the Jews. The
emotional and religious significance of Zion derive from the importance of the city of Jerusalem to Jews as the city of King
David—the greatest of Jewish kings—and as the city of the Temple.

A rocky knoll in the city of Jerusalem known as the Temple
Mount is held in the highest regard by Jews, Christians, and Muslims as the holiest of holy sites. For Muslims the mountain is where
the Dome of the Rock shrine is built. Islamic tradition teaches that
Allah went up to Heaven from this spot after he created all things.
Christians teach that the Temple Mount is the site where the baby
Jesus was dedicated and where the young Jesus confounded the
elders. When Jesus died, the New Testament records that the veil
of the Temple separating its most sacred rooms from the outside
was torn from top to bottom.

Judaism teaches that Abraham, the father of the Hebrew people, took his son Isaac to sacrifice him on the Mount. Later in the
history, King David purchased a threshing floor on the Temple
Mount that became the First Temple, thereafter the spiritual center
of Jewish culture and history. The First Temple was destroyed in
586 B.C., but was later rebuilt on the same site. The Second Temple
also was eventually destroyed. For more than 2,000 years the Jews
lost control of Jerusalem and the Temple Mount, until 1967 when
they won it back in war. Israeli authorities returned the Temple
Mount to the Muslims, but many Jews would like to see it returned
to Israeli control and a Third Temple built. Many millennialists
believe that when the Jews rebuild the Third Temple, the Messiah
will return.[2]

Jerusalem (Zion) is the place where Yahweh, the God of Israel,
lives, the place where he is king, and the place where God installed
his earthly king, David. Zion is thus the seat of action in the history

of the Jews; it is either being destroyed by enemies or delivered by God back to the Jews. After Jerusalem was destroyed by the Babylonians in 586 B.C., the Israelites could not forget Zion (Ps. 137). In Jewish prophecy after the Babylonian exile, Zion became the scene of Yahweh's messianic salvation. It is to Zion that the exiles will be returned (Jer. 3:14), and where they will find Yahweh (3:31).

While the name Zion is rare in the New Testament (it appears seven times, mostly in reference to the Old Testament), it has frequently been used as the designation for the heavenly city and for the earthly city of Christian faith. Jerusalem, or Zion, is both the metaphor and the actual site for those awaiting the return of the Messiah and the creation of a heavenly city on earth. For Jews, Zion has come to mean the Jewish homeland, symbolic of Judaism and Jewish nationalist and spiritual aspirations, hence the name Zionism for the nineteenth- and twentieth-century movement to establish a Jewish national state in Palestine.

Zionism developed in Eastern and central Europe in the latter part of the nineteenth century, but it is a continuation of the deeply felt attachment Jews have always had to a homeland in Palestine, the "promised land," where one of the two hills of ancient Jerusalem was called Zion. The word Zion appears to be a pre-Israelite Canaanite name of the hill upon which Jerusalem was later built; the name "Mountain of Zion" is common. In biblical literature "Mountain of Zion" is often used to designate the city of Jerusalem, rather than the hill itself.

In the sixteenth and seventeenth centuries a number of "messiahs" came forward to show the way back to Zion. Occasionally a movement such as the Haskala ("enlightenment") of the late eighteenth century would appear and urge Jews to accept exile and assimilate into the modern secular culture. The Haskala reflected the experiences of Jews whose contact with European civilization through business and education heightened their desire to become part of the larger European society.[3] Into the nineteenth century it was primarily Christian millennialists like the Adventists who kept alive the interest in a Jewish repatriation of Palestine, an event that would fulfill Scripture and bring on the millennium.

Beginning with the Babylonian exile in 586 B.C., and flourishing in Alexandria in the first century A.D., when an estimated five million Jews lived outside of Palestine, Jews have lived in the Diaspora—the scattered settlements of Jews throughout the world. Thereafter, the main centers of Judaism shifted from country to country (e.g., Babylon, Persia, Spain, France, Germany, Poland, Russia, and the United States). Gradually, many of these Jewish communities developed distinctive traits in adaptation to their new homes, some submerging themselves in gentile culture and losing their own traditions. However, Jews did not always assimilate in these new lands, nor were they allowed to, as they were often the targets of anti-Semitism, such as the czarist pogroms in Eastern Europe. In reaction to these attacks, a group of Eastern European Jews formed the Hoveve Zion ("Lovers of Zion")—an organization to promote a settlement of farmers and artisans in Palestine.

Zionism took a political and secular turn when Austrian journalist and Jew Theodore Herzl, who had regarded assimilation as the best way to dissolve the social problem of anti-Semitism, changed his mind. While working in France as a journalist, Herzl continued to see the deep resentment that many Europeans harbored and the persistent anti-Semitism even among some of the most educated and democratic peoples. Herzl often said it was the Dreyfus affair that made him a Zionist. In 1894, Alfred Dreyfus, a highly placed Jewish army officer, was falsely accused of treason. His innocence was questioned by an anti-Semitic press, resulting in a controversy that threw French society into turmoil.[4] Herzl came to believe that the only hope for the Jews and the world was to build a homeland for the Jewish people.

In 1897 the first Zionist Congress was convened by Herzl at Basel, Switzerland. The congress drew up the Zionist program, which stated that "Zionism strives to create for the Jewish people a home in Palestine secured by public law."[5] The Zionist Congress met every two years until 1901, at which time the Ottoman Empire refused to allow Herzl's request for autonomy for Palestine. The Zionist movement found support from the British government in 1903, which offered the Zionists 6,000 acres in Uganda for the homeland. The Zionists held out for Palestine and continued to agitate for their cause. They published pamphlets and their own newspaper, *Die Welt* (*The World*), and they helped to create a Jewish "renaissance" in the arts and sciences, a worldwide movement backed not only by Jews but also by Jewish sympathizers everywhere. While he lived to see the Zionist movement spread its wings, Theodore Herzl, at the age of 44, died in 1904, 44 years before the birth of the new state of Israel.

The wave of repression against Jews that followed the Russian Revolution in 1905 caused the migration of large numbers of young Russian Jews to Palestine as pioneer settlers. 90,000 Jews were living in Palestine by 1914.[6] With help from the French Jewish philanthropist Baron Edmund de Rothschild, settlers built dozens of agricultural communities, or communes. World War I reignited Zionist aspirations, and some political influence passed to Russian Jews living in England. Chaim Weizmann and Nahum Sokolow helped to obtain the Balfour Declaration from Great Britain (1917). The Declaration promised British support for a Jewish homeland in Palestine. Zionists celebrated in 1922 when Great Britain included the Balfour Declaration in its League of Nations mandate following World War I, giving the Allied victors authority to settle disputes in the former theater of war, including Palestine.

Jewish settlements and culture began to grow, so that by 1925 the population was officially estimated at more than 100,000. By 1933 the population had increased to more than 200,000, 20 percent of the population of Palestine at the time.[7] Immigration remained relatively stable until the rise of Hitler and the start of Jewish internment in Germany. By then immigration had increased to such a degree that Arabs were now worrying that all of Palestine might really become a Jewish-controlled state. The Arabs bitterly began to oppose Zionism and the British for supporting it, calling on the British government to mediate Arab claims.

With the extremism of Hitler, especially directed at the Jews, European Jews sought refuge in Palestine with fellow Jews. Jews in other nations, including the United States, began to intensify their support for Zionism. Arab–Zionist conflicts continued to increase and Great Britain attempted to find a solution in a proposal to split the country between the Arabs and the Jews with Jerusalem as a kind of "international" center. The State of Israel was instituted on May 14, 1948. This brought on the Arab–Israeli war of 1948–1949. With victory over the Arabs, Israel gained more land than the original UN resolution gave them. Fifty years after the first Zionist Congress, Zionism, both in its secular and religious forms, was able to achieve its goal of creating a Jewish state in Palestine.

The creation of the State of Israel in 1948 fulfilled prophecies made by many observers, but not all in the same way. To Jews, it was the crowning glory of 50 years of Zionist movement for the creation of a Jewish homeland in Palestine, the ancient biblical land of the Jews. For religious Jews, it was the fulfillment of the ancient prophecies of Isaiah and Psalms, in which the homeland of God's chosen people would be Jerusalem, or Zion.

To many Christians it meant much the same thing. Hal Lindsey, in his 1970s bestseller, *The Late Great Planet Earth*, writes of the creation of the Jewish homeland as the fulfillment of Revelation and a prelude to the coming of Christ. To others, on the far right, the creation of Israel was a revelation of a different sort; it was fulfillment of prophecies showing that the "heaven stormers" of Lucifer and the Jewish Antichrist were in control of the Babylonian Empire. They viewed this as a major accomplishment for the forces of evil in their plan to build a new world order controlled by, and for the benefit of, the Jews. It was the plan revealed in the infamous forgery known as the *Protocols of the Learned Elders of Zion*—the Jewish conspiracy to take over the world and impose a new world order.

*Awake, and arise from the dust, O Jerusalem; yea, and put on thy beautiful garments, O daughter of Zion; and strengthen thy stakes and enlarge thy borders forever, that thou mayest no more be confounded, that the covenants of the eternal father which he hath made unto thee, O house of Israel, may be fulfilled.* (THE BOOK OF MORMON, MORONI, 10:31)

As we noted earlier, Columbus' discovery of America was heralded in millennial terms, first by Columbus himself and later by the Puritan settlers and down through American manifest destiny to the present. America continues to be seen as Babylon by some and a millennial land by others, a confusion that is part of the fragmentation and adaptive nature of the millennial myth.

Historians have labeled the period 1830–1860 in the United States an Age of Reform because so many new religious and secular social movements developed that were oriented toward social reform, communal utopias, and millennial expectations. It was another of the many "awakenings" that have dotted popular American culture since its inception.[8] Many of the groups organized a strong community, focused on collectivist values and an emphasis on a spiritual or intellectual "perfectionism." At the same time that the Industrial Revolution was in full swing and American capitalism was becoming so frenzied that some observers called it the nation's true religion, tens of thousands of Americans flocked to an array of movements and communities dedicated to spiritual and secular uplift.

Some of the more millennial groups included the Oneida community, also called the "perfectionists," because of their belief that God had already returned to earth in A.D. 70. Human redemption and liberation from sin had already occurred, they taught, thus we were living in the prophesied millennial period, a time of "perfection."[9] Also, as noted earlier, there were the "Millerites," later to become the Seventh-Day Adventists and to inspire Charles Taze Russell and the Jehovah's Witnesses.

Another popular millennial church was the United Society of Believers in Christ's Second Coming, or Shakers, who branched off from the Quakers. Named because of their ecstatic behavior and wild dancing and shaking, the Shakers also practiced celibacy and communal living. The Shaker doctrine, as it became known in the United States, was formulated by Mother Ann Lee, an illiterate textile worker from Manchester, England, who had been converted to the "shaking Quakers" in 1758. Mother Ann had a series of revelations in which she came to regard herself as the female aspect of God's dual nature and the second incarnation of Christ. She established celibacy as the cardinal principle of the sect and then migrated to the United States where she instituted her millennial church in Niskeyuna (or Watervliet), New York, later moved to Lebanon, New York. The Shaker movement reached its zenith during the 1850s, when about 6,000 members were enrolled in the church.[10]

The more secular communitarian movements concentrated on finding a better way to live—"perfection" in study, intellectual and spiritual investigation and experimentation, quiet contemplation, and shared work and responsibilities. Some of the more well-known utopian groups included the New England "transcendentalist" experiments known as Fruitlands in Concord, Massachusetts, and Brook Farm in West Roxbury, Massachusetts.[11] Brook Farm was a communitarian experiment begun by Unitarian minister George Ripley, along with poet Ralph Waldo Emerson and educator Bronson Alcott. Writers Herman Melville, author of *Moby Dick*, and Nathaniel Hawthorne, who penned *The House of the Seven Gables* and *The Scarlet Letter*, were also members for a brief time.

The transcendentalists were loosely bound by an idealistic system of thought based in a belief in the essential unity of all creation, the innate goodness of man, and the supremacy of insight over logic and experience for the revelation of the deepest truths. Eclectic and cosmopolitan in its sources, the transcendentalist spiritual quest rejected the conventions of eighteenth-century thought. Advocating reform in church, state, and society, they contributed to the rise of free religion, the abolition movement, communitarian experiments, and a renaissance in American literature.

There's no general agreement as to why such a rage for reformist, perfectionist, and communitarian experimentation occurred in the antebellum United States. The revival of Protestant evangelism and a reform spirit, which included at various times abolitionism, temperance, women's rights, pacifism, and prison reform, spread throughout the Anglo-American community, especially in the Northeast. It may have been a reaction to the "perfectionism" and universal human progress of the Enlightenment, which saw in science, industrialization, and the free and competitive market-place an erosion of civilized behavior, humanitarian concerns, and spiritual or transcendental meaning.

The millennial revival certainly was spurred by the industrialization and increasing complexity of American life at the time. The movements served as a response to the many new social stresses caused by rapid social and cultural changes going on in society. The importance of these movements derives from neither their size nor their achievements, since few of them had much longevity. The reformist spirit of many of these movements reflected the sensitivity of a segment of Americans to the problems in American life incurred through industrialization. In a sense, the reformers were voices of conscience, reminding their materialist countrymen that the American millennial dream was not yet a reality for many, as they pointed to the gross inequalities that persisted in society.

Perhaps the most successful of the religious revitalization movements in the United States, and one that placed a great deal of emphasis on building an earthly millennial paradise, or Zion, was Mormonism. As we've seen, Zion is alternately Jerusalem, Israel, the Jewish people, or the Jewish homeland. Zion can also refer to Heaven, or some other utopian world reflecting a paradise on earth. Salt Lake City, Utah, is the American Zion of the Mormons. The Church of Jesus Christ of Latter-day Saints, better known as the Mormons, represents an American millennial movement of the Age of Reform that has enjoyed great success in this country in its attempt to build an American Zion.

In 1823, Joseph Smith, Jr., son of a poor New England farmer, was living in upstate New York in a region known as the "burned over district" because of its popularity among fire-and-brimstone-preaching ministers and barnstorming evangelists. In this district of revivalist zealotry, the young charismatic Smith began to claim to have had revelations from God. In a scene reminiscent of John's revelations at Patmos, one evening while in prayer, Smith claimed he was visited by an angelic messenger, "exceedingly white and brilliant," called Moroni. Moroni, who supposedly was a resurrected being, told Smith that there was a sacred book written on gold plates buried in fields in the county. The book, Moroni said, related the story of God's dealings with the ancient inhabitants of the Americas, as well as additional revelations concerning the Second Coming of Jesus Christ that should serve as an addendum to the Old and New Testaments.[12]

Presumedly, the book had been passed down through the generations by revelation and prophecy, and Moroni's father, Mormon, who had been a great prophet and historian, had translated the text carved into the gold plates. Smith had been chosen by God to be the next prophet to reveal God's further plans to the world. There also were two stones in silver bows fastened to a breastplate with the golden plates. The stones, which were called the Urim and the Thummim, were "peep stones," crystals used by seers and diviners to decipher omens or locate buried treasure.

Smith claimed that the angel Moroni led him to the highest hill in the county, and then to its western side. There he discovered the "gold plates" and the Urim and Thummim. Smith's translation of the plates became the *Book of Mormon*. Three associates of Smith—Oliver Cowdery, David Whitmer, and Martin Harris—also claimed they saw the angel Moroni and the golden plates. They became Smith's first converts and thereafter claimed also to have supernatural revelations.[13]

The *Book of Mormon* is accepted as scripture by the Church of Jesus Christ of Latter-day Saints. First published in 1830, the *Book of Mormon* relates the history of two tribes of Hebrews who migrated from Jerusalem centuries before the birth of Christ. One tribe, the Jaredites, left Jerusalem during the period when God confounded the tongues of people at the Tower of Babel. Around 600 B.C. another tribe migrated out, and after years of wandering separated into two tribes—the Nephites and the Lamanites. After many thousands of years, all but the Lamanites were destroyed. Led by a prophet Lehi, the Lamanites eventually ended up in America. The final glory of the *Book of Mormon* is the appearance of Jesus Christ among the Lamanites in America, soon after his resurrection. As he had in Palestine, Jesus reveals to the Lamanites the doctrine of the Gospel, what they must do to receive salvation, and prophecies for the end times.[14]

Smith and his early followers gathered together and decided to form a church, eventually settling upon the name the Church of Jesus Christ of Latter-day Saints ("Latter-day" refers to the Western hemisphere period of scriptural history, when Christ appeared to the inhabitants of the American continent). Perhaps because it was American in both setting and theology, the church boomed, gaining 1,000 members within a year. However, persecution was also visited upon the Mormons by angry mobs, who saw the new church as strange and dangerous. New York authorities arrested Smith repeatedly for disturbing the peace.[15]

Smith and his converts fled to Kirtland, Ohio, established the communistic order of Enoch, and began spreading the word with some success. They were able to convert a prominent minister, Sidney Rigdon, and many members of his church, to the new religion. They continued on to Missouri, but there, too, they encountered trouble. Mobs attacked them and even tarred and feathered Joseph Smith. Despite the turmoil that Smith and his young Mormon flock evoked, the church grew. Continued conflict, however, caused several thousand Mormons to leave Missouri in 1839. Smith built the new city of Nauvoo in Illinois, and he became mayor and an official in the militia.

Mormon beliefs, particularly Smith's teachings about and practice of polygamy, provoked more attacks from outraged critics. Smith's own questionable handling of church funds and his bad dealings in land caused several members to dissent and call for Smith to step down. On June 27, 1844, while in a Carthage, Illinois, jail with his brother Hyrum and two other Mormon officials, Smith and his brother were shot by a mob, while the other two Mormons barely escaped the same grim fate. After the death of Joseph Smith, rivalry erupted in the church hierarchy. Finally, the majority chose as their new leader Brigham Young, who had been president of the Council of Twelve Apostles. Young gathered together 143 "saints" into a "pioneer band" and set out westward along the north fork of the Platte River in 1846–1847. They turned south across the Wasatch

Mountains, emerging on the shores of the Great Salt Lake (Utah), where Young decided they would build their "desert Zion."[16]

Brigham Young felt that the Mormon Church would need thousands of followers abroad, so missionary work became a central function of the church. In addition to the United States, early missionaries went to Canada, Britain, Scandinavia, Germany, Italy, Spain, and China. The missionaries proved very successful in converting Europeans to Mormonism, with the most converts and migrants to America coming from Britain and Scandinavia.

In 1849 the Mormons established the provisional state of Deseret, with Young as governor. The next year this area became part of the state of Utah, and Young became the territorial governor. Young made polygamy legal in the state in 1852. The propensity of the Mormons to establish their own social and political system led them into open conflict with the federal government. In 1857, President James Buchanan, believing the Mormons were in a state of rebellion, ordered warrants for Young's arrest. He also ordered 2,500 soldiers to Utah to depose Governor Young, which led to the "Utah war." A Mormon militia was organized to defend themselves and their church from federal troops. In one instance, Mormon settlers fled from northern Utah, burning the crops at Fort Supply and Fort Bridger in advance of U.S. federal troops who were coming to arrest Young. Also during the year 1857, the so-called mountain meadow massacre occurred, when a group of non-Mormon settlers bound for California were attacked and murdered by Mormon zealots. The campaign against Brigham Young and the Mormons became known as "Buchanan's blunder," but it ended Mormon control of Utah. Polygamy officially ended in 1890.[17]

It is the theology of the *Book of Mormon* that most interests us for our inquiry, especially its focus on the millennium and the heavenly city. The *Book of Mormon* describes several different millennial kingdoms. In 1888, Joseph Smith had a revelation of three postresurrectional kingdoms—the celestial (a heavenly kingdom), the terrestrial (an earthly kingdom), and the telestial (an underworld kingdom for liars, adulterers, and other unrepentant sinners). Smith revealed that the return of Christ to earth will lead to the first resurrection and the millennium, the main activity of which would be preparing the way for the celestial kingdom and the final judgment, or "temple work," such as baptism on behalf of the dead. After this period the second resurrection would occur, and the earth would become part of a celestial kingdom, at which time the final judgment is made.[18] In the meantime, Smith tried to temper the expectations of the eternal kingdom and its revivalist excesses by focusing on building the terrestrial kingdom, or earthly Zion. He called on the faithful to gather and work together to build Zion in the great western desert as a new social and spiritual order.

The Mormons, needless to say, have flourished to the point that their sect has been transformed into a religious denomination—a large and complex organization with wealth, political clout, and respectability. Today the Mormons are the biggest, richest, and strongest homegrown faith.[19] The largest concentration of Mormons remains in the state of Utah, where Mormonism is a major force in the local culture. Mormon Church policy has always advocated self-sufficiency and survival preparation in anticipation of difficult times. Like other millennial churches, many Mormons also feel that a bad time is on the horizon, so preparing in advance of lean times has taken on increasing significance. The practice of survivalism is now a part of church doctrine.

*Arise, take up thy bed, and go into thine house.* (MATT. 9:2, KJV)

In recent years a variety of groups and movements has been searching for a utopian world in the near future. Another major site for the expression of the millennium is the New Age movement and the subculture of newfangled "spiritualism." New Age is a term that was coined in the mid-1980s to describe a nebulous, quasireligious set of beliefs and practices that are part of an outgrowth of the 1960s countercultures and the 1970s "human potential movement." New Age consciousness encompasses a wide array of beliefs and practices, including astrology, out-of-body experiences, reincarnation, unorthodox psychotherapeutic applications of the "healing powers," "UFOlogy," and spiritualism.

Spiritualism, a system of religious beliefs centered on the belief that communication with the dead or with other "spirits" is possible, has been recorded throughout history, especially in the ancient Near East, Egypt, and India. Anthropologists believe that achieving a state of mental transcendence from ordinary experience, where one can communicate with other-worldly spirits, exists in some form in all cultures. In its modern sense, spiritualism traces its origins to the widespread popular appeal it attained in the 1850s and 1860s, when American newspapers began to report on all kinds of strange happenings, including table levitations, instances of extrasensory perception, "automatic writing," and the appearance of ghosts or "ectoplasmic" matter.

All of the phenomena was attributed to hyperactivity in the spirit world by the numerous mediums who began to crop up. Early supporters of spiritualism included American journalist Horace Greeley, British author Sir Arthur Conan Doyle, and British scientists Sir William Crookes and Alfred R. Wallace (who, independently of Charles Darwin, formulated the theory of evolution).[20] It is important to remember that this was the continuing Age of Reform, which had begun in the 1830s with the evolution of many social reform and millenarian movements in the United States.

One interesting example of the spiritualism craze of the time is the case of Margaret Fox and her two sisters. In 1848, at their parents' farmhouse near Hydesville, New York, the Fox sisters began communicating with spirits. To questions posed to them, the spirits would respond by making "rapping" sounds through the children. The Fox sisters became local celebrities, performing numerous demonstrations. The family moved to Rochester, New York, and found a wider audience and profit in the "spiritual" capacities of the girls. Soon their fame spread throughout the country and across the Atlantic, inspiring a host of imitators. Later in life, Margaret Fox admitted that she had produced the rapping sounds herself by manipulating her joints.[21] The spiritualism trend eventually subsided when many mediums were shown to be fakes.

However, some individuals were not so easily dismissed and turned their original experiences with the spirit world into full-fledged churches that exist to this day. Mary Baker Eddy and the Church of Christ Scientist, or Christian Science, is one such example. In February 1866, at the age of 45 and recently divorced, Mary Baker Patterson slipped and fell on an icy street in Swampscott, Massachusetts, sustaining serious injuries. Fearing her death was near, a neighbor summoned a minister, while neighbors and friends waited by her bedside. Mary, in quiet meditation, read her Bible. After awhile she miraculously recovered, rose from her deathbed, and announced that she was completely well. She said later that while reading Matthew 9:2—"Arise, take up thy bed, and go unto thine house"—she had been healed.[22]

Claiming to have discovered the principles by which Jesus healed the sick and raised the dead, she began teaching metaphysical healing in the late 1860s and later set up a college. Her first published statement of the subject appeared in 1875, entitled *Science and Health*. As a philosophy, Christian Science declares that all matter is unreal, with God and man being infinite. It also believes that the condition of the unreal material body can be brought into harmony with the real spiritual form of man, who, in the image of God, should manifest perfection. It is the "true knowledge" of Jesus' healing powers, they believe, that alone heals sickness. To achieve this spiritual treatment, mental affirmation of these propositions through prayer and "mental work" may be undertaken by oneself or with the support of a Christian Science practitioner.[23]

In 1897, after marrying for a third time to Asa Eddy, a sewing machine salesman, Mary Baker Eddy established the Church of Christ Scientist, in Boston, as the mother church. This set forth a dual structure for Christian Science, by creating a system of therapeutics with accredited practitioners and a religious organization, the mother church, and its branches. Today, many associate Christian Science with downtown "reading rooms" in many American cities, the *Christian Science Monitor* newspaper, and the often controversial stands of some members in refusing modern medical treatments such as blood transfusions and cancer therapies, relying instead on the power of prayer.

During the late 1980s and early 1990s, the church faced serious problems, such as the highly publicized difficulties of its newspaper and television holdings, which suffered major financial cuts. Due in part to its aging membership, church membership has been declining for years. It reached about 270,000 in the mid-1930s, peaked, and has been settling down. Church membership is now down near 150,000.[24] As it consolidates its vast holdings, the church continues to survive, preaching that spiritual healing through God and Jesus are the proper treatments for medical and emotional sickness.

*Old things are passed away: behold, all things are made new.* (2 COR. 5:17, RSV)

*When the moon is in the seventh house, and Jupiter aligns with Mars, then peace will guide the planet and love will steer the stars. This is the dawning of the Age of Aquarius.* ("AQUARIUS," FROM THE MUSICAL *HAIR,* BY JAMES RADO AND JEROME RAGNI, 1969)

In the United States today spiritualism and New Age beliefs and therapies are once again the rage. The term New Age now alludes to unorthodox therapies, self-help programs, and the development of human potential, as well as to the expectation many practitioners have of a coming new spiritual age, in which humans will realize a more powerful and spiritual self and an awareness of their place in the universe.[25] The New Age movement encompasses a vast array of supernatural beliefs and practices, including spiritualism, astrology, out-of-body experiences, reincarnation, the occult, channeling, and UFOlogy, as well as alternative and unorthodox psychotherapeutic techniques and pseudoscientific applications of the "healing powers" of crystals, pyramids, and channeled spirits.

The "harmonic convergence" is one example of the modern millennial hope as expressed in the New Age movement. Forty-eight-year-old artist and historian Jose Arguelles prophesied that the human race would embark on a new age of spiritual harmony on August 16, 1987. Author of the New Age bestseller *The Mayan Factor*, Arguelles had predicted that on that day the heavens would align as they very rarely do—a "harmonic convergence"—that would coincide with the "end" of the 5,125-year-old Mayan calender, causing the transformation of the world.[26] Throughout the world there would occur numerous supernatural events, including devastating earthquakes, UFO landings, communication with extraterrestrials and other "spirit guides," and the return of the Aztec god Quetzalcoatl. He called on "144,000 true believers" to converge and form a human power grid to correct the earth's wandering frequency of 7.8 hertz, which would help usher in the new age.[27]

Worldwide, crowds gathered at the great pyramids, Stonehenge, Machu Picchu, and dozens of other "sacred sites" identified as places for believers to converge. In the United States 350 sacred sites were designated as official converging grounds, including Ohio's Great Serpent Mound, New York's Niagara Falls, and the Palace in Hollywood. On the big Sunday, there were some claims of supernatural events. At the pyramids some claimed to have seen flying saucers, while others said they saw images of the Virgin Mary. One medium in Santa Fe, New Mexico, channeled an angel on her television screen and set up a "video shrine" surrounded by dozens of crystals, which did give the shrine a kind of sun-reflected glory. Hundreds of pilgrims and curiosity-seekers came to witness and gawk at the celestial TV spook of Santa Fe. However, there were no mass landings of UFOs, no earthquakes rocked mother earth, and there was no sign of Quetzalcoatl. However, Arguelles and those in the New Age movement argued that the "harmonic convergence" was only the beginning of a new spiritual awakening that was now unfolding and would be accelerating as the new millennium dawned.[27]

Some of the New Age's rising stars over the past decade have included poet and "men's movement" guru Robert Bly, who encourages men to get in touch with their masculine instincts and warrior mythology. Mythologist Joseph Campbell unwittingly provided a certain amount of legitimacy to those on the New Age fringe with his scholarly depiction of universal myths and their power to affect individuals and cultures. On the shelves of New Age book stores, books by Campbell and by anthropologists covering the historical and cultural nature of myth and religious diversity reside near books by actress and New Age guru Shirley MacLaine, the channeled extraterrestrial spirit "Ramtha," and "official" Salem witch Laurie Cabot. There are also volumes on healings, spirit guides, UFOs, and even books on the great world religions, such as the *Bhagavad Gita*, *The Teachings of Buddha*, and the Bible.

The New Age subculture, like that of survivalism, is extensive and eclectic. In fact, a basic value among many New Age followers is that most anything goes, in a religious and spiritual sense. Witchcraft, Eastern religions, Christianity, shamanism, numerous forms of "paganism," and even UFOlogy—the study of UFOs, extraterrestrials, and the "relative" dimensions of time and space—oftentimes are combined to form a postmodern spiritual worldview that is culturally relative, global, and millennial. The New Age movement also blends elements from environmentalism, feminism, and, more recently, men's "primal heritage."

While there is tremendous diversity within the New Age movement, there is also the notion of "wholeness"; many New Age followers seek to build spiritual and communal relationships among the world's religions. Witches and other New Agers often speak of the holistic nature of their worldview, which includes an optimistic and "progressive" form of the millennial myth that looks forward to a new and better world. New Age belief is largely devoid of tribulations of decay, demonic dragons and beasts, and the carnage of Armageddon that so inspires Christian fundamentalists, survivalists, and other millennialists on the right. While avoiding specific dates, many New Agers feel that we are on the verge of a new millennium, when things will change dramatically throughout the world. Across the country New Age bookstores and even witch communities have sprung up in response to the New Age movement and its millennial aspirations and have begun to affect their surrounding communities.

*The best thing about Salem is that it's the latter part of Jerusalem, So, Shalom.* (ROCK 'N' ROLL PREACHER JACK, SALEM, MASSACHU-SETTS)[28]

*The connection with the New Age community in Salem has to do with the power center or lay line that is here—a spiritual core that has existed since the onset of time.* (LAURIE CABOT, "OFFICIAL WITCH" OF SALEM, MASSACHUSETTS)[29]

In some places the New Age presence has come to dominate the social, cultural, and economic environment of the community. Salem, Massachusetts, for example, is a place that has become a center for New Age consciousness, particularly that of modern-day witches. Why would a community notorious for a sensational "witch hunt" some 300 years ago now celebrate its witchcraft heritage? Salem reflects another conflict over the postmodern confusion between old and new religious beliefs and social changes reflecting new cultural values and the erosion of old ones.

While the incidence of witch hunting in seventeenth-century New England was not limited to Salem, nor does its occurrence compare with the witch pogroms of medieval Europe, it is the Salem experience that is of most interest to Americans. The hysteria is generally believed to have been triggered by Puritan Minister Samuel Parrish's Caribbean slave Tituba, who cared for and entertained the minister's daughter and her friends during the long winter months with tales of voodoo and examples of sorcery. A series of children's experiments in sorcery and magic followed, to which the Puritans overreacted.

The girls began to have fits, shaking violently and screaming in agony over real or imagined pains. They also began to experience hallucinations and claimed that they were possessed by demons. Examination of the children by a doctor could find no apparent cause, until they were asked, perhaps encouraged, to name those who were persecuting them. They accused three elderly women in the community, as well as Tituba, of afflicting them through witchcraft and being in league with the Devil. Civil magistrates, encouraged by the clergy, set up a special court and chose Samuel Sewall,

John Hathorne (ancestor of Nathaniel Hawthorne), and William Stoughton as judges. The finger pointing continued, while people were arrested and jailed on nothing other than accusations of witchcraft.

The Salem witch trials commenced in May of 1692 and ended in the conviction of several individuals on the basis of "spectral evidence"—the visions of witches, demons, and devils conjured up by young girls influenced by fits of hysteria, hallucination, and adult supervision. At the height of the hysteria over 200 people were imprisoned, including the wife of Governor William Phipps. In the course of the year of 1692, 19 "witches" were hanged, tradition has it, from trees on Gallows Hill, their bodies unceremoniously dumped in rocky crevices deep in the surrounding hills. Others died in prison, and one, Giles Cory, was pressed to death for refusing to admit guilt. The last hangings took place on September 22, 1692. In the end 24 members of the Massachusetts Bay Colony (17 women, 6 men, and 1 child) were dead as a result of the hysteria. Eventually, public opinion began to condemn the witch hunt, and legal action eventually put an end to the trials. The General Court (legislature) adopted a resolution for repentance (December 17, 1696), including a fast day on which Sewall publicly admitted the injustice of the trials.[30]

Historians point to the underlying social changes in Salem that contributed to the conflict, including the economic tensions between the farming community of Salem Village and the more prosperous and growing town of Salem.[31] Others have pointed out that most of the accused and executed were women over 40 years of age, whose personal and family lives were different from the norm, in that most most stood to inherit or did inherit larger portions of property and wealth than male heirs. Such analysis points to the fear of strong women as resting at the heart of the Salem hysteria.[32]

Over the years Salem was branded with the name "Witch City," an insult to the community that failed its members so miserably. But 300 years later, the name "Witch City" has returned, not in a negative light, but in a positive and commercial one. Today

Salem has become a kind of Disney World of witchcraft. Indeed, Witch City attracts over a million visitors a year and its major industry—tourism—centers on witchcraft. Salem celebrates the legacy of ignorance, hatred, and superstition with a month-long Mardi Gras-like "haunted happenings" during the Halloween season, as well as an annual "witches' ball." The Witch Dungeon, The Witch Museum, The Witch House, and The House of the Seven Gables compete with witch shops, tarot card readers, and New Age bookstores for tourist dollars. Salem has become a commercial "heritage industry" of witchcraft "museums," shops, and other tourist attractions, proudly proclaiming itself the "witchcraft and Halloween capital of the world."

The reinscription of Witch City has gone even further with the evolution of a witchcraft community in Salem. Salem's most famous modern witch, Laurie Cabot, helped bring New Age witchcraft to Salem in the early 1970s. In her shop, Crow's Haven Corner, now run by her daughters, who are also witches, she reads tarot cards, convenes her coven, and lobbies on behalf of witches, witchcraft, and the future of the New Age movement. She is also author of three books on witchcraft and sorcery, including *Power of the Witch* and *Pagan Seasons.*

In 1978 Cabot was named "official witch of Salem" by then Massachusetts governor Michael Dukakis. Laurie Cabot, now in her sixties, is a black-robed, former Californian who first came to Salem in 1978, and has been the most visible of an estimated 3,000 witches living in and around Salem. Cabot is founder of the Salem-based Witches' League for Public Awareness, "a proactive educational network dedicated to correcting misinformation about witches."[33] With Cabot's help Salem has become a local center for New Age consciousness and the numerous occult businesses and practitioners that have arisen with the New Age tide. Astrologers, palmists, tarot card readers, channelers, and seers abound in Salem and in many nearby towns. The New Age Bookstore, the Occult Book Shop, the Crystal Chamber, Laurie Cabot's Crow's Haven Corner, and even a shop devoted to angels called Angelica of the Angels cater to the local witchcraft and New

Age community, as well as to the larger witchcraft tourist mecca that Salem has become.

In addition to the Salem witchcraft history and the memory of its victims, who she views as martyrs, Cabot came to Salem because of its supernatural significance. "There is a power here, not present in most other places," she says. "It has a center of energy that other towns along this coast do not have, and that's what attracts people who are spiritually inclined." She also believes that "there is a supernatural undercurrent that runs through this area and causes it to be charged, and to be a very spiritual place." On the subject of a new age of spiritual bliss and harmony, Cabot's views mirror those of the greater New Age community. "Indeed, we are on the cusp of an Aquarian Age," Cabot says, referring to the predictions of some spiritually minded counterculturalists back in the 1960s, "and Salem is a good place to be."[34]

A place like Salem, then, with its historical and magical significance to witches and others attuned to the New Age movement, is of significance to those awaiting a more perfect age. This is apparent in the Salem New Age Center, a clearing house for information about Salem's New Age subculture and the practices and cosmologies of the larger New Age movement. The center promotes the belief that our planet and its entire population are literally moving into a new age of harmony, progress, higher consciousness, and spiritual awakening.[35]

Many New Agers point to the approach of the "photon belt" as the cosmic force that is going to alter the earth and its inhabitants and usher in the new age. Proponents of the theory claim that during the closing years of the twentieth century our solar system is due to pass through a massive photon belt—an area of outer space that has high-energy properties similar to a field of charged particles, like the plasma in the atmospheres of stars or the Aurora Borealis. Reportedly, the photon belt is a massive band of intense photon (light) energy that is on a collision course with earth. Supposedly, our solar system enters this area of the galaxy once every 11,000 years, and stays in the photon band for 2,000 years.[36]

To many New Agers, the photon belt first appeared during the 1960s (the beginning of the Aquarian Age), when scientists began to see further into the universe, detecting new galaxies and other cosmological wonders. Proponents of the photon belt theory point out that many scientists are fully aware of the astronomical event, but do not appreciate its spiritual significance. In the advancing science of astronomy, pseudoscientists and astrologers of the newly emerging New Age movement also see altered planetary alignments, "harmonic convergences," and cosmic transformations. As the millennium approaches, they predict, so will the photon belt. And when it gets here, things will change dramatically.

According to photon belt theory, during the early stages of the photon belt eclipse, around the time of the millennium, there will be an increase in seismic activity worldwide and dramatic changes in global weather patterns. Predicted are periods of extended darkness, mass UFO landings, psychic abilities for all humans, and physical and spiritual transformations of our bodies. Many believers in the theory point to the recent interest in channeling, witchcraft, UFO sightings, messianic cults, and the anticipated arrival of a "fifth dimension" as evidence of photon belt influence. It is an exciting time, argue many of Salem's New Agers, and we should be optimistic toward the millennium because we are on the cusp of a new and better age of physical and spiritual enlightenment and transformation.

There are those in Salem, however, who not not see the New Age millennium as predicted by Salem's "occult" community. In the Salem witches and the larger New Age movement, they see signs of the decadence of modern society and the evils wielded by demonic forces in the world today—especially in places like Salem. A visible and vocal Christian fundamentalist community is opposed to the presence of the New Age and witchcraft communities in Salem. For much of the past decade, several local churches, mostly small nondenominational sects, have routinely organized in opposition to the witches by confronting them on street corners and in shops and by holding "anti-Halloween" services on Halloween night, which is one of the witches' most important spiritual days.

Those opposed to the witchcraft community in Salem on religious grounds include the Reverend Russell Ely, a local fundamentalist minister who believes that along with promoting their business of witchcraft, local witches are promoting a diabolical religion. He and others have accused local witches of "experimenting with demonic forces" and warns of a "national epidemic of the occult."[37] Over the years, Ely and some of the more vocal religious critics of Salem witchcraft have promoted antiwitch crusades and produced and disseminated literature warning of Salem's occult problems. Members of these local groups often protest in front of witchcraft or New Age boutiques, handing out leaflets such as "The Dark Side of Halloween" and "The Truth about Salem Witchcraft." Small nondenominational churches hold seminars on cults and bring in "experts" and "deprogrammers"—oftentimes members of affiliated churches—who claim to be consultants to law enforcement agencies in their investigation of occult groups. Followers of these Christian groups go into the New Age and witchcraft stores citing Scripture and warning of the demonism behind the religion of witchcraft and the New Age heresy. In several instances police have had to be called in when protesters disrupted business in the stores.

Local fundamentalist ministers also like to point out the true meaning of the name Salem, which was given to the village by Puritan pilgrims. In a reference to Jerusalem and the promised land, earlier Puritans had referred to what is now Boston as the "city on the Hill." In 1626, Roger Conant led a small band of pilgrims from Cape Ann to a small, sheltered coastal area to the southeast (north of Boston), popular among local Indians for its fishing. Incorporated as a town in 1630, the new Puritan community called itself Salem, "the city of peace," a biblical allusion to Salem in Zion, but also popularly identified with Jerusalem.

Today, witches and Christians battle it out in the local newspapers, revealed in such lurid headlines as "Religious Zealots Hunt Witches," "Paganism, Unlike Christianity, Has Nothing to Hide," and "Religious Fanatics Use Hate Campaign against Witchcraft." The other side counters with "Demonic Activity behind Witchcraft," "Witchcraft: A Cult Deserving of No Recognition from Salem," and "Claim Disputed about Witchcraft Being Oldest Religion."[38] The conflict between the witches and fundamentalists erupts from time to time, such as during Salem's summer festival, "Heritage Days," when the town has traditionally celebrated its history. In recent years the witchcraft hysteria, and how to interpret it—"to celebrate or commemorate"—has politicized the event. Local witches, for example, now march in the parade and proudly proclaim their faith.

In 1991, during the Heritage Days parade, a group of about 20 local Christians surrounded and verbally assaulted marching witches with biblical quotations aimed at the witches, including the verse, "We bind the powers of darkness." The witches quickly formed their own inner circle and began singing and bestowing blessing upon the Christians, some of whom thought they were being cursed by demons. To modern witches and followers of the New Age, Salem is a spiritual and magical place. To some Christian fundamentalists, Salem is not a spiritual utopia, but a demonic center, its apocalyptic significance that of the Battle of Armageddon against the forces of evil.

*What is at stake here is a big idea. It's not about one small country. It's about a new world order.* (GEORGE BUSH, STATE OF THE UNION ADDRESS, JANUARY 24, 1991)

*If I am elected President of the United States, the minute I raise my hand to take that oath of office that new world order comes crashing down.* (PATRICK BUCHANAN, NEW HAMPSHIRE PRIMARY VICTORY SPEECH, FEBRUARY 15, 1996)

*But as for the cowardly and unbelieving, and abominable and murderers, and fornicators and sorcerers, and idolaters and all liars, their portion shall be in the pool that burns with fire and brimstone, which is the second death.* (REV. 21:16–23, ACE)

Nineteen hundred and ninety was an auspicious year for the cause of democracy and the hope for a more peaceful new millennium. In addition to the end of the Cold War and Soviet communism, the year witnessed democratic elections held from Poland to

Nicaragua. Nelson Mandela was freed, and the leader of the Soviet Union won the Noble peace prize. Economics and trade across world markets seemed the exclusive arbiters of fate and fortune for the future. While some analysts spoke of the "relative economic decline" of the United States, others spoke of a "multipolar world" where the United States and the Soviet Union would cooperate with new and diverse world powers. The two superpowers formed an alliance to enter space programs together and vowed to forge other political and cultural alliances. Multinational companies, now calling themselves "global corporations," jockeyed for position to enter lucrative new markets formerly closed to them. The international effort to take on the villainy of Saddam Hussein also demonstrated that new global cooperation could be achieved.

Despite the greater complexity of the matter of Saddam Hussein and his annexation of Kuwait—including the history of the region, the increasing stratification between wealthy oil-producing nations and poor ones, and American and European complicity in the "making" of Saddam Hussein—the entire matter was defined by Bush more simply: Saddam was evil, and he had to be stopped in order to preserve the new world order. So George Bush dispatched a military force to the Persian Gulf while Secretary of State James Baker hustled together an international alliance, won the support of the Soviet president, and turned to the United Nations Security Council.

The UN authorized economic sanctions, an embargo, and then military action. Thirteen nations sent troops to the Gulf and several others dispatched supplies, equipment, and money. Such broad solidarity among nations had been unmatched since the end of World War II. Was this the stuff of the new world order? After five months of military buildup, political posturing, and some last-minute negotiations, Bush gave Saddam an ultimatum: Get out of Kuwait by January fifteenth or else! Bush had "drawn a line in the sand."

On January 16, 1991, the United States and its allies launched a massive and devastating air attack on the Iraqi armed forces and much of the Iraqi infrastructure that would topple Saddam, or so we thought. After a month of continuous air assault, aimed at "softening up" the enemy, the ground assault began. Militarily, Operation Desert Storm was meticulously planned and unhesitatingly executed by General H. Norman Schwarzkopf, his coalition counterparts, and half a million soldiers. It was "won" quickly and with an astoundingly low number of allied casualties and an equally astoundingly high number of enemy killed. However, several years later, Saddam is still in power and Iraq is on the verge of attaining nuclear capabilities.

The policies that guided the Bush administration during the early months of the Gulf conflict saw the president move shakily from one justification to the next. First, the safety of American oil was the reason for checking the aggression of Iraq. But when critics called that self-serving, Bush switched tactics and said that Kuwait and Saudi Arabian democracy were at stake. However, once it was pointed out that neither nation was a democracy, the president quickly moved on to another strategy. Finally, he hit upon the idea of the preserving the "new world order." This was the phrase that stuck, a millennial phrase that struck at the heart of American political mythology. It also resonated with the momentous changes continuing in Europe since the end of of 1989. The Persian Gulf War provided a test of these secular millennial changes. It resonated in a different way, however, to conspiracy theorists on the right, who want to destroy the new world order. For them, George Bush had it backward. But, of course, many of them also believed that George Bush was part of the conspiracy.

The victory over the tyranny in the Gulf was heralded by Bush and most Americans as a positive sign of the future world order that was emerging, a world of greater cooperation between nations, of shared responsibility for the protection of the earth's natural resources, and of the peace, security, and freedom of the world's citizens. In the phrase "new world order" was also the hope that on a political level the nations of the world would be able to solve their differences peacefully. If not, then the decision of the "world body" or "world government" would enforce its mandate, just as the United Nations had done in the Gulf. The language of the new world order became a millennial call to build a new global cooperation on earth, however secular it might be.

In the images and meanings of the new world order we find another symbol of the millennium, a worldview based on the values of greater cooperation between nations, a larger world community, and shared responsibilities. One thing the Persian Gulf War did was demonstrate that Americans could work together with old and new allies to bring to heel a world-class tyrant. Indeed, the interactions between and among nations today is unprecedented in the history of the world. Technology has allowed communications between individuals and groups anywhere in the world in a matter of seconds. The Internet is the most spectacular of the recent communications technologies to reflect that power. Globally, economies are becoming more linked and interdependent. What happens on the other side of the world can affect us here too.

In the vast social changes that are breaking down the walls that used to separate the great variety of cultures in the world, other groups see signs of disaster. While some may speak of the new world order in optimistic terms, others perceive evil designs and a conspiracy on the part of certain groups to promote an immoral, non-Christian, and "un-American" world, a world that might destroy their own "American" way of life, a life they've grown to revere and love. The militias see this evil in unrestrained government law enforcement and believe the new world order to mean the erosion of an ethos and an American way of life—a belief that may be a myth itself.

To white supremacist survivalists, the new world order is viewed in terms of multiculturalism, cultural relativism, political correctness, and "polyglot mud people"—immigrants and minorities despised by the Aryan Nations and other white supremacists and viewed as henchmen to the Jews. They point to the *Protocols of the Learned Elders of Zion* and to the belief in the mythical Jewish-led conspiracy to take over the world, a truly apocalyptic event. Not surprising, perhaps, is the fact that some racist groups support Louis Farrakhan and other black "separativists," who have advocated the separation of the races.

On the Christian right, the new world order is seen in terms of "secular humanism" and its threats to Christianity. In the widespread cases of homosexuality, legalized abortion, New Age cults, cultural hedonism, crumbling families, and sexually explicit and violent popular culture, the Christian right sees demons' hands, the golden calf of capitalism, and the decay of the American Babylon. And there is Theodore Kaczynski, the alleged Unabomber, who is convinced that the complex industrial and technological world we have created is about to collapse, so let's help it along by hurling bombs at the "system." The new world order for these groups is a "global Babylon" in the last stages of life, bound to fall, but from its ashes will arise a promised land to those who can survive it.

Both conservative Christians and right-wing "Patriots" have found a champion for their causes in Patrick Buchanan. In light of the widespread changes sweeping the world and their effects on the United States, we can better understand Buchanan's "America-first" attitude, which seems to unite so many on the ultra-right wing in American society today. Heralded by conservative leaders such as Pat Robertson and Jesse Helms, the "America-first" philosophy is becoming a nationalist movement. Patrick Buchanan—political commentator, former Nixon speech writer, and perennial presidential candidate—is a Washington insider and the longtime "bulldog" of the Republican party.

However, Buchanan has distanced himself from the mainstream Washington "elite" in the Republican party and has allied himself with disgruntled, mostly white Middle Americans suffering the strains of economic restructuring, supposedly caused by government and international schemes. In their name he trumpeted "America first" and said that if he were elected president, he would to stop illegal immigration, abolish affirmative action, restrict imports, halt foreign aid, and pull the United States out of the United Nations.

Buchanan has also reached out to the Christian right, who have welcomed the conservative Roman Catholic into their flock, particularly Ralph Reed, GOP lobbyist for the Christian right and spokesman for Pat Robertson's Christian Coalition. Like Jerry Falwell's Moral Majority of the 1980s, the Christian Coalition builds bridges between various conservative Christian organizations, promoting Christian causes and candidates, and it serves as a spiritual and political action committee for the religious right. Buchanan champions their moral crusades against abortion and the "abominations" of gay and lesbian marriages and adoptions in America. Alongside many fundamentalists, he advocates returning prayer to the public schools and never misses an opportunity to refer to the United States a "Christian nation." "Praise the Lord and shut down the borders, the barbarians are at the gate," seems to be Buchanan's rallying cry.

Unlike George Bush, who promoted the idea of a new world order in millennial terms, Buchanan spins yarns of conspiracy theory, just like those of the survivalist right. In stump speeches and on talk shows he rails against the United Nations, the World Bank, and the World Trade Organization for usurping the United States' sovereignty. During the 1996 presidential primary in New Hampshire, which Buchanan won, the "longshot" candidate addressed the New Hampshire legislature and said, "If I am elected president of the United States, the minute I raise my hand to take that oath of office that *new world order* comes crashing down" (italics mine). "I give my word," he told New Hampshire voters, "I know that those folks in Tokyo, New York, Paris, Bonn, Brussels—they love this idea of world government."[39]

Perhaps what the "new world order" really means is that in many issues the United States is no longer strong enough to impose its wishes unilaterally. Globalization makes dialogue, not dictate, the only way to build international consensus. In the eyes of the American administration, the Gulf War provided the context for converting this cooperative spirit into decisive action. If and how it will hold remains to be seen. It may be that Bush was right, although not to the extent that he may have imagined. The Persian Gulf War may represent the final remnants of the old world order, but that old world order also might include American hegemony in the world and the American millennial myth.

Although the Gulf crisis seems to have undermined the notion that the United States is in decline, in a curious way it does confirm the assertion of Paul Kennedy (1987) that the United States may be overreaching, like other empires before it, by acting as a kind of global police officer, gaining short-term advantage but long-term disadvantage. It is interesting to note how Bush's new world order echoes a line in Kennedy's cautionary book, *The Rise and Fall of the Great Powers*, that "the only serious threat to the real interests of the United States can come from a failure to adjust sensibly to the newer world order."[40]

We are coming to live in a new world order, though I'm not sure how orderly it will be. But a type of global society is evolving, providing new opportunities and new dangers. At the same time that a more connected and thus smaller world is evolving, we are also learning how different we are from each other. We may all watch CNN, but we do not watch from the same perspective, which is dictated by our experiences and everyday lives. Still, a new world *something* does appear to be emerging. Change is more rapid and wide reaching than ever before. Will it mean greater world order or greater world chaos?

W hile the millennium is an arbitrary mark on the calendar and may mean little to non-Christians, it is nonetheless pregnant with historical symbolism and mythical power. The approaching millennial year 2000 is calculated from the birth of Jesus Christ in Bethlehem, in the year when Caesar Augustus sat on the throne of the Roman Empire. A millennial observation had occurred only once before—in the year 1000. One early commentator, a Burgundian monk born about 975 by the name of Raoul Glaber, wrote in his *Histories* that during the year 1000 there was tremendous panic and millennial expectation in medieval Europe, Jerusalem, and throughout the holy land. Glaber spoke of signs and omens occurring in the holy land: People claimed to see the devil in many different shapes; to see a giant dragon descending from northern skies; to see crucifixes and Virgin Mary statues weeping, and great earthquakes, hail storms, and hurricanes plagued the massive crowds of pilgrims converging on Jerusalem.[1]

Except for Glaber's *Histories*, there is little historical or geological evidence to support his fantastic assessment of the apocalyptic events during the year 1000. A few years earlier, in the year 993, Mount Vesuvius had erupted, which caused great panic and destruction. But the damage was not as great as that caused by the eruption on August 24, A.D. 79, which destroyed the ancient Italian cities of Pompeii and Herculaneum, covering them with up to 23 feet of volcanic debris. In those days Rome had not yet become Christian, so no millennial significance

was attached to that great event. The Roman Empire continued to expand. By 993 Rome had been Christian for almost 600
years and still, according to the available historical records,
no major figures drew any particular connection between the
eruption of Mount Vesuvius in 993 and the approach of the
first millennium.

Between 993 and 1000, a number of prominent kings and
clergy passed away, including Pope Gregory V in 999. But the
millennial significance of these events also went unnoticed by the
pope and the Council of Bishops of Rome, and by the Roman
Emperor Otto III, who began governing late in the year 1000. Most
contemporary historians now believe that little of great religious
significance actually occurred at the time of the first millennium
A.D. The year 1033 seems to have been more apocalyptic. Marking
2,000 years after Jesus' death, pilgrims amassed in the holy land in
unprecedented numbers. But they too were isolated to that year
and to the holy land. Not until 200 years later, with the onset of the
Crusades, was truly millennial rage unleashed with a power to
dramatically alter societies.[2]

Some have made the argument that the twenty-first century
does not begin technically until 2001, so there is no real millennial
significance to the year 2000. While they are right, it makes little
difference to everyone else, millennialist or not. Two thousand is
the big round number; it is the one with apocalyptic significance.
Also, we shouldn't expect millenarian movements and apocalyptic
prophecies to cease once the year 2000 is over. We can expect the
millennial zeal to roll on well into the following decade.

Still, this millennium is a special one, given the amount of time,
thought, and exuberance surrounding it. The reach of the millennial myth is worldwide now because the global scope of communications and the economic and cultural interdependence of
nations make it so. The world is so much aware of its various parts
and its connectedness that the shared experience of reaching a
major milestone like a millennium causes many of us to pause and
contemplate the past 1,000 years and wonder about the next. Given
the extent of communications technology, the dawn of the millen-

nium promises to be an event of global proportions, simultaneously observed all around the world.

In fact, the Millennium Society, founded by American college students in 1979, has already scheduled a global extravaganza to welcome in the new millennium. The 6,000-member international organization has booked the Queen Elizabeth 2 to transport 1,750 people from New York City to Alexandria, Egypt. The celebrants will continue their millennial quest on the ground to the great pyramids at Giza. Invited guests, who have paid $10,000 each (most of which will go to a charity for international student exchange programs) will include former presidents Reagan and Bush and their wives, former Beatle Paul McCartney, as well as hundreds more of the rich and famous.[3]

As the millennium emerges, the millennial rage and zeal will be played out through a multitude of symbolic forms, be they rituals of birth, life, decay, death, or afterlife. It is a grand myth that provides a huge picture—a frame of reference— concerning our place in the universe and the meaning of life through the ages. The millennium also forces us to ponder what is beyond the year 2000. This question of what lies ahead sends our religious and secular prophets and futurists into a frenzy, and there is no shortage of prognostications for life in the twenty-first century. As always, there are the doomsayers and the undeterred optimists.

From the apocalyptic warnings of Christian fundamentalists to New Age aspirations for a holistic world community to the paranoia of militias and survivalists over the supposed global conspiracy to bring about the collapse of society and a new world order, the millennial myth thrives in the United States. It is a deep-seated religious tradition that prophesies the final events in the history of humankind, and it informs the beliefs and practices of these and many new and revitalized social movements and cultural trends in the United States. But the flames of the millennial rage are fanned by widespread, fast-moving social and cultural changes that are truly transforming people's lives and bringing about some kind of new world order or disorder. The fact that this change coincides with the turn of the millennium may only be a coincidence, but it focuses attention on the historical moment and enhances the expectations of some for utter devastation or a new beginning.

The sweeping social and cultural changes that are creating a more globally oriented world have transformed the apocalyptic beliefs of the small towns, rural villages, and colonial outposts of earlier periods into the millennial rage of the middle-class sectors of our modern industrial societies. Today, millennial expressions are myriad and fragmented, appearing in messianic movements like the Branch Davidians, as well as in the most contemporary images of the mass media and popular culture. Seemingly unconnected trends such as survivalism, messianic cults, extraterrestrial abductee groups, witchcraft, New Age consciousness, and post-apocalyptic films all play a role in the widespread "pop apocalypticism" that has evolved in our culture.

In addition to the "classical" religious forms, the millennial rage has taken in Christian fundamentalism, for example; secular or nonreligious forms are flourishing as well, such as "boy scout" survivalists, patriot "constitutionalists," and the militia movement. Secular millenarian movements read into the contemporary social problems of society, government ineptitude, villainy, and a conspiracy to impose a tyrannical new world order on unsuspecting Americans. The current social system has become viewed through an apocalyptic lens, where the American government or the United Nations become symbols of Babylon; its leaders and architects become demonic characters like the beast, the dragon, and the Antichrist; and a deteriorating environment and rapidly changing world are the signs of the decay and destruction foretold in the seven seals of Revelation.

There is a strong relationship between revolutionary and nationalist movements and the millennial myth. While their aspirations may be purely political, movement leaders often incite doomsday predictions or a utopian millennium in order to provide a credo and motivation for followers, as well as to bring legitimacy to their sometimes questionable words and actions. From the apocalyptic "manifest destiny" of the expansionist United States in the ninteenth century to George Bush's clarion call to preserve the new world order in the Gulf, American nationalist and cultural movements have been fueled by millennial rhetoric.

For much of this century, more than a quarter of the world's population was controlled by political movements and organizations that prophesied their own millennial paradises on earth. Stalin, Mao, and Hitler were all intensely nationalistic. They also used millennial symbolism to render their actions legitimate and to provide meaning for their followers, as they attempted to build their own communist- or nationalist-inspired kingdoms—secular equivalents of the earthly paradise of Revelation. While not always overtly apocalyptic, they were as much millennial as the more conventional religious movements. The millennial myth has always left its mark on the nationalist social movements and political revolutions that have developed throughout history.

Often in the spirit of those millennial dreams, national or revolutionary movements have committed genocide, the deliberate and systematic destruction of entire peoples—often the citizens of their own nation—because of their race, religion, political ideology, or ethnic identity. In the twentieth century there have been many examples of genocide perpetrated in the name of communism, fascism, and ethnic purity. For example, at the outbreak of World War I, Turkish authorities deported the whole Armenian population of about 1,750,000 to Syria and Iraq. Removal of the Armenians to these desert regions resulted in the loss of an estimated 600,000 lives en route by exposure, starvation, and massacre. Hitler would later consciously emulate the Turks' tactics through his own "final solution" to ridding the world of Jews and other undesirable peoples, including gypsies, Catholics, and homosexuals.

The rule of Joseph Stalin, head of the Communist Party and state leader of the Soviet Union for over a quarter of a century (1929–1953), also used brutal repression, mass killings, and genocidal mania. In 1928, as part of his massive plan for social reorganization, Stalin launched an intensive industrial and agricultural campaign that included the massive relocation of whole communities and repressive measures to control dissidents. During the reorganization, millions of innocent peasants and other laborers perished through relocation, hard labor, harsh prison sentences, torture, and executions. During the 1930s, Stalin also supervised the purges of the Communist Party, which ended in the execution of most of those revolutionaries who in 1917 had begun the Russian Revolution. In the 1930s and 1940s the "cult of personality" that had evolved around Stalin, and that he himself cultivated, took on the proportions of a national religion. Official propaganda played upon populist legends and ranked Stalin next to the great czars Peter and Ivan and other heroes of Russian history, and thus the natural inheritor of absolute authority.

Genocidal mania continued into midcentury; for example, in Cambodia following the American withdrawal from Vietnam. Pol Pot and his Khmer Rouge killed an estimated one million Cambodians beginning in 1975, the revolutionary "Year Zero." More recently thousands have been slaughtered in Rwanda, the result of ethnic rivalry, civil war, and the legacy of French and Belgium colonialism. And in the aftermath of the collapse of the Soviet Union, nationalist politicians fanned the embers of ethnic and religious tension between the Serbs, Bosnians, and Croatians in the former Yugoslavia that exploded into civil war, including the mass killings of Bosnian Muslims and Croats by Serbian nationalists through a program of "ethnic cleansing."

While we may never know the precise number of casualties due to the Bosnian civil war, U.S. officials have suggested as a conservative number 250,000 dead or missing, mostly innocent noncombatants, including thousands of children. In certain ways the millennial myth provides both inspiration and justification for those who commit genocide. In our own country there are those who see in this international turmoil and genocidal mania one more sign of the tribulations that are to accompany the end times. To the extent that such a view explains these tragedies, it may also serve to reduce the believers' outrage, perhaps even to condone such brutality, since these kinds of events were predicted in the Bible, and we need to pass through the bloody crucible to reach the glorious millennium.

During the 1995 New Hampshire primary, word leaked out that presidential candidate Patrick Buchanan's campaign cochairman, Larry Pratt, allegedly had connections to some of the most racist, anti-Semitic, and heavily armed organizations on the far right. Pratt has insisted that he "unknowingly" associated with these groups, but Kenneth Stern of the American Jewish Committee has chronicled many sightings of Pratt within the paramilitary subculture. Not only was Pratt attending these meetings, according to Stearn, but he was also speaking before them and promoting the philosophy of "Buchananism" to groups such as the Aryan Nations, the Ku Klux Klan, and countless other paramilitary and militia groups, whose heroes Bo Gritz and Mark Koernke were reportedly in attendance.[4]

Pratt appears to have many connections. He is commandant of Gun Owners of America, a political action group that gave money to 19 Republican campaigns for the House or Senate in 1994. The biggest check went to Steve Stockman, a Texas freshman who backed the militia movement after the Oklahoma City explosion. Pratt has been seen in the company of Pete Peters, the Christian Identity leader who warns that Jews are children of the devil. Peters also claims that racial minorities are subhuman. He has also been tied to the religious right group the Committee to Protect the Family (CPF), which has warned of gay terrorists intentionally contaminating the blood supply to spread AIDS. The CPF has also raised funds for Randall Terry's militant antiabortion organization Operation Rescue.[5]

Finally, Pratt is affiliated with the Council for National Policy, an umbrella organization of right wingers that includes House majority leader Dick Armey, House majority whip Tom Delay, Senator Jesse Helms, G.O.P. strategist and executive director of the Christian Coalition Ralph Reed, the Reverend Pat Robertson, head of the Christian Broadcast Network (CBN) and founder of the Christian Coalition, and the Reverend Donald Wildmon who, like Pratt, was a cochairman of Buchanan's 1996 presidential campaign. Amid a flurry of accusations and bad press, Larry Pratt was forced to take a leave of absence from his cochairmanship of the Buchanan campaign. But he symbolizes an important segment of Patrick

Buchanan's populist appeal among right-wing fundamentalists, white supremacists, and new world order conspiracy theorists. That these grassroots groups could grow into a larger nationalist "America first" movement—a kind of American millennial fascism—is a speculation we might seriously consider.

Buchanan's American first campaign also underscores how the classical, or more clearly religious, forms of millennialism have adapted secular elements to the current social and political issues. This is the way the millennial myth works, by providing the stories of apocalyptic texts and interpreting current events through them. When Christian fundamentalists Jerry Falwell and Pat Robertson suggest that nuclear war, environmental degradation, or AIDS may be God's way of fulfilling Scripture—as in the "plagues" unleashed by the seven seals—a rational understanding of these secular issues becomes challenged by a supernatural or apocalyptic one.[6] Conversely, when militias, survivalists, or *Soldier of Fortune* enthusiasts apply apocalyptic language and imagery to their interpretation of current events, they are also transforming the secular into the sacred. In the process there has occurred a melding of apocalyptic scenarios of the classical religious groups with those of secular millennial types.

The American survivalist subculture provides one area where contemporary forms of the American millennial myth are expressed in both religious and secular ways. I have defined survivalism in terms of cultural "sites," which encompass survivalists, their literature, products, practices, conventions, and Internet activity. These "sites" provide the forum for the dynamic process in which the myth is communicated, fragmented, and reproduced. Although altered in form to fit the meaning of its users, symbols and images of the millennial myth such as the Apocalypse, Armageddon, and Babylon are appropriated by *Soldier of Fortune* magazine, the Patriot movement, the militias, and white supremacist groups.

In important ways survivalism represents the downside of the millennial myth, the part that predicts decay, mass destruction, and mass death. But it also prophesies "redemption" in the manner of surviving "the great cosmic battle" and living on to build a "new world," though not that of supposed one-world-government conspirators or the fictitious Jewish Elders of Zion. For survivalists the collapse of civilization will require adaptation to a preindustrial way of life, where independence, individualism, small communities, and greater autonomy will be the rewards; such is the postindustrial world envisioned by the Unabomber.

Like the classical myth, this important dual nature is always present. In Revelation we see the terrible side of the myth in the decay of tribulations and the destructive war of Armageddon. But we also witness the hope of salvation in the return of the Messiah and the dream of a utopian kingdom in the millennium. This duality provides flexibility for the myth and allows for a wide range of interpretive meaning and staying power. It is also important to point that out the the millennial myth is not "monolithic," with a single meaning influencing all in the same way. The power of the millennial myth rests in its protean adaptation to change and its ability to mirror the experiences of many different groups, as the American version of the myth has done throughout American history.

The survivalist ethic is a part of the American millennial myth, the myth of the "individual" and of the pioneer who holds in his hand the destiny of the nation, expanding the "rim of Christendom" by carving a civilization out of the wilderness. Through the millennial myth, many survivalists, militiamen, "Patriots," and "Christian survivalists" see America as the "redeemer nation"—the primary defender of freedom, democracy, Western civilization, and Christian heritage in the world. When used to justify or legitimate a cause, as in the case of the war with Iraq, the millennial myth becomes a tool for ideological and social control.

In this way we can see how the war with Iraq, fought in the name of the new world order, was an American version of the millennial myth. It served to legitimate the actions and practices of the state, particularly those that press for American economic, political, and military hegemony in the world, and a continued vigilance against evil forces. For President George Bush, employing the millennial call to build and preserve a new world order became a master stroke in the contemporary political application of the myth, though he probably failed to realize its opposite effect on the survivalist and conspiracy-minded right wing. While the new world order was never really defined by the president, for many Americans it seemed to provide the best justification for taking on Saddam Hussein, even if they had only a vague idea of what it meant. To many on the far right the new world order takes on a more ominous meaning, especially in the wake of Oklahoma City and the rise of the militia movement.

At the same time, the millennial myth is familiar to Americans in terms of the sensational exploits of apocalyptic cults like the Branch Davidians, the People's Temple, and the Moonies—and their messianic leaders David Koresh, Jim Jones, and Sun Myung Moon. We are also familiar with less sensational examples of apocalyptic thinking in our society, from the door-to-door evangelizing of Jehovah's Witnesses to the Bible-thumping, doomsday lamentations of fundamentalist preachers and televangelists. The millennial myth is so flexible in its ability to adapt to modern times that it has been invoked by many groups and even by the mass media and popular culture to explain contemporary events, as in the news stories with apocalyptic themes during the Persian Gulf War and in the live television coverage of the "Apocalypse at Waco."

To some members of the survivalist subculture the millennial myth becomes a set of organizing principles for making sense of a world that they see as out of control. In a general sense, the language and symbols of survivalism (if only in fantasy) express fear of the imminent decline of civilization, the vigilant war with "Satanic forces," and the necessity of developing survivalist strategies in order to live on—through individualism and a survival-of-the fittest philosophy—in a new world not of peace, harmony, and global cooperation but of mass destruction.

However, for those even further to the right, the myth has fractured in quite a different fashion. Here survivalism has evolved into a haven for religious cults, would-be mercenaries, white supremacists, right-wing anarchists, and apocalyptic thinkers. This combination of survivalism and apocalyptic thinking, which is on the increase, is a dangerous mix. While we have yet to learn the depths of the the Oklahoma City bombers' religious and political beliefs, we know enough about the subculture of survivalism that seems to have produced them to link them to a violent form of millenarian movement in the United States. To this segment of the survivalist subculture, talk of a new world order hearkens back to the *Protocols of the Learned Elders of Zion* and the supposed Jewish-led conspiracy to take over the world.

The paranoia of the survivalist right of the new world order, in contrast to George Bush's embrace of it during the Persian Gulf War in 1990, further reflects the often contradictory nature of contemporary expressions of the millennial myth. With the help of the mass media, which further obfuscates its history and meaning, the myth is freed up and its meaning goes up for grabs, to be manipulated by certain individuals and groups as they see fit or to be lodged in other sites in the culture, as in movies and popular music. In any case Americans are receptive to the symbols and images of the millennial myth, if only in fragmented and obscure expressions. Indeed, as we have seen with messianic sects like the Branch Davidians, in the Unabomber's secular analysis of global collapse and revolution, in the bombing in Oklahoma City, and in the deadly Amtrak derailment by the "sons of Gestapo," apocalyptic thinking's effects can blow up, quite literally, on the rest of society.

Just as there are various shades of survivalism, there are other forms of millennialism, not all of which are militaristic or survivalist in their understanding or approach to the millennium. Some of these represent millennial interpretations in opposition to both the dominant myth and to survivalism as well. Such movements may be "progressivist," seeing in Revelation metaphor and allegory, but in the real world, history is progressing through human action and creation. Such groups may espouse a millennium not reached through mass destruction but through its prevention and in the formulation of new beliefs and practices, as in the New Age movement. New Agers compose a millenarian movement that, like survivalism, fears the current "deteriorating" state of the world. However, they differ from survivalists in that they do not accept destruction as inevitable and, on the contrary, offer solutions in which self-initiative, creativity, civic action, and an openness to alternative lifestyle practices will lead to a new and better world. In these ways their interpretation of the millennial myth flies in the face of survivalists, militias, and white supremacists.

To the extent that buying crystals and practicing modern witchcraft have become New Age ways to "self-actualization," reminiscent of "the power of positive thinking," they may in fact only serve the extreme individualism of Americans and thus mirror the individualism and isolationism of the survivalist right. When environmentalists speak of the destruction of the ozone layer or the "greenhouse effect" in images of "environmental holocaust," they too may be buying into the destructive myths of survivalism and millennialism. At those moments when environmentalists and ecologists intersect the survivalists by defining our era's critical environmental problems in apocalyptic terms and through images of mass destruction, they may be, to some extent, defusing their own potential for strong oppositional and positive social change. But if they can retain and build upon the progressive and optimistic dimensions of the myth, as in the millennium and the "new Jerusalem," they may better serve their cause and enlist support.

Millennium rage reaches beyond the subcultural practice of survivalism into the American popular culture. In American television and film, in popular music, and in toys, games, and other leisure time activities, survivalism and apocalyptic themes and images permeate our popular culture. We all partake of the millennial myth at different moments and at various places. While fundamentalist Christians continue to heed the words of "fire-and-brimstone" preachers and to look for scriptural concordance between Revelation and current events, the general public is glued to its television sets watching the "Apocalypse in Waco," following the antics of militias, survivalists, and white supremacists, or viewing "postapocalyptic" films such as *Waterworld* (1995) and *12 Monkeys* (1996) and "alien invasion" films such as *The Arrival (1996)* and *Independence Day* and television shows such as *The X-Files, Alien Nation, Dark Skies,* and *Millennium.*

The point is not that we are all strongly influenced by the apocalyptic images in our culture, but that we are exposed to them continuously, and thus have become familiar enough with them to understand their basic meanings. So we do plug into the myth, and it plugs into us. If we pay attention, we can see the millennial myth as a floating framework for understanding one's life and destiny, and that of this nation and the world. It also provides the grist for the mill of cultural commentary and criticism. The myth is a transcendent entity, almost supernatural, in the life it has taken on, a life that we have given and continue to give it.

The resurgence of the millennial myth now should not surprise us. In the past, millennial movements often arose during periods of intense social change coinciding with the end of a century or an era. In many ways contemporary expressions of millennialism are a reflection of the major social changes the world is currently undergoing. The United States and much of the world are at a turning point. The fact that it is coinciding with the end of one millennium and the beginning of another may be only a coincidence, but it helps fulfill the prophecy that as the millennium approaches, so does a new era. But what kind of a new era is developing?

In important ways the world is different now than it was during periods in the past that faced tremendous change and upheaval. It is only since World War II that total world annihilation, whether through nuclear war or moribund environmental pollution, "has come to pass" as a real and palpable threat. Both the destructive potential of current world flare-ups and the mass communication of their horrifying images are two principle factors promoting millennialism in American society today. Famine, war, terrorism, and pollution have taken their place as the common fare of television news, film drama, literature, popular music, and even toys and games.

The real issues behind these images of nuclear devastation, economic collapse, and environmental pollution have intensified the belief, however subconsciously, of total world annihilation. What is more perplexing, and of primary concern, is that such massive disasters are not natural but manmade; a catastrophe could therefore be avoided if we heed the warning signs. Such disasters are no longer bound to a single town or locality but are global in their effects. Apocalyptic visions are all too real at the end of the twentieth century, and one does not have to be on the millennial fringe to appreciate them. These actual worldwide dangers account for the secularization of the millennial myth in apocalyptic terms.

For millennialists, the year 2000 looms, and we are already witnessing the increase in apocalyptic activity. In the past, millenarian movements often developed into radical and revolutionary social movements. In the 1960s, for example, many young counterculturalists were also inspired by millennial dreams of bringing down the establishment and creating a communal utopia in an "Aquarian" new age. Some of the more extremist countercultural groups of the era, such as the Weather Underground, also planted bombs in government buildings that resulted in tremendous property damage and the deaths of innocent people.[7] Other "people's armies," such as the Black Panther Party for Self Defense and (later) the American Indian Movement, aggressively protected their civil rights and violently resisted local police and government law enforcement, which often sought to undermine these radical groups through violent measures and illegal means; in the process many died.[8]

Still, the counterculture had a significant impact on society in the 1960s and after, overturning discriminatory laws and institutions and initiating a liberalism that was more in tune with the pluralist and increasingly multicultural society that America had become. Today the militant antigovernment counterculture is coming from the right, with a different set of values and a different millennial worldview. In fact, in many ways the right wing revolutionaries of today seek to overthrow the gains made by the civil rights, women's, gay and lesbian, and environmental movements of the 1960s and 1970s. Should the antigovernment, antiforeigner, anti-Semitic, and Christian supremacist values and beliefs of right-wing survivalism continue to develop in American society, the potential for future Oklahoma Cities, or worse, is almost assured.

There are those who suggest that classical myths are self-ful-filling. As with David Koresh and the Branch Davidians, who helped engineer their own apocalypse, the bombers in Oklahoma City were acting on their own interpretation of the millennial myth. For many survivalists social collapse and the practice of survival-ism are contemporary signs of Armageddon and the Millennium. The confusing and rapidly changing events of the day allow the survivalist to draw on his own often marginal social status and position to interpret trends and events as he sees fit. Survivalists and other millenarian movements will continue to "act" upon the myth, fulfilling what becomes their own prophecies or those of the group. In this sense, we cannot ignore such "marginal" and post-modern expressions of the millennial myth.

Finally, as long as many Christians accept the text of the Bible as the word of God, and as long as people search and hope for a better and more humane world, the millennial myth will continue to evolve, adapting to changing periods, influencing the beliefs and actions of people, and enduring.

# Notes

## Preface

1. Philip Lamy and Jack Levin, "Punk and Middle-Class Values: A Content Analysis," *Youth and Society*, Vol. 17, No. 2, 157–170 (December 1985); Harold Levine and Steven Stumpf, "Statements of Fear through Cultural Symbols: Punk Rock as a Reflective Subculture," *Youth and Society*, Vol. 1, No. 4, 417–435 (June 1983). The apocalypticism of punk music is not surprising, since the countercultural critique through which popular music, especially rock, has often been interpreted is that of the Romantic tradition—of nihilism or "negative classicism"—and of literary and academic critiques of the mass society and mass culture concerning the decline of "true" art, culture, and civilization. See Patrick Brantlinger, *Bread and Circuses: Theories of Mass Culture as Social Decay* (Ithaca: Cornell University Press, 1983).

   In reggae, punk, new wave, New Age, heavy metal, and rap music, apocalyptic and millennial themes and meanings are common to the music and, often times, to its subculture as well. Thus to speak of "punk prophets" of the Apocalypse, or to note the obvious millennial themes in punk music, punk films, and the punk and New Wave subculture, is to note similar mythical interpretations of society in emergent areas in popular culture such as music. See also Richard Miller's *Bohemia: The Proto-culture, Then and Now* (Chicago: Nelson Hall, 1977).

2. John G. Mitchell, "Waiting for Apocalypse," *Audubon* Vol. 85, 18–24 (1983).

## 1. Millennium Rage

1. Four biblical texts provide the apocalyptic references for this study: the King James (Authorized) Version (KJV) (London and New York: Cassell, Peter, and Galpin, 1866); the Revised Standard Version (RSV) (New York: Harper and Brothers, 1952); the Authorized Catholic Edition (ACE) (New York: Guild Press, 1963); and the New Testament in Modern English: Revised Edition (NTME), translated by J. B. Phillips (New York: Macmillan, 1976). Although these (and many other) Bible translations differ in interpretation in various ways, the primary components of the apocalyptic or millennial myth are persistent across translations.

2. Jim Robbins, "Sect Ready for Soviet Attack," *Boston Globe*, March 19, 1990.

3. Ibid.

4. Ibid.

5. Timothy Egan, "Thousands Plan Life Below, after Doomsday," *New York Times*, March 15, 1990, sec. B6, p. 1.

6 Jim Robbins, "Sect Ready for Soviet Attack."

7. Yonina Talmon, "Pursuit of the Millennium: The Relation between Religious and Social Change," in William Lessa and Evon Vogt (eds.), *Reader in Comparative Religion: An Anthropological Approach* (New York: Harper and Row, 1979); Kenelm Burridge, *New Heaven, New Earth: A Study of Millenarian Activities* (New York: Schocken, 1969); Norman Cohn, *The Pursuit of the Millennium* (Fairlawn, New Jersey: Essential Books, 1957) and *Cosmos, Chaos, and the World to Come: The Ancient Roots of Apocalyptic Faith* (New Haven: Yale University Press, 1993); E. J. Hobsbawm, *Primitive Rebels: Studies in Archaic Forms of Social Movements in the Nineteenth and Twentieth Centuries* (New York: Norton, 1959); Otto Friedrich, *The End of the World: A History* (New York: Coward, McCann and Geoghegan, 1982); Yuri Rubinsky and Ian Wiseman, *A History of the End of the World* (New York: William Morrow, 1982); James A. Aho, *This Thing of Darkness: A Sociology of the Enemy* (Seattle: University of Washington Press, 1994).

8. Sacvan Berkovitch, *The American Jeremiad* (Madison: University of Wisconsin Press, 1978); Ernest Lee Tuveson, *Redeemer Nation. The Idea of America's Millennial Role* (Chicago: University of Chicago Press, 1968); Nathan O. Hatch, *The Sacred Cause of Liberty in Republican Thought and the Millennium in Revolutionary New England* (New Haven: Yale University Press, 1977); James West Davidson, *The Logic of Millennial Thought: Eighteenth-Century New England* (New Haven and New London: Yale University Press, 1977); Perry Miller, *Errand into the Wilderness* (Cambridge: Harvard University Press,1958); Michael Rogin, *Ronald Reagan, the Movie: And Other Episodes in Political Demonology* (Berkeley: University of California Press,1987), Paul Boyer, *When Time Shall Be No More: Prophecy Belief in Modern America* (Cambridge: Belknap/Harvard University Press, 1992).

9. Barbara Grizzuti Harrison, *Visions of Glory: A History and Memory of Jehovah's Witnesses* (New York: Simon and Schuster, 1978).

10. Data collected at the September 1990 *Soldier of Fortune* Convention and Exposition, Sahara Hotel and Casino, and the 1995 20th *SOF* Convention and Exposition at the Sands Hotel and Casino, Las Vegas, Nevada.

11. To respect the privacy of the respondents in this study, all names of participants in the *Soldier of Fortune* conventions, among survivalists and others I have interviewed have been changed, unless otherwise noted.

12. Barry Sadler, *Casca: The Eternal Mercenary #1* (New York: Charter Books, 1979).

13. Jerry Ahern, *The Survivalist: The Nightmare Begins*, back cover quote (New York: Kensington, 1981).

14. *Soldier of Fortune Magazine: The Journal of Professional Adventurers* is published by Omega Group Publications/Omega Group Limited/Soldier of Fortune Magazine, Inc., Boulder, Colorado. Issues cited in this book include: Feb. 1980; July 1980; Jan. 1983; Oct. 1983; March 1983; April 1984; May 1984; Sept. 1984; July 1984; Aug. 1984; May 1985; Aug. 1985; Oct. 1985; Sept. 1985; July 1986; Oct. 1986; Feb. 1987; July 1987; April 1988; Jan. 1989; Oct. 1989; Feb. 1990; March 1990; April 1990; May 1990; June 1990; Aug. 1990; Sept. 1990; Oct. 1990; April 1991; July 1991; Aug. 1991; July 1992; Jan. 1993; March 1994; June 1995; August 1995; Oct. 1995.

15. John Yemma, "Building the World's 'New Order'," *Boston Globe*, March 3, 1991, p. 1.
16. John Yemma, "Bush Addresses Christian Broadcasters." John H. Yoder, "In Search of the 'Just War,' " *Boston Globe*, January 27, 1991, Focus Section, pp. 73–74.
17. John Yemma, "Building the World's 'New Order'." Delia Boylan and Richard Feinberg, "The 'New World Order' and the Third World." *Boston Globe*, March 10, 1991, sec. A, p. 26.
18. Stephen Kurkjian and John Mashek, "State of the Union Gives No Promise of a Quick Victory," *Boston Globe*, January 30, 1991, p. 1.
19. Robert K. Brown, "Command Guidance" (editorial), *Soldier of Fortune*, October 1990, 1.
20. Robert K. Brown, Comments inside 1995 *Soldier of Fortune* Conventioneers packet.
21. E. J. Hobsbawm, *Primitive Rebels: Studies in Archaic Forms of Social Movements in the Nineteenth and Twentieth Centuries* (New York: Norton, 1959). In William A. Lessa and Evon Z. Vogt, *Reader in Comparative Religion: An Anthropological Approach* (New York: Harper and Row, 1979), 441.
22. John Naisbitt, *The Global Paradox* (New York: Avon, 1995).

## 2. Apocalypse: A History of the End of the World

1. Rev. 6:1–8:6; 12:1–13,18; 15:1–16, 21; 17:1–19:10; 19:11–21:8.
2. Stephen L. Harris, *Understanding the Bible: A Reader's Introduction* (Mountain View, California: Mayfield, 1985).
3. Other texts that include strong apocalyptic themes include Amos 2.6–8, 3.9–15, 5.10–13; Zechariah 1.2–18, 2.4–15; Joel 2.18–28; Ezekiel 30; Daniel; Jeremiah; and 2 Timothy.
4. Otto Friedrich, *The End of the World: A History* (New York: Coward, McCann and Geoghegan, 1982).
5. Mircea Eliade, *The Myth of the Eternal Return* (New York: Harper and Row, 1965).
6. Joseph Campbell, *The Masks of God: Vol. 1. Primitive Mythology* (New York: Doubleday, 1959).
7. Roland Barthes, *Mythologies* (New York: Hill and Wang, 1972).
8. Michael Grant, *Jesus: An Historian's Review of the Gospels* (New York: Charles Scribner's Sons, 1977).
9. Robin Lane Fox, *Pagans and Christians* (New York: Alfred A. Knopf, 1986).
10. While the term *millenarian* has been used in many of the earlier historical and anthropological accounts of such movements, the term *millennial* (according to my own survey of the literature) is the more commonly used term now. Millennial (and millennialism) also has a wider descriptive ability, defining not only religious and other social movements but also ideas, images, literature, etc. Therefore, I will use the term millennial throughout this study, while retaining the use of the term "millenarian movement."
11. Fox, *Pagans and Christians*; Yuri Rubinsky and Ian Wiseman, *A History of the End of the World* (New York: William Morrow, 1982).

12. Friedrich, *The End of the World*, p. 77.

13. Ibid. Friedrich explicitly states that these invaders were *not* soldiers, but general riff-raff.

14. Ibid.

15. Bernard McGinn, *Visions of the End: Apocalyptic Traditions in the Middle Ages* (New York: Columbia University Press, 1979).

16. Columbus, Christopher, "Discovery of the New World," *The Annals of America*, Vol. 1, pp. 1–5 (1493) (Chicago: Encyclopedia Britannica, 1976).

17. Rubinsky and Wiseman, *A History of the End of the World*. See also Kirkpatrick Sale, *The Conquest of Paradise: Christopher Columbus and the Columbian Legacy* (New York: Penguin, 1991).

18. Rubinsky and Wiseman, *A History of the End of the World*, p. 91.

19. McGinn, *Visions of the End*, p. 284.

20. Stephen Foster, *The Long Argument: English Puritanism and the Shaping of New England Culture, 1570–1700* (Chapel Hill, University of North Carolina Press, 1991).

21. Ibid.

22. "The Mayflower Compact," *The Annals of America*, Vol. 1, p. 64 (1627).

23. Perry Miller, *Errand into the Wilderness* (Cambridge: Harvard University Press, 1958).

24. Sacvan Berkovitch, *The American Jeremiad* (Madison: University of Wisconsin Press, 1978), p. xi.

25. Peter Bulkeley, "A City Set upon a Hill," *The Annals of America*, Vol. 1, pp. 211–212 (1651).

26. Berkovitch, *The American Jeremiad*, p. xi.

27. James West Davidson, *The Logic of Millennial Thought in Eighteenth-Century New England* (New Haven and New London: Yale University Press, 1977); Charles M. Wiltse, *The New Nation: 1800–1845* (New York; Hill and Wang, 1961); Ernest Lee Tuveson, *Redeemer Nation: The Idea of America's Millennial Role* (Chicago: The University of Chicago Press, 1968).

28. Colonel David Humphreys, "A Poem on the Future Glory of the United States," lines 15–20, in Tuveson, *Redeemer Nation.*

29. Frederick Jackson Turner, *The Frontier in American History* [New York: Holt, Rinehart & Winston, 1962 (1920)].

30. Herbert Bolton, *Rim of Christendom: A Biography of Eusebio Francisco Kino, Pacific Coast Pioneer* (New York: Macmillan, 1936) and "The Mormons in the Opening of the West," *Utah Genealogical and Historical Magazine*, XVI:41–72, 1926. Also see Ray Allen Billington, *Westward to the Pacific: An Overview of America's Westward Expansion* (St. Louis, Missouri: Jefferson National Expansion Historical Association, 1979); Walter Prescott Webb, Eugene Barker, and William Dodd, *The Story of Our Nation* (Evanston, Illinois: Row, Peterson and Company, 1928); Wilbur Jacobs, John Caughey, and Joe Frantz, *Turner, Bolton, and Webb: Three Historians of the American Frontier* (Seattle: University of Washington Press, 1965).

31. Ralph Linton, "Nativistic Movements," *American Anthropologist* 45:230–240 (1943); Anthony F. C. Wallace, "Revitalization Movements," *American Anthropologist* 58:264–281 (1956); Bryan R. Wilson, *Magic and the Millennium: A Sociological Study of Religious Movements of Protest among Tribal and Third-World Peoples*

(New York: Harper, 1973); David Aberle, *The Peyote Religion among the Navaho* (Chicago: Aldine, 1966). The anthropologists Ralph Linton, Anthony Wallace, and David Aberle have used various terms to describe the religious movements of dispossessed cultures, including nativistic, transformative, and revitalization movements. Linton used the term "nativistic" to refer to any religious movement that sought to build social solidarity in times of crisis, particularly during periods of rapid social change. Wallace spoke of "revitalization" movements as seeking to reform society by building an ideology that would be relevant to changing cultural needs. Aberle used the term "transformative" to refer to movements that preached withdrawal from society.

32. Anthony F. C. Wallace, *The Death and Rebirth of the Seneca* (New York: Alfred A. Knopf, 1970).

33. Ibid.

34. Vincent Harding, *There Is a River: The Black Struggle for Freedom in America* (New York: Harcourt Brace Jovanovich, 1991).

35. Tuveson, *Redeemer Nation*, p. 198.

36. J. C. Furnas, *The Road to Harper's Ferry* (New York: W. Sloane, 1959).

37. Abraham Lincoln, "Second Inaugural Address," *Annals of America*, Vol. 9, pp. 555–556 (1865).

38. Robert N. Bellah, *The Broken Covenant: American Civil Religion in a Time of Trial* (New York: Seabury, 1975) and "Civil Religion in America," *Daedalus* 96 (Winter):1–21 (1967); Nathan O. Hatch, *The Sacred Cause of Liberty in Republican Thought and the Millennium in Revolutionary New England* (New Haven: Yale University Press, 1977), and "The Origins of Civil Millennialism in America: New England Clergymen, War with France, and the Revolution," *William and Mary Quarterly* 31:417 (1974). The secular millennial thesis has been adopted by Hatch, who applied Bellah's (1967) civil religion thesis to the study of millennialism and thus spoke of "civil millennialism." Secular religion and millennialism has been defined and identified in a wide variety of subcultures and social and political movements. See Norman Cohn, *The Pursuit of the Millennium* (Fairlawn, New Jersey: Essential Books, 1957); Edward Hyams, *The Millennium Postponed: Socialism from Sir Thomas More to Mao Tse-tung* (New York: Taplinger, 1974); Robert Jewert and John Lawrence, *American Monomyth* (New York: Doubleday, 1977); Greil Arthur L. And Thomas Robbins, "Between the Sacred and the Secular: Research and Theory on Quasi-Religion." *Religion and the Social Order* Volume 4, pp. 1–23; (Greenwich: Jai Press, 1994); Rodney Stark and William Sims Bainbridge, *The Future of Religion: Secularization, Revival, and Cult Formation* (Berkeley: University of California Press, 1986).

39. Tuveson, *Redeemer Nation*, pp. 73–77.

40. Edward Deming Andrews, *The People Called Shakers* (New York: Dover Publications, 1963); Constance Noyes Robertson, *Oneida Community: An Autobiography, 1851–1876* (Syracuse: Syracuse University Press, 1970); William Kephart and William W. Zellner, *Extraordinary Groups: The Sociology of Unconventional Lifestyles* (New York: St. Martin's Press, 1982).

41. Robin M. Wright and Jonathan D. Hill, "History, Ritual and Myth: Nineteenth Century Millenarian Movements in the Northwest Amazon," *Ethnohistory*, 33(1), 31–54 (1985); Kenelm Burridge, *New Heaven, New Earth: A Study of*

*Millenarian Activities* (New York: Schocken, 1969); Vittorio Lanternari, *The Religions of the Oppressed: A Study of Modern Messianic Cults* (New York: Mentor, 1963); Peter Worsley, *The Trumpet Shall Sound: A Study of Cargo Cults in Melanesia* (London: MacGibbon and Kee, 1957); Bryan R. Wilson, *Magic and the Millennium: A Sociological Study of Religious Movements of Protest among Tribal and Third-World Peoples*; Wallace, "Revitalization Movements"; Linton, "Nativistic Movements."
The rise of millenarian movements and "cargo cults" among populations indigenous to Melanesia following the end of World War II offers further examples of the diffusion of the millennial myth. During this period Melanesians often suffered violent repression, which spurred them to anticolonial actions and native millennial upheaval. The cults predicted a future time when ancestors would return in steamships and airplanes bringing European goods (the cargo) and initiating a reversal of the social order. Anthropologists have undertaken many important studies of emerging forms of millennialism and have provided cross-cultural evidence for the globalization of the millennial myth. They also have shown how traumatic social changes in the forms of cultural contact and colonialism can incite the millennial spirit. Finally, they have demonstrated that millennial movements can induce social change.

42. Edward Hyams, *The Millennium Postponed*; Tuveson, *Redeemer Nation*.

## 3. Tribulation: Survivalists and Soldiers of Fortune

1. The discussion with "Abe," the urban survivalist, is based on a series of interviews conducted between 1990 and 1991 at Abe's apartment in a modern, low-rise complex in a small city northeast of Boston, Massachusetts.

2. Daniel Boone (1734–1820), frontiersman and legendary American hero, helped blaze a trail through the Cumberland Gap, a notch in the Appalachian Mountains near the border between Virginia and Tennessee. Zebulon Pike (1779–1813) was a U.S. Army officer and explorer for whom Pikes Peak in Colorado is named. In 1805 Pike led a 20-man exploring party to the headwaters of the Missouri to discover the source of the river, negotiate peace treaties with Indian tribes, and assert legal claim of the United States to the area. Pike also explored the Southwest and Spanish territory. Pike served in the War of 1812 and was killed in action on April 27, 1813. Davy Crockett (1786–1836), frontiersman, politician, and Indian fighter, was a legendary figure who made a name for himself in Tennessee during the Creek War (1813–1815). In 1821 he was elected to the Tennessee legislature, winning popularity with homespun yarns and humor. When he failed to win election to the U.S. Congress he headed west to Texas and joined the American forces against the Mexicans. In 1836 he and fewer than 200 Texas volunteers were killed by 4,000 Mexican soldiers at the eighteenth-century Franciscan mission in San Antonio known as the Alamo. Purportedly a real trapper and mountain man living in the mid-19th century, Jeremiah "Liver Eatin' " Johnson (so-called because of the way he devoured his victims) was made famous by the Sydney Pollack film *Jeremiah Johnson* (1972) starring Robert Redford. Jeremiah Johnson was writted by John Milius, author of *Apocalypse Now* and *Red Dawn*.

3. Two decades of legal squabbling and unruly protests turned the Seabrook, New Hampshire, nuclear power plant into a symbol of everything that was wrong with atomic energy in the United States during the 1980s. After years of start-ups, shutdowns, and protests that led to more than 2,500 arrests since the mid-1970s, the beleaguered power plant continues to operate, but at a lower level.

4. James Coates, *Armed and Dangerous: The Rise of the Survivalist Right* (New York: Hill and Wang, 1987); Stephen N. Linder, "Survivalists: Ethnography of an Urban Millennial Cult" (Unpublished Ph.D. thesis: University of California, Los Angeles, 1982); John G. Mitchell, "Waiting for Apocalypse." *Audubon* 85:18–24 (1983); Kevin Flynn and Gary Gerhardt, *The Silent Brotherhood: Inside America's Racist Underground* (New York: Free Press, 1989); Richard G. Peterson, "Preparing for Apocalypse: Survivalist Strategies." *Free Inquiry in Creative Sociology* 12 (1):44–46 (1984); James William Gibson, *Warrior Dreams: Violence and Manhood in Post-Vietnam America* (New York: Hill and Wang, 1994).

5. Spencer Weart, *Nuclear Fear: A History of Images* (Cambridge: Harvard University Press, 1988).

6. Philip Lamy, "Millennialism in the Mass Media: The Case of *Soldier of Fortune* Magazine, *Journal for the Scientific Study of Religion* 31: 408–424; (December 1992); Coates, *Armed and Dangerous*; Peterson, "Preparing for Apocalypse."

7. There are (and have been since before World War II) other American military-type magazines, including serviceman and veterans magazines. Although these deal with the military, weaponry, and international politics, they cannot be called gun magazines. Nor do they bear even passing resemblance to the paramilitary magazines of today. There is also a gun and war history genre that primarily concerns antiques and popular history. The popular history and the hobby content, however, do show correspondence with the paramilitary magazines. In the 1950s there were examples of military and masculine literature such as *True, Journal of the Foreign Legion,* and *Stormtrooper Magazine* (mid-1960s), a publication of the Ku Klux Klan. *Stormtrooper* now exists as a "home page" on the Internet. The sport/hunting magazines have continued on, largely unaffected by paramilitary literature. If anything they may have profited by the general interest in guns. Some of the changes that have occurred have been in the direction of paramilitarism and survivalism. For example, survival products are commonly advertised in *American Hunter, Guns and Ammo,* and *Sports Afield.*

8. James William Gibson, *Warrior Dreams: Violence and Manhood in Post-Vietnam America* (New York: Hill and Wang, 1994).

9. *Soldier of Fortune Magazine (SOF)*, January 1984, 97.

10. *SOF*, October 1985, 106.

11. *SOF*, January 1983, 79.

12. *SOF*, October, 1985, 89.

13. On the revisionist history of the Vietnam experience, see Gibson, *Warrior Dreams*; Susan Jeffords, *The Remasculinization of America: Gender and the Vietnam War* (Bloomington: Indiana University Press, 1989); William Broyles, Jr., *Brothers in Arms: A Journey from War to Peace* (New York: Knopf, 1986); and the "Vietnam War" issue of the *Journal of American Culture* 4 (1989).

14. According to *Soldier of Fortune* former assistant editor Susan Max (*SOF* field notes; September 15, 1990), *SOF* art director (since 1979) Craig Nunn was a

born-again Christian whose religious values strongly influenced the graphic look of the magazine. A member of a Christian motorcycle club, Nunn was killed in a motorcycle accident in 1989 (*SOF*, October 1990).

15. *SOF*, October 1982, 75; October 1983, 110.
16. *SOF*, March 1990, 14.
17. *SOF*, May 1983, 85.
18. *SOF*, February 1983, 88.
19. *SOF*, October 1983, 85.
20. *SOF*, April, 1991, 94–100.
21. *SOF*, August 1994, 108.
22. *SOF*, April 1983, 70; May 1984, 25; October 1985, 109; August 1995, 97.
23. *SOF*, October 1983, 110–111; August 1984, 108; April 1988, 103; July 1991, 103; May 1984, 109.
24. *SOF*, April 1987, 105; June 1990, 95; August 1995, 98.
25. Similar books in the apocalyptic genre include Billy Graham's *Approaching Hoofbeats: The Four Horsemen of the Apocalypse* (1984); Mike Evans' *The Return* (1986); Corrie Ten Boom's *Marching Orders for the End Battle* (1969)—to name but a few. Mike Evans, who has appeared on ABC News' *Nightline* as a media spokesman for American Christians, runs a ministry for evangelical outreach and has a newsletter and elaborate mailing system, which warns in each mailing of the coming Apocalypse, including detailed accounts of news events with their scriptural correlations. The Mike Evans Ministry has also produced a variety of other media and multimedia presentations concerning "the return" of Christ, including films and videos, audiotapes, and a wealth of books and other literature.
26. Eric Zency, "Ecology and the Peril of Doomsday Visions," *Utne Reader* 31: 90–93 (Jan/Feb 1989).
27. Weart, *Nuclear Fear*.
28. Ravi Batra, *The Great Depression of 1990* (New York: Simon and Schuster, 1987). Barry Brumett, "Popular Economic Apocalyptic: The Case of Ravi Batra," *Journal of Popular Culture* 24:153–163 (1990); Robert R. Prechter, Jr., and A. J. Frost, *Elliot Wave Principle: Key to Market Behavior* (7th ed.) (Gainesville, Georgia: New Classics Library, 1995).
29. Christine Ward Gailey, "'Rambo' in Tonga: Video Films and Cultural Resistance in the Tongan Islands," *Culture: Journal of the Canadian Ethnological Society* 9:21–32 (1989).
30. John G. Cawletti, *The Six-Gun Mystique* (Bowling Green, Ohio: University Popular Press, 1975).
31. Michael Barkun, *Disaster and the Millennium* (New Haven and London: Yale University Press, 1974).

## 4. Dragons, Beasts, and Christian Soldiers

1. For a full account of the Ruby Ridge incident see Jess Walters, *Every Knee Shall Bend: The Truth and Tragedy of Ruby Ridge and the Randy Weaver Family* (New York: Harper, 1995).

2. Adrian Walker, "Idaho Fugitive Weighing Surrender, Negotiator Says," *Boston Globe*, August 30, 1992, p. 16.

3. The government did not admit to doing anything wrong in the Weaver case. *Facts on File*, August 24, 1995.

4. Eric Larson, "A Painful Purge at the FBI" ("ATF under Siege"), *Time*, July 24, 1995, 20–29.

5. Stephen Harris, *Understanding the Bible: A Reader's Introduction* (Mountain View, California: Mayfield Publishing, 1985).

6. Daniel Junas, "The Rise of the Militias," *Covert Action Quarterly*, Spring 1995, 20–25. See also the ADL special report *The Militia Movement in America*, 1995. The ADL national survey also lists 40 states with organized militias, with active membership at 15,000.

7. Thomas Jefferson, "The Declaration of Independence," *The Annals of America*, Vol. 2, p. 447 (1996).

8. Jim Robbins, "Sect Ready for Soviet Attack," *Boston Globe*, March 14, 1990.

9. Robert Henry Goldsborough and Daniel Lawrence Cuddy, *The New World Order: Chronology and Commentary* (Baltimore, Maryland: The American Research Foundation), 28.

10. Linda Thompson, "Declaration of Independence, 1994," From the Patriot archives on the Internet.

11. A copy of Thompson's "Declaration" can be found on the Internet and is located through the many militia and Patriot archives and home pages. Included is a petition to sign and send to Thompson's organization, the American Justice Federation.

12. Goldsborough and Cuddy, *The New World Order*, 37.

13. Robert K. Brown, "One to the Groin, Two to the Head," *Soldier of Fortune*, October 1995, 72.

14. David Van Biema, "Message from Mark Koernke," *Time*, June 26, 1995.

15. Ibid.

16. Ibid.

17. Jill Smolowe, "Go Ahead, Make Our Day," *Time*, May 29, 1995.

18. Ibid.

19. Ibid.

20. Ibid.

## 5. Antichrist: The Myth of the Jewish World Conspiracy

1. James Coates, *Armed and Dangerous: The Rise of the Survivalist Right* (New York: Hill & Wang, New York), 7.

2. Ibid.

3. Ibid, 3.

4. Norman Cohn, *Warrant for Genocide: The Myth of the Jewish World Conspiracy and the Protocols of the Elders of Zion* (New York: Harper and Row, 1966), 21-22.

5. Ibid, 283. *World Conquest through World Government: The Protocols of the Learned Elders of Zion*, translated from the Russian by Sergei A. Nilus (Chulmleigh,

England: Britons Pub. Co.). *The Protocols* can be found on the Internet, accessed through various right-wing, Patriot, and militia home pages.

6. Cohn, *Warrant for Genocide*, 25.
7. Ibid, 61.
8. Ibid, 189.
9. Ibid, 189.
10. Ibid, 160–163; James Coates, *Armed and Dangerous: The Rise of the Survivalist Right* (New York: Hill and Wang, 1987).
11. Cohn, *Warrant for Genocide*, 164.
12. Ibid, 229–230.
13. Ibid, 284.
14. James Corcoran, *Bitter Harvest: Gordon Kahl and the Posse Comitatus—Murder in the Heartland* (New York: Viking-Penguin, 1990), 75, 152.
15. Ibid, 38, 137.
16. Ibid, 40, 152–153.
17. Ibid, 11.
18. Ibid, 34.
19. Ibid, 34–35.
20. Ibid, 35.
21. Southern Poverty Law Center, Klanwatch Special Reports: Outlawing Hate Crime (Montgomery, Alabama, 1989).
22. Other organizations that track the development of racist and anti-Semitic groups include the Anti-Defamation League of the B'nai B'rith, the Center for Democratic Renewal (Atlanta, Georgia), and the National Institute against Prejudice and Violence (Washington, D.C.), as well as various government agencies.
23. Corcoran, *Bitter Harvest*, 36.
24. William L. Pierce (alias Andrew MacDonald), *The Turner Diaries* (Hillsboro, West Virginia: National Vanguard Books, 1978).
25. National Vanguard Books, catalog 12 (Hillsboro, West Virginia: National Vanguard Books), 1.
26. National Vanguard Books, catalog 12.
27. Ibid, 32.
28. Ibid, 32.
29. Michael Barkun, *Religion and the Racist Right: The Origins of the Christian Identity Movement* (Chapel Hill: University of North Carolina Press, 1994) and "Militias, Christian Identity and the Radical Right," *The Christian Century*, August 2, 1995, Vol. 112, p. 738.
30. Edward Hines, *Identification of the Ten Tribes of Israel with the Anglo-Celto-Saxons* (Vancouver, Canada: The Association of Covenant People, 1970).
31. Ibid; Corcoran, *Bitter Harvest*, 38–39; Coates, *Armed and Dangerous*, 82.
32. Corcoran, *Bitter Harvest*, 38–39.
33. Ibid, 39.
34. Jack Levin and Jack McDevitt, *Hate Crimes: The Rising Tide of Bigotry and Bloodshed* (New York: Plenum Press, 1993); James Aho, *This Thing of Darkness: A Sociology of the Enemy* (Seattle: University of Washington Press, 1994).

## 6. "Babylon Is Fallen": America at Century's End

1. Stephen Kurkjian and John Mashek, "State of the Union Gives No Promise of a Quick Victory," *Boston Globe*, January 30, 1991, p. 8.

2. Ibid.

3. Unabomber's manifesto, complete text, as it appeared on the Internet. The document is referenced throughout this section by paragraph (i.e., para.).

4. "Peter Jennings' Journal," ABC Information Radio Network, September 19, 1995.

5. "Unabom Press Release," UNABOM Task Force, FBI home page on the Internet, June 30, 1995.

6. Two very good sources of the literary and cultural use of apocalyptic mythology can be found in Patrick Brantlinger, *Bread and Circuses: Theories of Mass Culture as Social Decay* (Ithaca, New York: Cornell University Press, 1983); and Frank Kermode, *The Sense of an Ending: Studies in the Theory of Fiction* (London: Oxford University Press, 1966). The authors demonstrate the inspiration and application of the millennial myth in the philosophies and writings of dozens of luminaries, from Aristotle to Heraclitas, Marx and Engles, the existentialists Kierkegaard and Nietzsche, the literary critics Arnold, Eliot, Orteqa y Gasset, and Mark Twain, the "cyclical historians" like Spengler, the psychoanalysts Freud and Jung, and modern critics of mass culture such as Christopher Lasch and Daniel Bell.

7. Theodore W. Adorno, Else Frenkel-Brunwik, Daniel Levinson, and R. Nevitt Sanford, *The Authoritarian Personality* (New York: Harper and Brothers, 1950); Herbert Marcuse, *One Dimensional Man* (London: Sphere, 1968); Max Horkheimer, "Authoritarianism and the Family Today," in R. Ansden (ed.) *The Family: Its Function and Destiny* (New York: Herder and Herder, 1949); M. Horkheimer and T. Adorno, "The Culture Industry: Enlightenment as Mass Deception," in James Curran *et al.*, (eds.), *Mass Communications and Society* (London: Edward Arnold, 1977); Leo Lowenthal, "Historical Perspectives of Popular Culture," in Bernard Rosenberg and David White (eds.), *Mass Culture: The Popular Arts in America* (New York: Free Press, 1964).

8. Brantlinger, *Bread and Circuses*. Also see Adorno *et al.*, *The Authoritarian Personality*.

9. Brantlinger, *Bread and Circuses*, 18. As Brantlinger suggests, the way to get beyond the apocalyptic theorizing about mass culture is to root one's analysis in the specific artifacts of the mass culture and mass media. But like Brantlinger, I am interested in the apocalypticism of the mass cultural argument, as well as the mass cultural artifact. Indeed, apocalypticism increasingly has moved beyond cultural criticism to the mass media and mass culture, where it has becomes a basic theme or form. For example, films like the *Mad Max* trilogy (1979, 1981, 1985) are mass cultural artifacts whose primary theme is the post apocalypse. In the 1990s we see it in the films *Waterworld* (1995), *Strange Days* (1995), and *The Prophecy* (1995) and after this in the "alien invasion" films *The Arrival* (1996), and *Independence Day* (1996).

Another way to get around the mass culture dead end is to consider "popular culture" as a different entity, as an emergent form of cultural expression arising from the various social groups that make up "the masses." Popular culture may draw its symbols from the dominant or mass culture, but it can mold these symbols and meanings to suit its unique social reality. In the popular culture what comes down from the top may be adapted and altered in form by subcultures within the "masses." In other words, popular culture is dynamic and may be the site of resistance and social change.

10. Concerning the CNN poll that showed that 14 percent of respondents believed that the war with Iraq was the prelude to Armageddon, a Jehovah's Witness informant pointed out to me the numerological similarities between the 14 percent and 144,000 who will be caught up with Christ in the "rapture" just prior to the destruction of everyone else. He reminded me of 1 Thessalonians 4:16–17: "Those who have died in Christ will be the first to rise, and then we who are still living (the 144,000) will be swept up with them into the clouds to meet the Lord in the air."

11. It is interesting that while the numbers of Americans killed during Desert Storm were low (376 according to the *Boston Globe*, June 9; 1991, p.1), they were generally made public by the administration throughout the course of the war. On the Iraqi side (at least from my observation) numbers were hardly ever given. To date, the Pentagon has refused to make official estimates of Iraqi war dead on the grounds that it was impossible to keep accurate numbers. The peace and environmental group Greenpeace has estimated that 200,000 Iraqis died in the war and its aftermath (*Boston Globe*, June 9, 1991, p. 1).

12. The clear line between good and evil were also apparent in the missile war, which pitted the "Patriots" against the "scuds." These names could not have been better scripted. In a photograph published nationwide, President Bush congratulates the management and employees at the Raytheon Plant in Massachusetts, which makes the Patriot missile system. On a stage framed by two actual-size Patriot missiles sits Bush and Raytheon officials. The erotic symbolism of the props in the photograph filled the discussion of radio talk shows the following day.

13. William Kornhauser, "The Politics of Mass Society," in Marvin Olsen (ed.), *Power in Societies* (New York: Macmillan, 1970), 403–417.

## 7. Messiah: "Many Will Say They Are Me"

1. Michael Riley, Richard Woodbury, Julie Johnson, and Elaine Shannon, "Tragedy in Waco," Special Report, *Time*, May 3, 1993.

2. Jill Smolowe, "February 28: Sent into a Death Trap?" Special Report, *Time*, May 3, 1993, 33.

3. James D. Tabor and Eugene V. Gallagher, *Why Waco?: Cults and the Battle for Religious Freedom in America* (Berkeley: University of California Press, 1995). See also James Lewis, ed., *From the Ashes: Making Sense of Waco* (Lanham, Maryland: Rownan & Littlefield, 1994).

4. Tabor and Gallagher, *Why Waco?* 53–54.

5. Stephen L. Harris, *Understanding the Bible: A Reader's Introduction* (Mountain View, California: Mayfield, 1985).

6. Gorden Melton, *Encyclopedia of American Religions*, (Detroit, Michigan: Gate Publishing, 1994).
7. *Survival into a New Earth* (New York: Watchtower Bible and Tract Society of Pennsylvania, 1984), 2.
8. Leonard Barret, *The Rastafarians* (Boston: Beacon Press, 1988).
9. William F. Lewis, *Soul Rebels: The Rastafari* (Prospect Heights, Illinois: Waveland Press, 1993).
10. Grace Halsell, *Prophesy and Politics: Militant Evangelists on the Road to Nuclear War* (Westport, Connecticut: Lawrence Hill, 1986).
11. ABC News Special, "Waco: The Decision to Die," with Peter Jennings, April 20, 1993.
12. Gordon Melton, *Encyclopedia of American Religions*.
13. Tabor and Gallagher, *Why Waco?* 33–38.
14. Ibid, 38.
15. Ibid, 38–39.
16. Ibid.
17. Ibid, 40–41.
18. Ibid, 41.
19. Ibid, 42.
20. Ibid, 42–43.
21. Ibid, 43.
22. Thomas Robbins, *Cults, Converts, and Charisma* (London: Sage, 1988).
23. Tabor and Gallagher, *Why Waco?* 12.
24. Ibid.
25. Ibid.
26. Militarization of Law Enforcement," presentation, *Soldier of Fortune* Convention, Las Vegas, Nevada, September 29, 1995.

## 8. Armageddon: "Kill Them All, Let God Sort Them Out"

1. Soldier of Fortune (*SOF*) magazine subscription advertisement, September 1985, 16; Philip Lamy, "Millenialism in the Mass Media: The Case of *Soldier of Fortune* Magazine.".
2. Rex Applegate, "The Evil Empire Eyes the Big Enchilada," *SOF*, August 1985, 86.
3. "Apocalypse in America," review of film *Red Dawn*, *SOF*, September 1984, 28.
4. Advertisement for the Conservative Book Club, *SOF*, October 1990, 9.
5. *SOF*, October 1984, 91.
6. William F. Buckley, "Death Squads and U.S. Policy," *SOF*, May 1984, 24.
7. "Mouthful of Rocks: Modern Adventures in the French Foreign Legion," book review, *SOF* March 1990, 16.
8. Peter Douglas, "No Honor among Mercs," *SOF*, October 1990, 60.
9. "Onward Christian Soldiers," *SOF*, June 1990, 34.
10. *SOF*, May 1990; *SOF*, October 1990.
11. David Mills, "Abandoned Angola: FNLA's Uncertain Future," *SOF*, May 1985.
12. David Isby, "Harassing the Bear," *SOF*, September 1984, 41.
13. Sterling Seagrave, "Burma's Golden Triangle," *SOF*, May 1984, 38.

14. Ibid, 39.
15. James L. Pate, "Waco Hearings: Somebody's Lying," *SOF*, October 1995, 92.
16. Craig B. Hulet, "All the News That's Fit to Invent." *SOF*, August 1995, 56.
17. Craig B. Hulet, "Patriots or Paranoids?," *SOF*, August 1995, 43.
18. Ibid, 45.
19. Ibid, 45.
20. Robert K. Brown, "Command Guidance: Two Decades of Soldier of Fortune." *SOF*, October 1995, 3.
21. Ibid.
22. Ibid.
23. Ibid.
24. Robert K. Brown, *"Soldier of Fortune,* 1995 Convention/Expo Directory," p. 1.
25. Richard Normington, "Wargames," *History Today,* October 1986; Jon Freeman, *The Complete Book of War Games* (New York: Simon and Schuster, 1980).
26. Freeman, *The Complete Book of War Games.*
27. Ibid.
28. Normington, "Wargames."
29. Pamela Tuchscherer, *TV Interactive Toys: The New High Tech Threat to Children* (South Bend, Indiana: Pinnaroo Publishing, 1988).
30. Lindsey Gruson, "'Most Dangerous Game' Is Gaining as a Sport," *New York Times,* August 24, 1987: A12.
31. Kent Black, "It's Only a Game: Fighting Corporate Battles with Guns," *M,* April 1986, 83–88.
32. Lionel Atwill, *The New Official Survival Game Manual* (New London, New Hampshire: The National Survival Game, Inc., 1987).
33. Ibid, 2.
34. D. Keith Mano, "Skirmishing," Part II: *National Review,* October 19, 1984, 60–61.
35. Black, "It's Only a Game."
36. Ibid.
37. Ibid.
38. Gruson, "'Most Dangerous Game.' "
39. The data for this analysis were gathered from several studies of *Survival Game* play from 1989 to 1992, with two outings involving Northeastern University (NU) (Boston) college students who volunteered to participate in the project as part of a course on the sociology of sport. Methodology included participant observation, field interviews, questionnaires, and videotaping. While quantitative data were collected, the analysis relies more on the qualitative information provided by players, especially in their comments and written remarks about their experiences of playing the game. In the two Northeastern games, 46 players (out of 52) answered questionnaires, and in the second game, 36 (out of 41) did the same ($N = 82$). From the sample, 87% (71) of the players were males and 13% (11) were females. More than half of the NU players [52% (43)] were business majors (administration, management, finance, accounting, and marketing), and 29% (24) were engineering majors. The final 19% of the players (15) were liberal arts majors.
40. Jay Coakley, *Sport and Society,* 5th ed. (St. Louis, Missouri: Times Mirror/Mosby, 1995); Valerie DeBenedette, "Spectator Violence at Sports Events: What Keeps

Enthusiastic Fans in Bounds?" *The Physician and Sports Medicine* 16 (March); 202–211 (1988); John Hoberman, *Sport and Political Ideology* (Austin: University of Texas Press, 1984); M. Smith, *Violence and Sport* (Toronto: Butterworths, 1983); David Phillips, "The Impact of Mass Media Violence on U.S. Homicides," *American Sociological Review* 48 (August): 560–568 (1983); Tuchscherer, *TV Interactive Toys*; R. Hughes and Jay Coakley, "Player Violence and the Social Organization of Sport," *Journal of Sport Behavior* 1(1): 15–25 (1978); James Aho, *Religious Mythology and the Art of War: Comparative Religious Symbolisms of Military Violence* (Westport, Connecticut: Greenwood Press, 1981); Richard Sipes, "War, Sports and Aggression: An Empirical Test of Two Rival Theories," *American Anthropologist*, 75: 64–85 (1973); Lionel Tiger, *Men in Groups* (New York: Vintage Books, 1970); Elliot Chapple, *Culture and Biological Man: Explorations in Behavioral Anthropology* (New York: Holt, Rinehart & Winston, 1970); Stanislav Andreski, *Military Organization and Society* (Berkeley: University of California Press, 1968); Elton McNeil, "Personal Hostility and International Aggression." *The Journal of Conflict Resolution* 5(3): 279–290 (1961).

The research and debate on sports violence has centered on whether the violence in sporting events serves as a cure or cause of aggressive or violent behavior in participators and spectators. The debate has also focused on the nature of warlike sports, and the militaristic culture of a society. Richard Sipes provides a useful framework for this debate by contrasting "Drive Discharge" and "Culture Pattern" models of war, sports, and aggression. The Drive Discharge model proposes that aggression and warfare are basic human drives or instincts. The discharge or cathartic function of sport has also been seen in terms of "militant" energy or "enthusiasm," ultimately defining sports and war as functional equivalents of, or alternatives to, one another (Coakley, 1990; Tiger, 1969). By contrast, the Culture Pattern model argues that learned, rather than instinctive, behavior explains cultural patterns, i.e., that aggressive behavior is learned and shows up in consistent patterns across the various dimensions of a society's culture (Sipes, 1976). Where social institutions like the government and the media promote or glorify war, warlike or aggressive qualities will more likely be learned by the members of the society (Andreski, 1968). Other studies have suggested a relationship between the societal acceptance of aggression and the existence of warfare (McNeil, 1961; Chapple, 1970). Sometimes referred to as the "enhancement" or "sport as cause" model, Culture Pattern theories also focus on the ways in which the structural components of sports involvement may induce aggressive or violent behavior in participants, spectators, or the general public (Hughes and Coakley, 1978). Some of these studies have suggested that the greater emphasis on violent roles, such as "hit men" or "enforcers," in professional sport (Smith, 1983), and "stimulus cues" like equipment can be interpreted as tactical weapons used to provoke violence (Coakley, 1995). Those who have controlled for other factors, including social class, sex, education, and, most importantly, types of aggression, have also found some support for the Culture Pattern model (DeBenedette, 1988). A large body of studies focusing on media violence and its effects on viewers also supports the Culture Pattern argument (Phillips, 1983; Tuchscherer, 1988). The more direct link between sport and military ideology is drawn by theorists who see sport as a type of combat "training grounds." DeBenedette (1988:205) has noted that "in an extreme cases, rioting at three soccer games between the national teams of Honduras and El Salvador escalated into war in 1969." Political violence has been induced by athletic contests between China and Hong Kong (Hoberman, 1984). A more interpretive approach to the meaning and nature of war games and sports would be to frame these issues in terms of a cultural reading. Like other social institutions, sport has been viewed by sociologists as an agent for the transmission of important social and cultural values; in American society, for example, participants in team sports are socialized in the instrumental values of competition, motivation, hard work, and achievement. Regular participation in sport is also believed to encourage participants in the development of physical and mental skills and in coping strategies adaptable to everyday life."

41. Black, "It's Only a Game."
42. Albert Gross, "Armageddon under the Christmas Tree," *Technology Review* 89: 73–74 (1986).

## 9. Millennium: New Age Harmony or New World Chaos?

1. Yuri Rubinsky and Ian Wiseman, *A History of the End of the World* (New York: William Morrow, 1982), 19.
2. Don Stewart and Chuck Missler, *The Coming Temple: Center Stage for the Final Countdown* (Orange, California: Dart Press, 1991).
3. Amnon Rubinstein, *The Zionist Dream Revisited: From Herzl to Gush Emunin* (New York: Schocken Books, 1984), 24.
4. Shlomo Avineri, *The Making of Modern Zionism: The Intellectual Origins of the Jewish State* (New York: Basic Books, 1981), 92–93.
5. Ibid, 88–100.
6. Rubinstein, *The Zionist Dream Revisited.*
7. Ibid.
8. Marshall W. Fishwick, *Great Awakenings: Popular Religion and Popular Culture* (New York: Haworth Press, 1995).
9. William Kephart and William Zellner, *Extraordinary Groups: An Examination of Unconventional Life-Styles* (New York: St. Martin's Press, 1994). Constance Noyes Robertson, *Oneida Community: An Autobiography, 1851–1876* (Syracuse, New York: Syracuse University Press, 1970).
10. Edward Deming Andrews, *The People Called Shakers* (New York: Dover Publications, 1963).
11. Perry Miller, *The Transcendentalists* (Cambridge: Harvard University Press, 1971).
12. Kephart and Zellner, *Extraordinary Groups.*
13. Ibid, 236.
14. *Book of Mormon*, translated by Joseph Smith and first published in English in 1830 (Salt Lake City, Utah: Corporation of the President of the Church of Jesus Christ of Latter Day Saints, 1981).
15. Kephart and Zellner, *Extraordinary Groups*, 241.
16. Ibid, 242–243.
17. Ibid, 249–251.

18. Grant Underwood, *The Millenarian World of Early Mormonism* (Chicago: University of Illinois, 1993).

19. Kephart and Zellner, *Extraordinary Groups*, 276.

20. Ruth Brandon, *The Spiritualists: The Passion for the Occult in the Nineteenth and Twentieth Centuries* (New York: Knopf, 1983).

21. Ibid.

22. Kephart and Zellner, *Extraordinary Groups*, 137.

23. Ibid, 151–152.

24. Ibid, 160.

25. Martin Gardner, *The New Age: Notes of a Fringe Watcher* (Buffalo, New York: Prometheus Books, 1988).

26. Jose Arguelles, *The Mayan Factor: Path beyond Technology* (Santa Fe, New Mexico: Bear and Company, 1987).

27. Jack Friedman, "Hum if You Love the Mayans," *People*, August 31, 1987, 4.

28. Interview with Preacher Jack, August 22, 1992, Salem, Massachusetts.

29. Interview with Laurie Cabot, September 15, 1991, Salem, Massachusetts.

30. Paul Boyer and Stephen Nissenbaum, *Salem Possessed: The Social Origins of Witchcraft* (New York: Delta, 1974).

31. Ibid.

32. Carol Karlsen, *The Devil in the Shape of a Woman: Witchcraft in Colonial New England* (New York: W. W. Norton, 1987).

33. "Witches' League for Public Awareness" pamphlet, 1993.

34. Interview with Laurie Cabot, September 15, 1990, Salem, Massachusetts.

35. "Building a New Age Together," Internet home page for the Salem New Age Center, Salem, Massachusetts, February 1996.

36. "Photon Belt Compilation," Internet home page for the Salem New Age Center, Salem, Massachusetts, February 1996.

37. Interview with Rev. Russell Ely, March 1991, Wakefield, Massachusetts.

38. All articles or editorials are from *The Salem Evening News;* Staff report, July 9, 1992; Michelle Kurnusky, April 21, 1992; Tina Sciola, December 3, 1991; Anonymous, March 3, 1992; Jacki Mari, January 30, 1992; Kenneth Russell Baldwin, December 26, 1991.

39. Associated Press, *New York Times*, February 2, 1996, p. D20.

40. Paul Kennedy, *The Rise and Fall of the World Powers: Economic Change and Military Conflict from 1500 to 2000* (New York: Random House, 1987).

## 10. Conclusion: A Fractured Millennium

1. Yuri Rubinsky and Ian Wiseman, *A History of the End of the World* (New York: William Morrow, 1982).

2. Ibid, 65.

3. Jill Smolowe, "Tonight We're Gonna Party Like It's 1999." Time, Special Issue: Millennium—Beyond the Year 2000. The Great Event, 1994, 10.

4. Kenneth S. Stern, *A Force upon the Plain: The American Militia Movement* (New York: Simon and Schuster, 1996).

5. Frank Rich, "The Pratt Fall," *New York Times*, February 17, 1996, p. 23.

6. Grace Halsell, *Prophecy and Politics: Militant Evangelists on the Road to Nuclear War* (Westport, Connecticut: Lawrence Hill, 1986).

7. Tom Bates, *Rads: The 1970 Bombing of the Army Math Research Center at the University of Wisconsin and Its Aftermath* (New York: Harper and Collins, 1992).

8. Daniel Brandt, "The 1960s and CONINTELPRO: In Defense of Paranoia," NameBase Newsline, No. 10, July–September, 1995.

# Index

**287**